THE FINE

DELIGHT

THAT

FATHERS

THOUGHT

Franco Marucci

❧ THE FINE

DELIGHT

THAT

FATHERS

THOUGHT ❧

Rhetoric and

Medievalism in

Gerard Manley Hopkins

The Catholic University of America Press
Washington, D.C.

Originally published as *I fogli della Sibilla:
Retorica e medievalismo in Gerard Manley Hopkins* by Casa editrice G. D'Anna, Messina-Firenze, 1981.

*Library of Congress Cataloging-in-Publication
Data*

Marucci, Franco, 1949–
    [Fogli della Sibilla. English]
    The fine delight that fathers thought :
rhetoric and medievalism in Gerard Manley Hopkins / Franco Marucci.
       p. cm.
    Translation of: I fogli della Sibilla.
    Includes bibliographical references and
index.
    1. Hopkins, Gerard Manley, 1844–
1889—Criticism and interpretation. 2. Medievalism—England—History—19th century. 3. Rhetoric—History—19th century. 4. Middle Ages in literature.
5. Rhetoric, Medieval.   I. Title.
PR4803.H44Z717313   1993
821'.8—dc20
92-39010
ISBN 0-8132-0778-9

To my children,
Lorenzo,
Francesca,
and Bernardo

CONTENTS

The present book, a revised and updated translation of my *I fogli della Sibilla. Retorica e medievalismo in Gerard Manley Hopkins* (Messina-Firenze: D'Anna, 1981), was conceived and written in the wake and at the suggestion of two innovative and seminal approaches to the literary text that came into prominence during the seventies. The first is that of the "new rhetoric," which, superseding the old-fashioned, taxonomic methods of description, put forward the possibility of a functional integration of rhetoric within the complexity of the literary text. The second is represented by the extensive research on semiotic theory and above all on cultural typology carried out by the Tartu school and by its most outstanding exponent, Jurij Lotman. While the relevant works of Heinrich Lausberg, of Roland Barthes, and above all of the Belgian rhetoricians of Groupe μ are still untranslated into English, the writings of Lotman, whom the Italian academic world precociously discovered and launched through timely and ground-breaking translations, only recently have been made available in English.

Needless to say, this book is anything but a deliberate adaptation of the text to the theory; rather, the twofold rhetorical and typological approach perfectly dovetails with peculiar, specific and genuine features of Hopkins's textuality. I use this general term, *textuality,* rather than *poetry,* because the latter has been alternatively the starting point and the goal of an investigation ranging from Hopkins's letters to his diaries, from his essays to his sermons and to his spiritual and theological writings. The only poetic specimen analyzed thoroughly here is, in fact, "The Wreck of the Deutschland."

Part One examines Hopkins's oeuvre *synchronically* (yet not statically), that is, as a self-enclosed poetic message provisionally cut loose from the cultural influences of his time. The aspect brought to a focus is the well-known rhetorical manipulation of poetic language, particularly at the phonological, rhythmical, syntactical, and above all tropical levels. Yet, what I have aimed to do is not so much to judge Hopkins's rhetoric on the basis of subjective taste, as has frequently been done, but to interpret it according to its function and to the communicative exigencies and finalities supporting and justifying its uses.

Part Two places Hopkins's oeuvre back within its cultural context and tries to see how it accords (or, more precisely, does not accord) with it. Hopkins's position in relation to the cultural type into which he was born is still an intriguing question, and one that has given rise to the most controversial and even fanciful hypotheses. The advantage of my argument is perhaps that, with the decisive help of Lotman, I have been working mainly with cultural and epistemic codes and models rather than echoes and borrowings from this or that writer.

As will be seen, I have taken into due and careful consideration the criticism of the decade elapsed since the publication in Italian of this book.* Much has appeared of general value and interest, and yet very little (excepting Harris's *Inspirations Unbidden* and Bump's *Gerard Manley Hopkins*) directly relevant to both Hopkins's rhetoric and medievalism. This is perhaps the best justification for this book.

---

*Brian Vicker's "Rhetoric and Functionality in Hopkins," in A. Mortimer, ed., *The Authentic Cadence* (Fribourg: Fribourg University Press, 1992), 73–141, which tackles Hopkins's rhetoric from the same functionalist perspective I have adopted, unfortunately appeared too late to be discussed here.

ACKNOWLEDGMENTS

I wish to thank Dr. John Moore and Dr. David Bridges for kindly reading the first draft of the English translation of this book; Dr. Mariella Gurato and Dr. Diana Zambardi, who were always ready to put promptly at my unlimited disposal books of my department library; my colleague and friend Professor Guido Fink and Mrs. Stefania Centenaro, who facilitated access to some bibliographical material. I am especially grateful to Dr. Emma Sdegno for her continuous and even last-minute assistance in tracking down and forwarding to me books and articles I needed.

The following abbreviations will be used throughout to identify Hopkins's writings:

J   *The Journals and Papers of Gerard Manley Hopkins*, edited by H. House and G. Storey. London: Oxford University Press, 1970 (first edition 1959).

L I   *The Letters of Gerard Manley Hopkins to Robert Bridges*, edited by C. Colleer Abbott. London: Oxford University Press, 1970 (first edition 1935).

L II   The Correspondence of Gerard Manley Hopkins and Richard Watson Dixon, edited by C. Colleer Abbott. London: Oxford University Press, 1970 (first edition 1935).

L III   *Further Letters of Gerard Manley Hopkins*, edited by C. Colleer Abbott. London: Oxford University Press, 1970 (first edition 1938).

P I   *The Poems of Gerard Manley Hopkins*. First edition. Edited by Robert Bridges. London: Oxford University Press, 1918.

P II   *The Poems of Gerard Manley Hopkins*. Fourth edition, revised and enlarged. Edited by W. H. Gardner and N. H. MacKenzie. London: Oxford University Press, 1970.

P III   *The Poetical Works of Gerard Manley Hopkins*, edited by N. H. MacKenzie. Oxford: Clarendon Press, 1990.

S   *The Sermons and Devotional Writings of Gerard Manley Hop-*

kins, edited by C. Devlin. London: Oxford University Press, 1970 (first edition 1959).

Other references will be given by author's name, date of publication, and page number (see Bibliography at the end of this volume).

English translations of passages and parts of books and essays not available in English are my own.

Except for customary cases (titles, Latin and Greek words and others in foreign languages, etc.), all italics in quotations (whether poetical or not) are mine unless otherwise stated in brackets or footnotes.

PART ONE

RHETORIC

I

✤ THE RHETORICAL VICE

Anyone aiming to investigate the function and functionality of Hopkins's poetic rhetoric finds very few valuable and comprehensive treatments of this subject in a bibliography grown at an exponential rate since 1918, when his poems were first published, and of which it is customary to praise the richness and variety of approaches. Rather, a kind of Bridgesian allergy to rhetoric and jesuitism (very often associated phenomena)[1] seems never to have left criticism, and to this day one occasionally meets with impromptu old-fashioned dismissals of Hopkins tending to reduce his poetry entirely to a clever and ingenious show of effects that cover an irreparable void of sense: terms and epithets such as "tricks," "oddities," "extravagances," "eccentricities," and "mannerisms" are still extensively used to define and refer to Hopkins's tropical practices and stylistic idiosyncrasies. In other words, the widespread critical approach to Hopkins's rhetoric still seems to be subjective, instinctive, and impressionistic, since rhetoric is seen, not as hypothetically substantial to his poetry, but as accessory and contingent; as a result, even in the best criticism one often finds nothing more than summary classifications—with different mixings from critic to critic—of good and bad, successful and unsuccessful effects, without any preliminary assessment of the communicative objectives and purposes and

1. According to his "spokesman" Claude Colleer Abbott, the Poet Laureate "had, and rightly, a profound distrust of the Society of Jesus" (Introduction to L I, xlv).

3

the linguistic and extra-linguistic context, all of which necessitate such an abundant recourse to rhetoric. It is just the frequency with which Hopkins's poetry has been presented in terms of pure extravagance and mannerism—not to say non-poetry—that has induced me to devote the entire first part of this work to an investigation of the "artificial" and rhetorical devices, not in terms of generic "support" and even less of mere accessoriness and contingency, but of functionality and contextuality—an investigation that is the only correct one, as in any nonformalistic analysis of the poetic signifier.

Before I proceed, however, a quick survey of the *status quaestionis*. As I hinted above, the critical reception of Hopkins's work was heavily affected by the biased editing of the first of his editors, Robert Bridges. Opinions about Bridges's editorial policy still vary widely. Retrospectively one cannot but be grateful to him for having involuntarily favored Hopkins's "explosion" in the twenties and thirties—which proved much more sensitive to his art than the decades in which he lived—but one can hardly forgive him for publishing only a selection of his friend's poetry of which he was the keeper—and a selection made according to debatable and subjective aesthetic criteria such as those expounded in a *Preface to Notes* (P I, 94–101), which soon asserted itself as a mandatory reference in all subsequent criticism. As is well known, Bridges—whose prestige, as Poet Laureate, was in 1918 at its height—gave credit to Hopkins for "great" and even "rare masterly beauties" (P I, 97, 101), but condemned very severely, in the name of a "continuous literary decorum" (97) and of an aesthetic canon based on an altogether subjective and abstract sense of proportion, some "errors of . . . taste" (such as the "perversion of . . . feeling," the "exaggerated Marianism" and the "naked encounter of sensualism and asceticism") and some "faults of style" and "extravagances" that could not but seriously threaten and impair the previously admitted "beauties" (96, 97). On the whole, Hopkins's poetry was for him negatively marked by artificiality, by a search for effects, by rhetorical exaggeration—as when he noticed an "affectation in metaphor" (96) and "freaks [of rhyme]" (99); or saw "efforts to force emotion into theological or sectarian channels" (96); or spoke of "passages where, in a jungle of rough root-words, emphasis seems to oust euphony" (100); or emphasized the supposed complacency with which Hopkins sought semantic "confusion" and made use of paradox.[2] And it was symptomatic that Bridges should regret, at the end of the Preface, the death of his friend just when he was probably preparing himself to "castigate his art into a more reserved style" (101).[3]

For at least two decades critics either assented to Bridges or repeated, through a different route or in an only slightly extenuated form, his strictures. John Middleton Murry, though less severe than Bridges, dangerously aggravated Bridges's error of approach when, in 1919, he maintained the supremacy of the pure musical line over meaning;[4] Edward Sapir, in 1921, ended one of the first non-hostile reviews emphasizing, however, how often Hopkins was prone to lapse into a gratuitous artificiality ("To a certain extent Hopkins undoubtedly loved difficulty, even obscurity, for its own sake"), and, again, into pure musicality ("his wild joy in the sheer sound of words").[5] From my perspective, the only appreciation from the twenties of real use and originality is the essay I. A. Richards wrote in 1926 in *The Dial*.[6] Richards not only disowned Bridges's rigor but turned into merits or at least into strictly necessary elements many of Bridges's "defects." In particular, obscurity, experimentalism, and the recourse to ar-

2. "Our author . . . would seem even to welcome and seek artistic effect in the consequent confusion. . . . It was an idiosyncrasy of this student's mind to . . . take pleasure in a paradoxical result" (99, 100).

3. It is indicative of Bridges's strictures that he should consider as stylistic blemishes both ambiguity and semantic pregnancy ("straining the meaning of . . . words" [99]), two phenomena unanimously recognized today as substantial and distinctive of the poetic practice.

4. " 'Inscape' is still . . . musical; but a *quality of formalism* seems to have entered with the specific designation. With formalism comes rigidity; and in this case the rigidity is bound to overwhelm the sense." Hopkins avoided rigidity, for Murry, only in the *terrible sonnets*. And again: "The communication of thought was seldom the dominant impulse of his creative moment, and it is curious how simple his thought often proves to be when the obscurity of his language has been penetrated. Musical elaboration is the chief characteristic of his work" (Murry 1919 in Bottrall 1975, 48–54).

5. Sapir 1921 in Bottrall 1975, 65–69.

6. Richards 1926 in Bottrall 1975, 69–77.

tifice were turned to account per se, no longer qualified as regrettable "vices": "It is an important fact that he is so often most himself when he is most experimental. . . . Hopkins was always ready to disturb the usual word order of prose to gain an improvement in rhythm or an increased emotional poignancy." The first sustained and unconditionally favorable evaluation of Hopkins appeared in 1932, written by F. R. Leavis in *New Bearings in English Poetry*. Although Leavis, developing Richards's critical premises, concurred in fostering another misunderstanding—that of Hopkins as a modern and even ideally contemporary poet[7]—the novelty of his essay consisted in a downright rejection of the then-current, Bridges-oriented attitude to Hopkins, who was for Leavis "the only influential poet of the Victorian age," indeed "the greatest" (156). The main target of Leavis's polemic was precisely Robert Bridges, against whose pseudo-theories he brought convincing objections, asserting the essentiality of Hopkins's obscurity and ambiguity and of what the Laureate had called "blemishes" and "faults of style": Hopkins had "positive uses for ambiguity," just because "every word in one of his important poems is doing a great deal more work than almost any word in a poem of Robert Bridges" (134).[8] In quick—or, as he admitted, "clumsy and inadequate" (145)—analyses Leavis exemplified the perfect integration of the formal and semantic levels—"the kind of function that the more obvious technical devices serve" (ibid.)—and therefore the strict motivation of artifices: "In ["The Leaden Echo and the Golden Echo" Hop-

7. "He is now felt to be contemporary, and his influence is likely to be great" (Leavis 1932, 156; see also 130, 136). On Hopkins's misunderstood "modernity" see below, Part Two, chapters 1 and 2.

8. For Leavis the "poetic" consisted in the "adequacy" of the verbal technique and the states of mind felt by the poet and communicated to the reader: "The only technique that matters is that which compels words to express an intensely personal way of feeling, so that the reader responds, not in a general way that he knows beforehand to be 'poetical', but in a precise, particular way. . . . To invent techniques that shall be adequate to the ways of feeling, or modes of experience, of adult, sensitive moderns is difficult in the extreme" (Leavis 1932, 28). Accordingly, Leavis saw in Hopkins "a genius . . . in which technical originality is inseparable from the rare adequacy of mind, sensibility, and spirit that it vouches for" (23), and in his poetry the capacity to provoke in the reader an "extremely complex response" (134).

kins] is elaborating and mastering his technical devices for more important purposes. It is not as mere musical effects (if such were possible in poetry)—melody, harmony, counterpoint—[Leavis was clearly alluding to Murry] that these devices are important; they are capable of use for expressing complexities of feeling, the movement of consciousness, difficult and urgent states of mind" (141–42). The "devices" are not a "mere musical trick," but serve "to increase the expectancy involved in rhythm and change its direction" (142); similarly, in "The Wreck of the Deutschland," "we do not feel of any element . . . that it is there for the sake of pattern" (144), and in the *terrible sonnets,* alliterations and assonances "serve to call the maximum attention to each word" (154).

Leavis's essay is very important because it is—though within the limits I have indicated—the first hint of a reading of Hopkins's poetry in embryonically semiotic terms of technical and stylistic functionality and, above all, because it is a veritable exception in the critical panorama until the forties. In an unfortunate page of his *After Strange Gods* (1934)[9] T. S. Eliot pronounced a new dismissal of Hopkins's poetry—as vitiated by "devotionality," unlike the work of a Baudelaire, a Villon, or even a Joyce—and associated him, for his showiness, his lack of "inevitability" and his "technical tricks," to his contemporary George Meredith. To Yeats, Hopkins appeared instead "the last development of poetic diction";[10] while Herbert Read sketched out a doubtful hierarchy of poems in which the first place was given to the "poetry which has no direct or causal relation to any such [religious] beliefs at all."[11] In the same years Claude Colleer Abbott, in his prefaces to the first two volumes of Hopkins's correspondence, published in 1935 and 1938, proved that Bridges's influence was far from exhausted. His introduction to L I (xv–xlvii)—a clear-cut essay on Hopkins's poetry—made it in fact immediately clear that he did not intend to stray in the least from Bridges's strictures and vetoes: "The fascination of what is diffi-

9. Bottrall 1975, 107–8.
10. In the Introduction to *The Oxford Book of Modern Verse* (1936), quoted in Hartman 1966, 1.
11. Bottrall 1975, 101–6.

cult and yet more difficult sometimes involved him in a struggle for technical conquest to the detriment of poetry. . . . Often in practice he takes complete freedom and dragoons words to fit his rhythm by a personal or capricious stress which has no more justification than a private symbolism" (xxii). It was again the failure to advert to any contextual relation and the lack of any investigation of the communicative model of this poetry—and at the same time the reliance on merely subjective taste—that made Abbott repeat Bridges's diagnosis of "excess" in the use of artifices and of "mannerism": "he is too greedy as poet and prosodist. . . . He feels no bar to the use of stress, alliteration, assonance, internal- and end-rhyme in the same poem. This excess is probably more often a loss than a gain. . . . [T]here are in his more experimental work weaknesses and violences belonging rather to mannerism than style" (xxii–xxiii). Such a position was naturally reflected in his judgments on single poems or groups of poems: the "Deutschland," for instance, could only be the object of a "qualified approval," as "marred by the something of propaganda and 'presentation-piece' that pervades it . . . excited, violent, over-pitched," and "handicapped by the academic [!] religious subject" (xxvi–xxvii).[12]

The forties were a period of normalization and accumulation for Hopkins criticism, yet the issue of Hopkins's rhetorical "vice" remained largely untackled[13] and subjective methods of evalua-

12. Abbott's judgment of Hopkins's post-"Deutschland" poetry up to the *terrible sonnets* was, besides, indicative of a more serious misunderstanding and distortion. Abbott ended up by praising Hopkins for the wrong reasons when he pointed to, and stressed, the subtle and half-hidden paganism, the repressed sensuality and the alleged religious deviance pervading many of those poems (such as "The Habit of Perfection" and "The Windhover"); it was symptomatic that Abbott should prefer "Spelt from Sibyl's Leaves," "tremendous and undoctrinal," to "Henry Purcell," "blending the parochial with the magnificent" (xxxvii).

13. One of the few instances of a functionalist approach in those years was V. Turner's essay "Hopkins: A Centenary Article" (Turner 1944 in Bottrall 1975, 126–39). Following Leavis, Turner emphasized Hopkins's orientation toward the receiver and the "total response similar in quality to his own experience and emotion" which he presupposes and seeks in the reader. If this "central line of communication" is cut, any aesthetic enjoyment comes to nothing. Turner perfectly sensed the aims of Hopkins's rhetorical strategy: "Inspired as it is by dogmatic beliefs that have entered into the very texture of his mind and give their 'selfbeing'

tion continued to prevail. This was confirmed by the Kenyon Critics' *Gerard Manley Hopkins* (Collections 1945), all the essays of which, though stemming from undoubtedly original and independent positions and from moderately encomiastic aims, surprisingly converged toward a global evaluation that still showed traces of Bridges's aesthetic criteria—or, more seriously, prejudices. Harold Whitehall, for example, began his long contribution on sprung rhythm with an erudite, convincing, and wideranging analysis of its nature, essence, and Anglo-Saxon origins, and came quite near to envisaging a functional approach: "In dipodic verse, alliteration is functional. It is used, as the rarer internal rhyme, word repetition, and assonance are used, to reinforce or 'overstress' the strong positions in the rhythmic pattern. . . . All the overstressing devices illustrated depend upon the same principle—anticipatory familiarization with certain sounds or sound combinations, so that, upon repetition, the reader is induced to give them slightly more emphasis than usual" (Whitehall 1945, 49–50).[14] This very useful notion of "overstressing" was, however, dropped without further inquiry whether it was applicable to Hopkins's poetry—whether, in other words, the recourse to rhythmic and phonological manipulations (to remain within the area examined by the critic) is required and motivated by corresponding semantic manipulations. Whitehall chose instead to remember that "[I]n the history of poetry . . . the functional often becomes ornamental"—a transition that he traced, and copiously, in Hopkins, who only in the "later poems . . . mastered the principle of functional overstressing" (51), whereas, in general, he "was anticipated by those medieval poets who, like him, were strongly interested in sound pattern, rather than in the lucid communication of ideas" (52). Whitehall actually ended by paraphrasing and at the same time amplifying Murry's judgment

---

to his feelings, there is something, I think, in Hopkins's poetry, that is outside the compass of many a reader's apprehension and sensibility; and there is much that baffles and shocks and alienates."

14. See Ong 1949 for another discussion of sprung rhythm, and in particular 145–47 for a criticism of Whitehall's theory of sprung rhythm as a "system of dipodies."

of Hopkins as an exquisitely "musical" poet.[15] But undoubtedly the most solemn dismissal of Hopkins's poetry came, in this symposium, from Austin Warren and his essay "Instress of Inscape," which, initiated on neutral or mildly eulogistic tones, ended with a series of scathing remarks, once again dictated by a dogmatic and rationalistic aesthetics of a Bridgesian type. It is worthwhile to quote the conclusion almost entirely:

Hopkins' poems intend, ideally, an audience never actually extant, composed of literarily alert countrymen and linguistically adept, folk-concerned scholars; he had to create by artifice what his poetry assumed as convention. "The Wreck" and "Tom's Garland" suggest, adumbrate, a greater poetry than they achieve. . . . In Hopkins' poems, the word, the phrase, the local excitement, often pulls us away from the poem. And in the more ambitious pieces, the odes as we may call them ("The Wreck", "Spelt from Sibyl's Leaves", "Nature is a Heraclitean Fire"), there is felt a discrepancy between texture and structure: the copious, violent detail is matched by no corresponding mythic or intellectual vigor. Indeed, both the Wrecks are "occasional," commissioned pieces which Hopkins works at devotedly and craftfully, as Dryden did at his *Annus Mirabilis,* but which, like Dryden's poem, fail to be organisms. Hopkins wasn't a story-teller, and he was unable to turn his wrecks into myths of Wreck: they remain historical events enveloped in meditations. "The Bugler-Boy" and the other poems suffer from the gap between the psychological *naïveté* and the purely literary richness. To try prose paraphrases of the middle poems is invariably to show how thin the thinking is ["how simple his thought often proves to be," Murry had said]. Hopkins' mind was first aesthetic, then technical: he thought closely on metaphysical and prosodic matters: his thinking about beauty, man and Nature is unimpressive. The meaning of the poems hovers closely over the text, the linguistic surface of the poems. The rewarding experience of concern with them is to be let more and more into words and their linkages, to become absorbed with the proto-poetry of derivation and metaphorical expansion, to stress the inscapes of our own language. (Warren 1945, 87–88; Warren's italics)

15. The parallels and the relationships he indicated were in this case even more improbable: "His verbal innovations exist merely to assure the precise ordering of the musical elements in his lines. As a poet, Hopkins was a half-musician writing a poetry half-music. . . . Like Pater, he came to understand that all art strives towards the conditions of music. Like Wagner [!], he eventually subordinated poetical to musical composition" (54).

W. H. Gardner's two-volume monograph, published between 1944 and 1949, had then undoubtedly the merit to rule out, from the outset, any pre-ordained divergence between signifier and signified in Hopkins, any "supposed autonomy of *matter* on the one hand and *form* on the other" (Gardner 1949, I, 77; Gardner's italics), and to point out repeatedly the need to consider Hopkins's artifices (from rhythm, meter, and sound to the rhetorical tropes and all the other syntactic, morphological, and grammatical manipulations) as semantic and functional (and therefore potentially communicative) factors.[16] In practice, however, Gardner did not go beyond acceptable and even in some cases ingenious insights and suggestions,[17] which were too soon abandoned or were eventually carried to modest conclusions. Gardner's approach, in fact, was more formalistic than structural or semiotic (an "*aesthetic* criticism" [II, 225; Gardner's italics], that is, an evaluative method studying the single poems with reference to a summary biographical, psychological, and theological framework). Failing to develop and activate, at the level of the analytical praxis, considerations regarding the communicative model and the semantic and rhetorical planning of Hopkins's poetic message—with the exceptional illumination that such an investigation could have given—Gardner substantially fell back within the compass of that subjective and impressionistic criticism and into those practices of separation of successful and unsuccessful effects at which I hinted above.[18]

16. See I, 47–48, 137, 140–41, 146, 149–51, 189–90 and II, 131, 135, 369.

17. See, above all, his observations on Hopkins's "gift for impassioned rhetoric" (II, 136), and on the effect of estrangement and surprise, so that the richness in figures of speech is the spontaneous choice of "a newer mode, a more brilliant *décor*, which will recapture the reader's or hearer's attention and direct his mind once more to neglected or forgotten matters" (II, 135; Gardner's italics); see also his observations on the "disintegration of language" and on the failure of communication in "Harry Ploughman" and "Tom's Garland" (I, 146) and, finally, on credibility in "Spelt from Sibyl's Leaves."

18. Here is a significant instance (on "Peace") of a certain cliché of textual criticism: "Having regretted, as most critics will, the affected inversion of 'own my heart' and the uncomfortably weak ending of line 6 ('. . . the death of *it*'), we can still pronounce this poem a success. The second line, which at first presents 'an irritating grammatical tangle,' resolves itself with familiarity into a thought-dramatization of subtle precision. The modified gerund 'round me roaming' is a complete poetic word, the delicate exactitude of which would have been de-

Ironically, the same year (1949) that saw the completion of Gardner's study also saw an almost unprecedented counterattack on Hopkins. Yvor Winters published as a review (and in 1957 reprinted without alteration in his *The Function of Criticism*) an essay that remains to this day one of the most sensational cases of incompatibility between Hopkins and his critics. Indeed, this essay lays exemplarily bare the basic misunderstanding found in much of Hopkins criticism, that of a rigidly abstract and rationalistic concept of the literary text (directly taken from Bridges's Preface to the 1918 edition, one would say), a concept where contextualization has no place, and (as I will try to demonstrate later on) one which, once applied to Hopkins's poetry, programmatically "confused" and anti-rationalistic,[19] cannot but give extremely disappointing results. Winters asserted the strict necessity in poetry for an inviolable "conceptual identity" between sign and reference, and that "[i]t is the business of the poet, then, to make a statement in words about an experience; the statement must be in some sense and in a fair measure acceptable rationally; and the feeling communicated should be proper to the rational understanding of the experience" (failing which a poem becomes "incomplete" and "very confused" [Winters 1949, 104]). From these premisses it was easy for Winters to establish the superiority of two poems, by Donne and by Bridges ("exact and powerful . . . definite . . . precise" [105, 106, 107]), over a sonnet by Hopkins, characterized by ambiguity, indeterminacy, and inconclusiveness (but of course only because he made no effort to contextualize the poem and to look for possible traces of functionality). These charges of scarce clarity and precision and of sheer disproportion

---

stroyed if Hopkins, in deference to conventional idiom, had written 'Your roaming round me end' or 'End your roaming round me'; for in these locutions 'round me' becomes syntactically confused with 'end', whereas it must exclusively limit 'roaming'. Similarly, 'under *be* my boughs' (on the analogy of 'under*lay*', 'under*lie*', 'under*prop*', etc.) carries an elemental sense of passive *being* which would be excluded by some more specific and facile word, such as 'rest', 'dwell', or 'live'. Again, the alliterative punning in line 5 is not mere musical ingenuity; it is an earnest 'running logic' of feeling linked with sound, other examples of which we have noted in Sophocles, Shakespeare, Sidney, and Rilke" (II, 285–86; Gardner's italics).

19. See below, Part One, chapter 2.

between form and content led to the assertion that Hopkins "conveys emotion for a moment, and conveys it with an illusion of motivation but with no real motivation" (108). In the second part of the essay, where many of Hopkins's other compositions were analyzed, Winters's dismissiveness touched unthinkable peaks of gratuitous categoricalness and critical obtusity. The logical conclusion of the essay was a literal demolition of "The Windhover," whose great difficulties and objective ambiguities could not but appear virtually insurmountable to a critic who, like Winters, abided by the criterion of the "real evidence" and of "what the poem says": the sonnet was for him—like the other poems analyzed—vague, inconclusive, grammatically incorrect (Winters's pedantry outdid even Bridges's), conceited, "over-wrought and badly wrought" (135), as it provides the "physical embodiment of the meaning, without the meaning, or with too small a part of it" (134). Some years later, Donald Davie's ingenious discussion of the embryonic critical system that can be drawn from Hopkins's letters[20] was completed by an old-fashioned reproposition of the "faults" and "flaws" of Hopkins's idiolect: "hysteria" and "sickness" pushed to the limit, "refinement and manipulation of sensuous appetite," "hectic intensity" (Davie 1952, 171), "excess of sensuous luxury" (172), "thinking . . . casuistical" (173), grammatical indiscipline and "no respect for the language . . . crammed, stimulated and knotted together . . . luxuriating in the kinetic and muscular as well as the sensuous" (175). Not even Giorgio Melchiori helped to make things clearer when in his *The Tightrope Walkers* (1956) he set Hopkins beside Henry James to show the "manneristic" and "euphuistic" attitude of both regarding language and style. Although Melchiori declared that he did

20. Davie, however, stated at the outset, and concluded most ungenerously, that Hopkins's critical system "can be dangerous" (160), and, surprisingly, that "however it may touch at several points upon modern criticism, [it] is violently at odds with what distinguished later poets have laid down in theory or implied in critical practice" (176). Of Hopkins's critical principles and of the underlying cultural codes I will speak at length in Part Two. Contrast, however, Davie's judgment with Grigson's: "Among those letters to Bridges, Dixon, and Patmore, which themselves add up to one of the most direct, strict, piercing, and convincing bodies of criticism in the English language, he establishes a test which does not, and never can, defeat his own poetry" (Grigson 1955, 31–32).

not associate any derogatory or Bridgesian connotation with the term "mannerism," his investigation of the specific motivations, both structural and semiotic, was—unlike that of the historical and epistemic ones—rather superficial and debatable. Hopkins's "mannerism," according to him, was constantly threatening to stray into the "conceit" or the "ridiculous," or in any case into "supreme preciosity" or "exalted artistry" (Melchiori 1956, 19).[21]

G. H. Hartman observed in 1966: "The manneristic element in Hopkins, whether nurtured by traditional rhetoric or by the force of the vernacular, is the dragon that lies in the gates of his verse. . . . After almost fifty years of close reading and superb editing, Hopkins' verse remains something of a scandal. For we continue to be uncertain as to whether Hopkins, like Spenser, 'writ no language,' or whether he coins a radically new idiom. The basic questions about his greatness, direction and even plain-sense are not yet answered" (Hartman 1966, 1). I would have some doubts about the "superb editing"; yet, with some notable exceptions, these statements apply perfectly to the criticism of the last thirty years. Boyle's *Metaphor in Hopkins* (1961) is, to a certain extent, one of the exceptions, though the linguistic and functionalist approach, announced in the introduction, is prevalently confined in

21. Melchiori inclines to identify diatonism with parallelism and chromatism with asymmetry, and to consider Hopkins's poetic expression more chromatic than diatonic (therefore, we are surprisingly to infer, non-parallelistic, and thereby innovative with respect to nineteenth-century poetry): indeed "an art expressing with the utmost intensity and closeness the intellectual reactions to sensations and emotions" (20). The relevance of this justly emphasized mimetic component is, in my opinion, quite contrary to that indicated by Melchiori: it is a diatonic, not a chromatic, element. The distinction between chromatism and diatonism may well be that between parallelism and asymmetry, but more accentuated by far is that between gradual and harmonic progression (chromatism) and marked and intervallary, "abrupt" progression, as the following statement unequivocally clarifies: "The division then is of abrupt and gradual, of parallelistic and continuous, of intervallary and chromatic" (J, 76). Hopkins adds eloquent examples taken from painting (chiaroscuro/contrasts of color) and music (change of note in violin/piano; see also J, 85, 104, 106). To assert, then, that in Hopkins there is "attention to details rather than to the structure as a whole," and that "details are worked out with a goldsmith's care, and this makes for an enormous gain in insight and precision—but the total effect is frequently lost sight of" (23), means in my opinion to neglect altogether one of the least controversial merits of Hopkins's poetry, its inscape. Cf., as a confirmation of my statements, Miller 1963, 277ff. and 345, and Sprinker 1980 ("Hopkins favors diatonism over chromatism" [23]).

short paragraphs to the end of each chapter, so that the "total context" (Boyle 1961, xix) for which he is searching is nothing but the pure conceptual and theological argument of each poem analyzed, highlighted, so to speak, by its dominant image(s). Bender's study was *really* "a new critical approach" (Bender 1966, vii) to Hopkins, its polemical hypothesis being that Hopkins was not that naïve and revolutionary poet, totally separated from tradition, whom the new theorists of an intuitionist aesthetics (among whom Richards, Empson, Day Lewis) exalted in the twenties and thirties, but, on the contrary, a most "derivative" poet. Such Hopkins was not with reference to English poetic tradition (which he indeed knew in a disorganic and lacunose way), but with reference to classical literatures. His poetry can be described, for Bender, as a "peculiar confluence of Jesuit, classical, and Victorian learning" (4); in particular: the Greek and Latin hyperbata are the source of the syntactic distortions and Martial of "the explosive word play congenial to Ignatian psychology," whereas from Pindar Hopkins took the non-logic structure of his poems (ibid.).[22] Bender applied at length this Pindaric key to the "Deutschland," focussing on and emphasizing the alleged obscurity of its principle of organization, the unlinked and unnecessary character of many of its sections, the "far-fetched" nature of its metaphors (84)—which "neither illuminate his meaning nor ennoble his sentiment" (ibid.)—and the flimsiness of the logical sequence. Bender's argument smacks of the specious *tour de force* and of the pre-established adaptation. The deliberate nature of Hopkins's obscurity is, for the reasons I shall give, untenable, and Bender was in any case on the wrong track when he saw rhetoric as prevalently *expressive* (i.e., an expression of the writer's emotion) and not also as *impressive* (i.e., provoking the emotion of the listener).[23] Furthermore, to maintain as Bender does (in his chapter IV) that Hopkins coldly and mechanically imitated classi-

22. Bender adds that Hopkins also shared some Victorian aesthetic inclinations with reference to the work of the mind and to mental associationism—such as, for instance, the "collage effect" theorized by H. Read, and F. M. Ford's concept of "unearned increment" (see below).

23. See for this distinction, Genette 1966, 217.

cal rhetoric is to decontextualize it and to considerably empty and enfeeble its semantic import, its communicative efficacy, and its semiotic functionality. E. Schneider, too, performed a similar decontextualizing of rhetoric when, in her *The Dragon in the Gate: Studies in the Poetry of Gerard Manley Hopkins* (1968), she viewed its occurrences—on the basis of purely personal taste—as a "residue" and a form of weakness and bizarreness, instead of a primary and substantial fact. She accordingly made a distinction between "baroque style" and "plainer . . . style" (Schneider 1968, 139ff., where several sonnets are analyzed), giving her preference to the latter category (where she included, surprisingly, the *terrible sonnets*).

Of the many books that appeared in the seventies and eighties only three, Milroy's, Robinson's, and above all Harris's, are relevant to my perspective. Milroy's dissection of Hopkins's poetic language, seen as a systematic "heightening" of common speech, is deliberately a taxonomic, formalistic operation which, splendidly performed though it is, except for a few sporadic hints[24] fatally leaves out any investigation of the extra-linguistic context. Robinson, on his part, echoes the old dilemma: Is Hopkins a poet all of us can enjoy, is he a universal poet, or is it necessary to share his faith to fully understand him? It is of course a pointless, absurd question, since every reading must be sympathetic and historicized. His method of evaluation too, aiming to separate the "strengths" from the "weaknesses" (Robinson 1978, 53, 107), savors of Bridges and of the old "anti-eccentricity school," and predictably hits the "Deutschland," where "sound appears to exist for its own sake so that the semantic core of a word has been lost and we are left dealing with the husk" (ibid., 61). Harris's book, *Inspirations Unbidden: The "Terrible Sonnets" of Gerard Manley Hopkins* (1982), is *dulcis in fundo,* being not only the last of a long series of variously useful and acceptable contributions on Hopkins's rhetoric but also by far the best and the

---

24. See, for example, this observation: "Hopkins was willing to use almost any phonological device that would help him to capture 'inscape'—to make his language sound and feel like the things he described, to 'tell' of them, to 'fling out broad' their *names*" (Milroy 1977, 126; Milroy's italics).

most valuable. It is, in fact, the only book in the whole Hopkins criticism that, however empirically, has tried to interpret Hopkins's poetry by measuring it against a contextual frame of rhetorical motivations and situations, namely, in terms of a progressive emptying out of its divine and human destination—a process that culminates in the *terrible sonnets*, the specific object of the critic's observation. Since his analyses tally in many points with mine, I shall have the opportunity of quoting from and discussing this work at length in the following chapters.[25]

25. One can reasonably assume that, had Hopkins had in Italy the same popularity and cultural resonance he had in the Anglo-Saxon world, his poetry would have sparked a literary debate analogous to that which long revolved around the confessional and oratorical, rather than truly artistic and poetic, value of Manzoni's *The Betrothed*. Until the seventies, despite an early essay by Croce in 1937 and the loving care of his first translator, Augusto Guidi, in the forties and fifties, Hopkins criticism remained sporadic and explorative, and only one book-length study was published, by Sergio Baldi in 1941. The only undoubtedly original Italian contribution remains that of A. Serpieri (Serpieri 1969), who, in an essay that touches on all the phases of Hopkins's production except the "Deutschland," carried out shrewd structural and functionalist analyses of a few "joyous" and "terrible" sonnets. Serpieri justly emphasized the emotional and above all "conative," "didactic and parabolic" and sermonistic components of Hopkins's message, adding that it is in the light of it that the " 'strangeness' of his poetry" is to be seen, a strangeness that "was certainly not due to motives of low formal or metrical indiscipline or of calculated obscurity, as Bridges, so distant from that expressive experience, thought, but to the perception of the inscape of an object, of its epiphany, which necessarily leads to that psycho-linguistic phenomenon which many years later Šklovskij would call 'estrangement' " (54).

2

❦ HOPKINS'S MESSAGE

AND ITS CONTEXT

As we have seen in the previous chapter, criticism has tended to decontextualize—or to contextualize imperfectly—the "artificial" aspects of Hopkins's poetry; as a consequence, the widespread critical approach has been subjective or roughly evaluative. What we need to do is therefore: (1) to make the due methodological adjustments and to go on to reconstruct the context, that is, the models, the communicative exigencies and finalities of Hopkins's poetry; (2) to formulate and then verify certain hypotheses about the functionality of rhetoric to those exigencies and finalities.[1]

The problem of the relation between meaning and the linguistic, rhetorical, technical, and formal artifices takes on, in fact, an immediately different aspect; at the same time, many discussions,

---

1. Among the texts that have proved most useful in this reconstruction are Roland Barthes's "L'Ancienne rhétorique," Lausberg's *Elemente der literarischen Rhetorik,* and also, for an investigation in a structuralist and semiotic perspective which has proved particularly useful in the final pages of this Part, Groupe μ's *Rhétorique Générale.* On the notions and terms of information theory and cybernetics hereafter used, see the texts quoted below in note 7. To emphasize and then study the eminently rhetorical features of a poetic message, and to point out, as I have done, their adequacy according to certain criteria of functionality, means, of course, to believe in the legitimacy and even necessity of the persuasive argumentation, and to take a stand against the centuries-long hegemony of a typically rationalistic, Cartesian argumentative mode. The fundamental study to which I will frequently refer is Perelman-Tyteca's *The New Rhetoric. A Treatise on Argumentation.*

arguments, and conclusions we have met with automatically lose much of their validity if, instead of a dogmatic, static, and rationalistic concept of the poetic text (such as that underlying Bridges's, Abbott's, Whitehall's, Winters's, and others' criticism), we correctly adopt a flexible, dynamic, and multi-level one.[2] While it is by now beyond dispute that personal taste and ideological leanings are factors that as much as possible should be left out of critical activity, in the attempt to make it closer to a scientific methodology, a widely admitted principle is that the constitutive elements of the literary text (sound, rhythm, meter, syntax, rhyme, meaning, etc.; better defined as *levels*) do not "live" in it inertly and separately—and consequently cannot be evaluated according to their abstract and autonomous activity—but interact and closely collaborate, and that, therefore, the artistic work consists of a series of "links," horizontal (between elements belonging to each single level) as well as vertical (between elements belonging to the same levels). This highlights the incorrect presuppositions with which criticism has mainly tackled our problem and which have made possible such tenacious and categorical presentations of Hopkins's poetry in terms of "pure musicality" and of patent *écart* between the logical and conceptual chain ("broken" and "evanescent") and the "unmotivated" multiplication of sound, rhythm, and syntactic "effects." The poetic text is not a prose+ornaments sum, and its meaning is not the logical nucleus to be extracted from the text and to be perfectly repeated in prose language; on the contrary, poetic communication is the transmission of a message that cannot be translated into a different code—under pain of its degradation to everyday speech. In this kind of message, therefore, the production of meaning is a

2. On the concept of the poetic text as a unity of levels see Ingarden 1960 and—for an exhaustive discussion and exemplification—Pagnini 1988. As regards the attitude of certain critical schools toward Hopkins's rhetoric, the following remarks of Perelman-Tyteca 1971 appear absolutely to the point: "If the writers who have concerned themselves with figures have been inclined to see only their stylistic aspect, this is due, in our opinion, to the fact that *the moment a figure is detached from its context* and pigeonholed, it is almost necessarily perceived under its least argumentative aspect. . . . *Only a more flexible conception, which considers the normal in all its changing facets,* can do full justice to the place argumentative figures occupy in the phenomenon of persuasion" (171).

complex and composite operation which avails itself, beside the semantic, of the decisive collaboration of all the other levels of the text. Hopkins himself was well aware of this when he affirmed nothing less than the accessoriness and contingency of the prosaic, logical, "denotative" meaning, and even its nature as pure material and starting point for the shaping of the "secondary," "connotative," poetic meaning:

Poetry is speech framed for contemplation of the mind by the way of hearing or speech framed to be heard *for its own sake and interest even over and above its interest of meaning.* Some *matter and meaning* is essential to it *but only as an element necessary to support and employ the shape* which is contemplated for its own sake. . . . Poetry . . . [is] speech wholly or partially repeating some kind of figure which is over and above meaning, *at least the grammatical, historical, and logical meaning.* (J, 289)[3]

If we admit then without being scandalized—as more than two thousand years of aesthetic debate, from Aristotle to the "new rhetoric," have proved, even if Hopkins's critics have evidently thought otherwise[4]—that rhetoric can be part of the literary text and can collaborate in some measure in the production of meaning, and that it therefore holds a potentially semiotic statute,[5] then we can synthetically enunciate the governing hypothesis of this first part of my book: In Hopkins, the *figure* is not only functional but also institutionally essential. We understand *figure* here

3. Milroy 1977 usefully points out that "the model for [Hopkins's] language was not *prose*, but *speech*" (20; Milroy's italics).

4. Walter Pater was in a sense a better theoretician than most ensuing Hopkins critics. In *Marius the Epicurean* Flavian observes that reading rouses in the reader a predilection for words as the main component and "instrument of the literary art"; yet he also discovers their potential rhetorical efficacy: he speaks of "secrets of utterance" capable of exerting an "effect upon others," of "over-aw[ing] or charm[ing] them to one's side" (here Pater hints at the use of *pathetic* rather than *ethic* figures: see my analysis of the "Deutschland" in chapter 3). While defending the expressive function of "euphuism," Pater admits that it may lapse into "mere artifice" and "fopperies and mannerisms" (88–93). See also, for further analogies and discrepancies, Melchiori 1956, Downes 1965 and, below, Part Two, chapter 3 notes 4 and 18; chapter 4 notes 1, 2, and 6; chapter 6 note 1.

5. Cf. the impassioned defense of the dignity of rhetoric and the refusal to de-class it to a mere expedient (provided it is proportioned to "things" and functional to an argumentative project), in Perelman-Tyteca 1971, in particular 1–10, 509–14.

in an extended sense: not only those operations recognized and classified by classical rhetoric but also any *écart* manifest both in the "inferior" levels—phonological, morphological, lexical, grammatical, syntactic, rhythmic, metrical, prosodic, etc.—as well as in the "superior" levels of the poetic text—enunciative, semantic, symbolic, etc.[6] The figure has, therefore, the task of semantically and emotionally intensifying a message that, without it, might become weaker or be condemned to "dispersion" on its way from the sender to the receiver, as bearer of a new and unheard-of *sense* which might be easily taken for a literal *counter-* or *non-sense*. The figure therefore rouses and keeps the reader's attention, saves him from intellectual routine, opens up deeper furrows for the penetration of the sense and helps the reader to appropriate it integrally. In the terms of information theory, Hopkins's message is characterized by a high rate of redundancy, made necessary by the particular nature of the content communicated: the figure not only establishes—or contributes to—the "security of canal," but also guarantees the complete intellection of the addressee. Though normatively arresting the flux of information, *this* redundancy becomes paradoxically informative, functioning as it does as a semantic and emotional amplification of the content.[7] And while the extensive use of estranging figures, such as paradox and oxymoron, or amplifying ones, such as repetition, metaphor, and simile, or emotional ones, such as anaphora and climax, appears highly functional to these objectives, it is im-

6. I take this distinction from Toporov 1979. For the concept of figure in this enlarged acceptation of *écart,* infraction of a rule of common language, see Lotman 1977 (26–31 and 204–8), Cohen 1966 (44 ff.), and Perelman-Tyteca 1971 ("a use that is different from the normal manner of expression and, consequently, attracts attention" [168]). Perelman-Tyteca 1971 emphasize the necessity of a functionalist analysis of figures within an argumentative frame, and introduce, on the basis of the effect that they have on the hearer, the useful distinction between *argumentative* and *stylistic* figures.

7. For a cybernetic and information theory approach to the rhetorical figure, see some excellent hints (here and there mixed with some verbosity) in Zareckij 1963. Regarding the notions of information theory here and hereafter introduced, see Eco 1972 ed. (which includes, besides the above-quoted essay by Zareckij, others by Eco, Bense, Arnheim, Moles, Coons, Kraehenbuehl, etc.) and Žolkovskij 1969.

portant to emphasize that phonological, rhythmic, prosodic, syntactic, and rhyme alterations and complications are by no means excluded by such a functionalization.[8]

The first proof that Hopkins's poetic text is therefore to be considered and decoded as a primarily *rhetorical* message is constituted by the unusually strong prominence that the success of its destination has in it. The integral intellection, the impassionate participation, the involvement and the sympathy of the receiver are in Hopkins not only the ultimate end toward which several textual practices converge, but also, as we shall see, the motivation *tout court* of the act of writing. Paradoxical as it may appear— in an author whose production was never published during his lifetime—Hopkins's poetry presupposes, postulates, and demands an addressee, *real* though *virtual*. His poetry was uncontestably an unpublished and unequivocally a destined poetry: that Hopkins, writing without the stimuli and feedback offered by an audience (which he, in any case, allusively and nostalgically often invoked: see for example L I 66, 270, 291), should have been induced to take refuge in a "private," esoteric, and extravagant poetry, altogether neglecting to establish points of contact with the external world, is to me an unacceptable interpretation.[9] That,

---

8. If, on the one hand, rhythm, sound, etc. do not slip into those forms of "asemanticity," "autonomy of the signifier," and "pure musicality" frequently stigmatized by critics, they do not on the other hand function exclusively in a phono-symbolic sense. To characterize them only or principally in such a way, as, among others, Boyle (1961) and Serpieri (1969) have done, seems to me to uncover only partially their great and decisive efficacy. Sound and rhythm, as we shall see, also and first of all perform an "aprogrammatic," propaedeutic function of signalling the hidden sense—indeed a rhetorical function. Something similar had already been noticed, as will be remembered, by Leavis (1932), Gardner (1969), and Whitehall (1945).

9. Equally unacceptable is Sulloway's statement that Hopkins "was giving the public what he thought it needed," that is, several "Victorian commonplaces" (217, note 19; but contrast 219, note 44). Hopkins wanted indeed to *shock* his "virtual" public, and to this kind of purpose we must retrace his poetic rhetoric. See Milroy 1977, 100–104, on Hopkins's disautomatizing poetic language. Harris (1982), in chapter 4 of his book (129–44), has made the strongest case so far for Hopkins's "real demand for an actual audience" and for the "implied" (129) or "hypothesized or fictive audience" (130) that props up and propels his poetic output until the *terrible sonnets*. This "fictive audience," he says, "although not characteristic of every poem preceding the 'terrible sonnets,' is yet unmistakably present" (134–35).

moreover, Hopkins's addressee was not conventional and in-
definite but historical and concrete, well identifiable and even lo-
catable, is proved by his geographical accuracy and by certain mimetic features of his language. Let it suffice to think of the Welsh
poems (P III, 130–31, 136), of the Welsh dialect words of the
"Deutschland," of the Lancashire words of "Ribblesdale," of the
Irishisms of "Spelt from Sibyl's Leaves," of the Scottish words of
"Inversnaid," and the Yorkshire words of "Henry Purcell."[10]

Hopkins had a personal awareness of this rhetorical structuring
of the poetic message, and more precisely of its perlocutory impetus (little as writers' confessions and programmatic statements
may count, compared to the evidence of texts themselves). Rhetoric is frequently referred to in his letters as the indispensable,
natural ingredient of poetic discourse, as the "common and
teachable element in literature, what grammar is to speech, what
thoroughbass is to music, what theatrical experience gives to
playwrights" (L II, 141), so that the ignorance or the absence of
it ("rhetoric . . . inadequate," "weakness [in] rhetoric," "poverty
of plan" [ibid.]) mars or enfeebles otherwise original and valuable
poetic experiments. Rhetoric thus becomes the main instrument
of that heightening of current language in which Hopkins saw
the essence of poetry: "The poetic language of an age shd. be the
current language heightened, to any degree heightened and unlike itself" (L I, 89). This is certainly not a metaphorical or unduly
hyperbolic heightening ("to any degree"): Hopkins, in the
youthful, well-known classification of poetic styles (L III, 215–
23), already describes the "language of inspiration" (that is, poetry at its highest level) as a "mood of great, *abnormal in fact, mental acuteness,* either energetic or receptive, according as the
thoughts which arise in it seem generated by a *stress and action of*

---

10. See also Gardner 1969, I, 134ff., and Boyle 1961, 175, and above all Milroy
1977, 27 and the whole of chapter 3, 70–98. In a letter written in 1876 to his
mother Hopkins says, when asked to suppress the accent marks: "I would gladly
have done without them *if I had thought my readers would scan right unaided* but I am
afraid they will not, and if the lines are not rightly scanned they are ruined" (L III,
138). On the necessity to select the audience on the part of the orator, see the apt
observations of Perelman-Tyteca 1971 in the paragraphs "The Speaker and his
Audience" (17–19) and "The Audience as a Construction of the Speaker" (19–23).

the brain, or to strike into it unasked" (L III, 216). It is no wonder that to such a concept of the essence of poetic communication, as far as the sender is concerned, there should correspond in the receiver the stimulation of an analogous and equally abnormal and acute mental and physical reaction: "In a fine piece of inspiration every beauty takes you as it were by surprise . . . every fresh beauty could not in any way be predicted or accounted for by what one has already read" (L III, 217). If the successful destination of the poetic message is here qualified simply as "touch" (although twice italicized out of the three times the word occurs: L III, 218, 219), elsewhere it is unmistakably compared to a sort of electric charge or an intense mental, physical, and muscular vibration. The poet must bear in mind, Hopkins wrote to Dixon, the ephemeral duration of the "enchanting power in the work" and the "shortcoming of faculty in us," so that "the mind *after a certain number of shocks or stimuli,* as the physiologists would say, *is spent and flags"* (L II, 38). Similarly, the penetration into Nature's mystery caused a shock to Plato and Wordsworth, in whom "when he wrote that ode human nature got another of those shocks, and the tremble from it is spreading" (L II, 148).

Summing up, Hopkins's message is therefore programmatically characterized by what Perelman-Tyteca (1971) define as the "feeling of the 'presence.' "[11] It is a communicative urgency that his poetic texts amply and unmistakably document, even on the basis of a rapid and summary survey, as is borne out first of all by the high statistical frequency of the conative function (imperatives, exclamations, interjections, apostrophes)[12] and by a series of operations pertaining to the sphere of the *pronuntiatio* and almost tending to overcome the limits and conventions of the written text. In his letters Hopkins constantly pointed out the necessity of a rhythmic and declaimed reading—with one's voice and

11. Perelman-Tyteca 1971, "Selection of Data and Presence," 115–120. *Presence* (a "notion . . . of paramount importance for the technique of argumentation" [119]) consists in "mak[ing] present, by verbal magic alone, what is actually absent but what [the speaker] considers important to his argument or, by making them more present, to enhance the value of some of the elements of which one has actually been made conscious" (117).

12. See, for a larger treatment, Motto 1984, 77–88.

not only with the eyes—of his poems: "To do the Eurydice any kind of justice you must not slovenly read it with the eyes but with your ears, as if the paper were declaiming it at you" (L I, 51–52). The demand for "presence" again causes Hopkins's poetry to share the nature—though it is doubtless much more than that—of heterogeneous linguistic performances such as the "party speech," the sermon (a genre of which Hopkins was professionally and vocationally an excellent and prolific author),[13] and even the drama and the melodrama (as is proved by the dramatic scaffolding of "A Soliloquy of One of the Spies left in the Wilderness" or of the *terrible sonnets:* see below, chapter 4). Hopkins felt these genres to be so congenial that he left from his adolescence countless dramatic fragments or simply projects (such as the wonderful "St. Winefred's Well") that his heavy extraliterary engagements prevented him from completing.[14] One can also remember the internal evidence provided by the argumentative or dialectic character of many of his poems (for example, "St. Alphonsus Rodriguez") and the copious use of such typical figures of classical rhetoric as the *sermocinatio* and the *percontatio*[15] (cf. again the sonnet "Thou art indeed just, Lord . . . ," and several sections of the "Deutschland," for example, st. 11, ll. 1–3, st. 24, ll. 5–8, and sts. 25–29). Like drama, poetry must have the indispensable chrism of "bidding":

Although on the one hand the action[16] is so good and its unity so well kept and on the other hand the style so beautiful I have doubts about the play's acting. Experience only can decide; but I do not think it has in a high degree a nameless quality which is of the first importance both in

13. A historical and comparatistic investigation of the homiletic elements of Hopkins's poetry has been carried out by Sulloway (1972) (see in particular chapter 4, 158–95). The "Deutschland," for her, aims "to kindle a homely and receptive answer in the ordinary Englishman's 'heart's charity's hearth's fire' " (194), and exploits aesthetically a commonplace of contemporary homiletics, the Apocalyptic premonition. I will return in Part Two, chapter 8, to this absolutely fundamental element of the poem. For a perceptive investigation of the techniques and rhetorical strategies of Victorian "sagistic" writing, and for a reconstruction of the context in which they must be placed, see also Landow 1989.

14. Bump 1982, 67.

15. Perelman-Tyteca 1971, "Figures of Choice, Presence, and Communion," 171–79, and Lausberg 1982, 142–43.

16. Hopkins is here referring to Bridges's verse-drama *Prometheus the Forgiver.*

oratory and drama: I sometimes call it *bidding*. I mean the art or virtue of saying everything right *to* or *at* the hearer, interesting him, holding him in the attitude of correspondent or addressed or at least concerned, making it everywhere an act of intercourse—and of discarding everything that does not bid, does not tell. (L I, 160; Hopkins's italics)[17]

Among the several consequences of poetics related to this communicative tension animating Hopkins's poetry we must include the abolition—at least as far as intentions are concerned—of any kind of *obscurity*.[18] Though it might seem otherwise, obscurity—excepting that modicum which is necessary to use as *licentia* to prevent an excess of perspicuity from becoming *platitudo* and to stimulate the interest and the collaboration of the reader[19]—is indeed for Hopkins the enemy *par excellence,* the capital vice to be avoided and fought.[20] For Hopkins as a Jesuit poet, obscurity is a

17. "Hopkins' style is as vocative as possible. This holds for sound, grammar, figures of speech, and actual performance. Tell and toll become cognates. . . . [Words] do not . . . exist in themselves or by some automatic virtue of revelation. On the contrary, they mimic, paint . . . , and participate in argument. Language is shown to be *contentio* in essence; there is nothing disinterested or general about it; its end as its origin is to move, persuade, possess. Hopkins leads us back to an aural situation (or its simulacrum) where meaning and invocation coincide" (Hartman 1966, 6, 7, 8). See also Ritz 1963: "L'intention du poète est claire: faire du langage un acte de relation, c'est tenir le lecteur ou l'auditeur en haleine, le contraindre à écouter et surtout à se sentir visé, et obligé de répondre à un appel. Il faut que le poète obtienne une réponse affirmative à la question qu'il pose avec chaque poème, et qui est exactement celle que nous l'entendons poser à son propre coeur dans *Le Naufrage du Deutschland*. . . . Pour que nous soyons touchés . . . Hopkins a recours au langage commun. Mais il le 'relève', lui donne une hauteur et une vigueur nouvelles en le modelant librement, en l'enrichissant de mille manières" (586–87). Ritz adds, apropos of the abnormal compound words, that Hopkins concentrates in them the need for a "vive synthèse qui offre une sorte de résistance à l'esprit du lecteur et empêche toute acceptation passive des mots," (611) and also for "une lutte constante contre la facilité, contre toute expression qui pourrait ne pas obliger l'esprit à participer à la vie du poème" (616).

18. See two interesting discussions of the relationship between clarity and obscurity in Noon 1949 and Milroy 1977, 5–14.

19. For Perelman-Tyteca 1971 "one wonders whether one of the benefits resulting from the obscurity of certain texts is not that it quickens the attention. . . . Sometimes a writer speculates that the reader will attach increased importance to a sign that belies his expectations" (145). The same function of surprise and semantic emphasis is attributable, as will be seen, to sprung rhythm and to puns, to solecisms and to dialect words.

20. There even seems to be, for Hopkins, a kind of equivalence or of direct proportion between intelligibility and artistic perfection, as can be seen from the following remark about the sonnet "Henry Purcell": "It is somewhat dismaying to find I am so unintelligible though, especially in one of my very best pieces" (L I,

downright strategic incoherence and, what is worse, a moral vice. Poetic perspicuity is connoted as a range of nuances going from truth (which is also, *in absentia,* beauty) to intelligibility, through seriousness, the being in earnest, realism: "A kind of touchstone of the highest or most living art is seriousness; not gravity but the being in earnest with your subject—*reality*" (L I, 225). It must immediately be made clear that *reality* and *realism* are not vague terms taken from the language of literary criticism, and that they mean a precise linguistic function of intensification of perspicuity, as they signify art's capacity for intimately and integrally interesting the reader, for charging the poetic structures with reality and truth in such a way as to invade and conquer his intellect as well as his sensibility.[21] Significantly, in painting and in poetry, realism is for Hopkins the truest and most valid of touchstones, and in the minute, detailed comments on paintings in the Journal, Greek sculptures and Michelangelo's frescoes, Pre-Raphaelite miniatures and Gothic architectural particulars are associated, diverse as they are, in the common denominator of realism. This realism is not just objectivity and adherence to things but a bold, overwhelming force brought to bear on the spectator, whether in the "touches of hammer-realism in the Entombment" of Michelangelo (J, 241), or in the "true bold realism" (J, 244) of B. Rivière and Millais, or in the "fiery truthful rainbow-end; green slimy races of piers; all clean, atmospheric, truthful, and scapish" of a painting of W. L. Wylie (J, 247).

In the domain of poetry, realism becomes a synonym for plasticity and palpability, vividness, graphicness, and highlighting of particulars,[22] so as to bring them into relief, almost to sculpture

---

171). However, as we shall see, in Hopkins's arguments in favor of the advocated exclusion of any institutional obscurity some most interesting observations of poetic theory are interwoven.

21. Such a demand for "presence" is traceable from Hopkins's youth. He writes for example in his essay "On the Signs of Health and Decay in the Arts": "The pleasure given by the presence of Truth in Art . . . lies in a (not sensuous but purely intellectual) comparison of the representation in Art with the memory of the true thing; and the truer it is, the more exact the parallel between the two, the more pleasure is perceived" (J, 74–75).

22. See also Robinson 1978, 55, 121. The highlighting of particulars—as well

them in natural size before the reader. As G. H. Hartman—one
of the few critics who has contrasted the prevalence of an exclusively intellectual approach—has written, Hopkins performs certain linguistic, grammatical, and syntactic solutions and manipulations (such as the verbal noun) just because they exalt

the freshness of a verbal root at the expense of a purely linguistic form
having no direct source in sense perception. . . . Hopkins, aware of the
atrophied or simplified sense-root of words, combines them to *suggest
their original identity in a physical percept.* . . . Moral and religious meaning
do not belatedly disclose themselves to reason, judgment or rationalization, *they are given in the very act of perception* . . . [italics mine]. Whatever
image we choose in Hopkins . . . there will be found in it a sensitivity if
not to actual stress then to touch, muscular action, and pressure. *The
sense of pressure or stress is the sixth and radical sense in the experience of Hopkins* [Hartman's italics]. It is evident to the tongue on reading his poetry
. . . thing and perceiver, thing and actor, tend in the sight of Hopkins to
be joined to each other as if by electrical charge; they are connected like
windhover and wind in terms of stress given and received. (Hartman
1954, 118, 120, 122, 123)

It is indeed according to this principle of "realism," applied in
these terms of even physical and muscular perception,[23] that
Hopkins frequently criticizes or advises his interlocutors, and it
is above all according to the observance of it that his own poetry,
too, is to be judged:

---

as many of the aesthetic categories mentioned here—is in Hopkins (at least initially) a clearly Pre-Raphaelite heritage: "The effect of verse is one on expression
and on thought, viz. concentration and all which is implied by this. This does not
mean terseness nor rejection of what is collateral nor emphasis nor even definite-
ness though these may be very well, or best, attained by verse, but mainly,
though the words are not quite adequate, vividness of idea or, as they would have
said in the last century, liveliness" (J, 84). Such an analytical bent, however, does
not remain in Hopkins an end in itself, but is counterbalanced by a spasmodic
synthetic tension, that global effect of the work of art which Hopkins called *inscape*. On the Pre-Raphaelite and Keatsian matrix see Miles 1945. Ong (1986, 8–
14) connects Hopkins's "fascination . . . with meticulously detailed, particular-
ized description[s]" with the Victorian "particularist aesthetics"; Bump (1982)
sees Hopkins's "minute fidelity to detail" as due to the "influence of science" (26)
and the progress of technology ("especially the invention of photography" [28]).

23. "The sounds and the rhythms of the language, with the nervous efforts and
the physical movements of lips, tongue, throat, the flow of air, etc., all enter into
the imagery and the poetry of Hopkins as a part of it, and an essential part" (Boyle
1961, 150).

Commonsense is never out of place anywhere, neither on Parnassus nor on Tabor nor on the Mount where our Lord preached; and, not to quote Christ's parables *all taken from real life,* but in the frankly impossible, as in the *Tempest,* with what consummate and penetrating imagination is Ariel's 'spiriting' put before us! all that led up and must follow the scenes in the play is *realised* and suggested and you cannot lay your fingers on the point where it breaks down. (L III, 374)

I want Harry Ploughman to be a *vivid figure* before the mind's eye; if he is not that the sonnet fails. (L I, 265)

Vividness, plasticity, suggestiveness, palpability, tactile and mimetic tension, verisimilitude: all these attributes are summed up and subsumed in the search for a spasmodic intelligibility or, better still, hyper-intelligibility,[24] stemming in the first place from Hopkins's didactic and explanatory vocation. If the Jesuit's mission is apostolic and pastoral, the Jesuit poet's mission (and Hopkins always is, when he writes poems—though dramatically—both Jesuit and poet)[25] is to establish the poetic communication as efficacious and persuasive teaching for a humanity become deaf to Truth ("in [the] public I regret . . . that it can no longer be trusted to bear, to stomach, the clear expression of or the taking for granted even very elementary Christian doctrines" [L I, 186]), enveloped in error and incapable of detaching itself "from what they have been taught and brought up to expect" (L II, 31). Hopkins writes in 1885 in a letter to Bridges: "we should explain things, plainly state them, clear them up, explain them; explanation—except personal—is always pure good; without explanation people go on misunderstanding; being once explained they thenceforward understand things; therefore always explain" (L I, 275). And he repeats to Dixon: "my hope is to explain things thoroughly and make the matter . . . as far as I go in it, perfectly intelligible" (L II, 139). Where intelligibility wanes or is missing, the sense does not "explode" and the poem fails: "The final cou-

24. As a poetic principle this hyper-intelligibility also means, of course, a censure on any margin of vagueness and indeterminacy. Hopkins remarks for example about a line by Bridges: "The present line is so vague, it might conceivably mean so many things, it stamps the mind with nothing determinate" (L I, 94).

25. On Hopkins's "double vocation" and its consequences on the poetic plane, see my study *Gerard Manley Hopkins. Il silenzio e la parola* (Marucci 1977).

plet, if I understand it, is a beautiful simile, but it is not explosive" (L II, 55). Or, as he wrote to Dixon: " 'Epigram' on the stage. It seems to me that it might be and ought to be more pointed and explosive" (L II, 62).

We are now able to tackle more closely the problem of the peculiar type of response on the part of the reader that Hopkins's message aims to achieve. As I hinted above, in Hopkins the poetic communication is not exclusively directed at the reader's intellect, but aims to involve his intellectual, emotional, and even physiological whole. As such, it is no arid exposition of concepts or ideas, but conveys a message of faith, thanks to the mediation and support of emotionally effective signals. This recourse to emotional mediation is witnessed in Hopkins's poems by the very frequent apostrophes to the heart, this most central of organs in his private cognitive system, often tacitly opposed to rational knowledge in the terms of the contrast stasis versus motion (ascent) and of a conflict in the interpretation of things.[26] The in-

26. On the central role of the heart as a cognitive instrument, and on the medieval derivation of this concept see Lewis 1964, 159–61. For examples of the functions and of the "hermeneutics" of the *heart* see below, chapter 3, the analyses of "God's Grandeur" and of the "Deutschland." Other significant occurrences can be found, however, in "*Nondum*" ("$_{49}$Speak! whisper to my watching *heart* / $_{50}$One word"), "Rosa Mystica" ("$_{20}$The *heart* guesses easily"; "$_{21}$well the heart knows") and the explicit, very clear lines 4–8 of "The Handsome Heart." In "Peace" the heart is an infallible instrument of revelation of truth ("$_3$I'll not play hypocrite / $_4$To own my heart") while in "To what serves Mortal Beauty?" ("$_{13}$heart, heaven's sweet gift") and above all in the "Heraclitean Fire" (l. 17) it is the heart that brings to light Nature's secret—and otherwise undecipherable—message. "[The Soldier]" in its turn unmistakably specifies the nature and type of knowledge ("confused" and "confusing," not certainly scientific and rigorous) brought about by the heart: "$_3$the héart, / $_4$ . . . gives a guess / $_5$That, hopes that, mákesbelieve . . . / $_6$It fáncies, féigns, déems, déars." The heart is also at the core of the *terrible sonnets:* in "[Carrion Comfort]" it is the heart, in the midst of the tempest, that wrings joy, strength and courage (ll. 11–12); to "To seem . . . " the heart is the organ from which once again (see above the quotations from "*Nondum,*" and, below, from the "Deutschland") words gush (ll. 11–12); in "I wake . . . " it is afflicted and impotent (l. 9); in "Patience . . . " it "$_9$grate[s]" on itself; in "My own heart . . . " it finally becomes the object of the poet's mercy. As for the coupling heart/ascent (absolutely prominent in the "Deutschland"), see "My prayers must meet a brazen heaven" (l. 5), "Hurrahing in Harvest" (ll. 5, 7, 13), "I must hunt down the prize" (l. 2), "The Elopement" (l. 35). See also a sermon entirely devoted to the heart (as the Sacred Heart and man's heart: S, 100–104). For other treatments of the cognitive functions and operations of the heart see Robinson 1978 (50), Motto 1984 (17–22) and Boyle 1961 (73–80).

telligibility of the message and the reader's intellection, therefore, do not necessarily imply a transmission of ideas through the simplicity and clarity of reasoning; they mean the attainment of the reader's total participation—both with his mind and with his senses—in the truth communicated, that is, the acquisition of an "intensified" meaning, which is transmitted by words but can even overcome and skip over them, occasionally detaching itself from logico-grammatical coherence and from syntactic norms, just because its task is to touch the "heart" of the reader's sensibility: in Hopkins, to use his own words, "the meaning shd. be *felt*" (L I, 72), not simply understood.

Rhetorical figures in Hopkins do precisely that: they are emotional rather than rational supports in his peculiar kind of poetic message.[27] We are thus nearing the true nerve center of Hopkins's communication, that semantic sense/non-sense (counter-sense) mechanism at which I hinted above. A strict observance of the Gospel word and a quasi-medieval intransigence—as will be seen much more amply in Part Two—not only admit the solely religious into the sphere of poetry but cause an unbridgeable fracture between faith and the world: the process of semantization is invariably spread apart. What is sense to the world's eyes—eyes that imply, as we have just seen, an erroneous, imperfect, approximate vision—is non-sense and counter-sense to the eyes of faith, and vice versa. The poet's mission is none other than helping the reader to give up the world's eyes and to take up those of faith, or, in other words, to perceive (to "disinter") the deep sense concealed by (and usually antithetical to) the superficial sense. Hopkins writes in a sermon: "To return then to where I began, this life is night, it is a night, it is a dark time. It is so because the truth of things is either dimly seen or not seen at all. . . . Or else things are seen, but not seen well" (S, 39). Hopkins again emphasizes this predominantly visual dimension of intellection when he complains to Dixon that "the world is full of things and events,

27. See, once again, Boyle 1961, 186: "The meters and rhythms, that structure of sound which frames the speech into a poetic object, spring from the heart of Hopkins rather than from his brain." One may add that, at the same time, they are also directed at the heart rather than at the *intellect* of the reader.

phenomena of all sorts, that go without notice, go unwitnessed" (L II, 7), or when he sees the exceptionality and superior genius of certain figures of the past, such as Plato and Wordsworth, in their "having had something happen to them that does not happen to other men, as having *seen something*" (L II, 147; Hopkins's italics)—in their having penetrated, that is, the most unfathomable and profound essence of Nature. And the successful unearthing of the counter-sense is to be gauged by the consciousness the reader has of it, as Hopkins once observed about Dixon's poetry, blaming him for "suggesting" only, in his poetry, "a deeper meaning behind the text without leaving the reader any decisive clue to find it" (L II, 177), the reader's consciousness of meaning being the truly conditioning requirement of every atom of the text. Quickly resuming now the thread of our argument, we will not have any difficulty whatsoever in admitting that Hopkins's type of poetic communication should take on distinctly "miracular" and unscientific characteristics of semantic and emotional confusion, diffusion, and amplification.[28] Hopkins's message faces, in fact, a problem of the credibility of its content, since it transmits, in the perspective of faith, a sense not easily acceptable as such (or even identified with a non-sense or counter-sense) by a mundane and purely rationalistic perspective. Boyle, and partially Bender, Schneider, and Sulloway, have noticed and analyzed this phenomenon:

Hopkins' mind tends towards expression through metaphor rather than through simile. . . . Simile is the expression of the detached mind observing and comparing beings. Metaphor is the expression of the mind thrusting itself into the white-hot center of one being and there fusing a new creation. . . . To a mind which prefers the clarity and order of con-

28. See what Žolkovskij 1969 writes of *amplification* in a cybernetic sense: " 'What is an amplifier? In general terms it is a device receiving something in a small quantity and emitting it unchanged in a great quantity' [quoted from W. Ross Ashby's *An Introduction to Cybernetics*]. . . . In the process of amplification a small quantity of energy, acting as a signal, sets in motion great masses of stored energy which, liberated, produces highly relevant effects. . . . The work of art is shaped with fragments of reality like a complex, multi-phase amplifier acting within the reader's consciousness. It works by short steps arbitrarily determined by the artist, each of which, *once the reader is willing to accept it as true,* acquires a far greater and unconditional importance by means of amplification" (94–95).

cept, simile is the natural expression. To a mind which hungers for the reality of being, even involved as being is in the darkness of unintelligibility, mystery, and confusion, metaphor is the natural expression. . . . Metaphor . . . is the core of [Hopkins's] creative operation. (Boyle 1961, 175, 185)[29]

If for "metaphor" we substitute "figure," Boyle elucidates its function and statute when he affirms its suggestive and antiscientific operation. Metaphor, in fact, produces

the psychological device of the miracle. The predication which it permits is clean and quick but it is not a scientific predication. For scientific predication concludes an act of attention but miraculism initiates one. . . . All other predications reduce reality to the level at which they can be grasped by our abstractive intellects; they reduce the real to the conceptual and are clear. Metaphorical predication reduces the mind to the thick and dark unintelligibility of material being. Metaphor attempts to drag the intellect into the imagination. In order to force the intellect to peer into material being just as it is, *the metaphor states that there is in that material being what is clearly not really there.* (Boyle 1961, 178)

Furthermore, metaphors, allegories, symbols ("the extreme[s] of metaphors"), "reconcile seeming contradictions because their terms can be 'different from' and 'the same as' simultaneously" (ibid., 179). If this is, synthetically, the operation of the "figure," we can accept Boyle's conclusion (despite the absence of any consideration of the destination of this communication, which is not, emphatically, a "contemplation" but an act of vibrating, dynamic participation): "Rhythms and sounds cannot be added to an argument as ornament and produce a living poem. . . . Hopkins' mature imagery is exact, profound, alive, predominantly meta-

29. Boyle however, as I have argued above, does not sufficiently exemplify these aspects in the texts. Bender maintains that rhetoric and above all tropes strengthen the reader's "assent" and make it more "forcible" (Bender 1966, 145), while Schneider emphasizes the "often supralogical" character of Hopkins's communication and its being prevalently addressed to the reader's "sensual imagination" (Schneider 1968, 12). Both Schneider and, above all, Sulloway have finally argued the presence of "miracular" elements in the "Deutschland." For both critics the heroic nun actually *sees* Christ coming to her on the waters (st. 28: see Schneider 1968, 18–19, 22, and Sulloway 1972, 182, 186). For Sulloway (1972) the whole poem hinges on the problem of credibility, presenting dogma "coupled with the power of passionate belief" (195).

phoric, with rhythms and sound which are components as essential as the meanings of word and sentence. The *function* of his imagery is primarily to contribute to the object of contemplation" (187, 190; Boyle's italics).[30] The rhetorical strategy is therefore justified in Hopkins by the necessity of breaking up common sense and the accepted notions of a spiritually "cold" or "lukewarm" and mentally lazy addressee, and thus facilitating the "explosion," not only in his intellect but also in his heart and his senses, of the "improbable" and "incredible" truths of faith. We can, then, with these observations, turn again to the problem of obscurity. Hopkins once criticized a poem by Bridges with these words: "The next quatrain is dark. One of two kinds of clearness one shd. have—either the meaning to be felt without effort as fast as one reads or else, if dark at first reading, when once made out *to explode.* Now this quatrain is not plain at first reading nor, if I am right in my taking of it, did that meaning explode" (L I, 90, Hopkins's italics). The distinction contained in this passage seems to me very important, as it silently bears the confirmation of what I have been hinting at concerning the dosage of perspicuity and obscurity in Hopkins's poetry. Hopkins, in other words, did admit to a certain superficial obscurity in his poems; it was an obscurity, however, that on a closer perusal would have been rent by the explosion of the sense—belated, but precisely because of this more efficacious and penetrating. It is, if anything, curious and in some aspects paradoxical that Bridges, Dixon, and Patmore, despite this deeply felt conviction on Hopkins's part, should have been at pains to hear the "sense-explosions" of their friend's poetry, and that they often should ask him for "cribs" or short prose paraphrases! The responsibility of Hopkins's obscurity falls in equal parts on the one hand on his excessive trust in the gifts of clarity of his poetic idiolect and his overestimating the

30. The functionality of the "figure" according to this principle of contextualization underlined by Boyle has also been appropriately perceived by Ritz: "*Pris séparément,* ces éléments [that is, the rhetorical ones] peuvent rebuter la logique et leur bizarrerie paraître choquante," were it not that "chaque poème assure son unité et interdit que l'esprit s'arrête à ce que l'analyse révèle ensuite d'audacieux et même d'artificiel" (Ritz 1963, 469–70).

receptive capacities of his audience, and on the other hand on the substantially rationalistic critical and aesthetic principles and the limited if not obtuse literary sensibility of many of his critics.[31] One touches here on one of the subtlest and most delicate points of the dynamics of sense and of its paths, as prefigured by an original and ingenious scientist of poetic language such as Hopkins was. Hopkins seems to postulate, besides a direct or at least linguistic semanticity, a kind of translinguistic semanticity, that is (once again in the terms of information theory), a non-logical, contentless information comparable to that of music. This effect is reached thanks primarily to the abundance of "figures." In other words, while at the first hermeneutic (logical) level the information may seem locally to decrease, at the second hermeneutic (emotional) level it is restored, and it is there more powerful and more informative. In this operation part of the meaning tends therefore to be transcoded into the contentless "language of sensibility." It is this type of production of translinguistic sense that I believe Hopkins had in mind when, as we have seen, he recommended frequent rhythmic and declaimed readings of his poems:

Granted that it ["The Wreck of the Deutschland"] needs study and is obscure, for indeed I was not over-desirous that the meaning of all should be quite clear,[32] at least unmistakeable, you might, without the effort that to make it all out would seem to have required, have nevertheless read it so that lines and stanzas should be left in the memory and *superficial impressions deepened,* and have liked some without exhausting all. I am sure I have read and enjoyed pages of poetry that way. Why, *sometimes one enjoys and admires the very lines one cannot understand,* as for instance 'If it were done when 'tis done' sqq., which is all obscure and dis-

31. Patmore writes for example in 1884: "I often find it as hard to follow you as I have found it to follow the darkest parts of Browning" (L III, 353). In general he has no difficulty in admitting to be a slow reader (L III, 352, 354–55).

32. Schneider explains this cryptic statement in terms of the "miracular" and incredible elements of Hopkins's poetry (see above, note 29): "It would not have been proper for him to proclaim a miraculous event explicitly, but there was nothing to prevent his suggesting it as he did, clearly though not quite explicitly" (Schneider 1968, 30–31). See also Sulloway 1972, 182–85.

puted, though how fine it is everyone sees and nobody disputes. And so
of many more passages in Shakspere and others. (L I, 50)

Even more allusive is the conclusion of the following long passage of another letter to Bridges, where Hopkins, answering new
charges of obscurity brought by his friend to "Harry Ploughman," implicitly envisages the necessity to skip over the words
and the syntactic norms linking them, too weak to bear the burden of the thought and of the experience they should communicate. In such an operation of semantic concentration, which exploits and exhausts the resources of language to such an extent
that it paradoxically makes it an instrument useless for communication, part of the sense (the logical, and the rationally and immediately graspable, one) must needs be "sacrificed":

The difficulties are of syntax no doubt. Dividing a compound word by
a clause sandwiched into it was a desperate deed, I feel, and I do not feel
that it was an unquestionable success. But which is the line you do not
understand? I do myself think, I may say, that it would be an immense
advance in notation (so to call it) in writing as the record of speech, to
distinguish the subject, verb, object, and in general to express the construction to the eye; as is done already partly in punctuation by everybody, partly in capitals by the Germans, more fully in accentuation by
the Hebrews. And I daresay it will come. But it would, I think, not do
for me: it seems a confession of unintelligibility. And yet I don't know.
At all events there is a difference. My meaning surely *ought* [Hopkins's
italics] to appear of itself; but in a language like English, and in an age of
it like the present, written words are really matter open and indifferent
to the receiving of different and alternative verse-forms, some of which
the reader cannot possibly be sure are meant unless they are marked for
him. Besides metrical marks are for the performer and such marks are
proper in every art. Though indeed one might say syntactical marks are
for the performer too. But however that reminds me that one thing I am
now resolved on, it is to prefix short prose *arguments* [Hopkins's italics]
to some of my pieces. These too will expose me to carping, but I do not
mind. Epic and drama and ballad and many, most, things should be at
once intelligible; but everything need not and cannot be. Plainly if it is
possible to express a subtle and recondite thought on a subtle and recondite subject in a subtle and recondite way and with great felicity and perfection, in the end, something must be sacrificed, with so trying a task,

in the process, and this may be the being at once, nay perhaps even the being without explanation at all, intelligible. (L I, 265–66)[33]

Bender had probably an inkling of this mechanism when he affirmed suggestively, on the basis of indications by Herbert Read and Ford Madox Ford, that Hopkins deliberately applied technical solutions of a collage or "unearned increment" type, which provide an "added emotional punch" through the juxtaposition of "logically unconnected items" (Bender 1966, 66–70). In such a way, according to Bender, "the juxtaposition of vital word to vital word [establishes] a sort of frictional current of electric life that will extraordinarily galvanize the work or art in which the device is employed" (106). Although, as I have argued above, Bender carries too far the alogical component of Hopkins's poetry, he has acutely brought to light the most acrobatic of its paradoxes, that of obscurity as an "explosive function" of meaning (161–62).[34]

33. Boyle evidently had these last statements in mind when, apropos of "The Windhover," he wrote that Hopkins expresses there what cannot be experienced, what "defies all logical explanations," and is "literally and even metaphorically inexpressible" (Boyle 1961, 102). In "As kingfishers catch fire . . . ," furthermore, "poetry attempts what would seem to exceed the power of human language—to express . . . to reveal and make vivid to human minds . . . not with scientific clarity but with metaphoric obscurity" (104).

34. Hopkins's poetic message can easily be framed, on the basis of the description here given of it and from the highlighting of its salient features, within an Aristotelian matrix, more precisely that of his *Poetics* and *Rhetoric*. There are good reasons to believe that these two books were profoundly and permanently assimilated by Hopkins. *Rhetoric* appears in a list of "Greats Books" (J, 49), and on it his essay "Rhythm and the Other Structural Parts of Rhetoric—Verse" (J, 267–88) is based. This makes it highly probable that it should have been the textbook for the course of rhetoric Hopkins held in 1873–74. Aristotle's *Poetics* is often quoted literally in the letters to Bridges and Dixon (L I, 210, 297 and L II, 140–41). However, considering the sense of proportion and the substantially balanced perspective of Aristotelian rhetoric, much stronger and crucial seem to me Hopkins's points of contact with Longinus—though no mention strangely is ever made of him by Hopkins. The physiological and "explosive" concept of Hopkins's "poetry of inspiration"—in the producer as well as in the receiver—is exactly the same as that of Longinus's "sublime" in poetry and oratory, which he repeatedly and significantly connotes with metaphors and similes of lightnings, hurricanes, storms, catapults, torrents, etc. (1.4; 12.4; 21.2). No one has described and better stressed than Longinus the enchantment, the capacity to seduce and to subjugate, to involve and sympathize, proper to poetry and oratory: "It is our nature to be elevated and exalted by true sublimity. Filled with joy and pride, we come to believe we have created what we have only heard" (7.2). It is a prominent characteristic of Longinus's "sublime," as much as it is of Hopkins's poetics, that

of seeking not so much the exact similarity with things, but "something higher than human" (36.3), and then to render credible, in some cases, the incredible (38.3–4). Hopkins's demand for vividness and immediacy is also among the prerogatives of the "sublime": the orator is not to aim at a factual and objective presentation, but uses expressions which, by means of enthusiasm and passion, "make the speaker see what he is saying and bring it visually before his audience (15.1). To this end Longinus repeatedly maintains the absolute necessity of "figures," which "are natural allies of sublimity and themselves profit wonderfully from the alliance" (17.1); accumulating them the orator "hit[s] the jury in the mind with blow after blow" (20.3). "The right occasions are when emotions come flooding in" and "bring the multiplication of metaphors with them as a necessary accompaniment," the metaphors' nature being that of "sweep[ing] and driv[ing] all these other things along with the surging tide of their movement" (32.1 and 4).

3

❦ AMPLIFICATION IN "GOD'S GRANDEUR" AND "THE WRECK OF THE DEUTSCHLAND"

"God's Grandeur," a sonnet Hopkins wrote a few months after "The Wreck of the Deutschland," between February and March 1877, can now be analyzed for a first verification of what I have been arguing so far concerning the motives and aims of Hopkins's poetic communication.

The first of a number of sonnets devoted to the illustration of nature's beauty and to its overflowing witness to God's presence, "God's Grandeur" belongs to a period of intense and stupefied enthusiasm on Hopkins's discovery of the unhoped-for usefulness of this theme for his newly revived poetic word. It was composed, as I have said, in the wake of the "Deutschland," in a moment in which the "therapeutic" and didactic perspective of art had become again, after a long silence, radiant and promising, and before the breaking up, and total collapsing, of the alibi of a poetry with a high religious content. For this reason it no doubt betrays a more composed and mediated pastoral urgency than the "Deutschland," but as with that poem its didactic nature and drift justify and require, in the poet's perspective, an elaborate rhetorical framing.

I have repeatedly observed in the foregoing pages how reality in general, but more than anything else the religious, tends to manifest itself in Hopkins, owing to the irredeemable conflict of the perspective of the world with that of faith, in terms of antithesis,[1] paradox, oxymoron:

He [God] brings together things thought opposite and incompatible, strict justice and mere mercy, free grace and binding duty. (S, 57)

It is one adorable point of the incredible condescension of the Incarnation (the greatness of which no saint can have ever hoped to realise) that our Lord submitted not only to the pains of life, the fasting, scourging, crucifixion, etc. or the insults, as the mocking, blindfolding, spitting etc, but also to the mean and trivial accidents of humanity. It leads one naturally to rhetorical antithesis to think for instance that after making the world He shd. consent to be taught carpentering, and, being the eternal Reason, to be catechised in the theology of the Rabbins. (L III, 19–20)

You will no doubt understand what I mean by saying that the *sordidness* of things, wh. one is compelled perpetually to feel, is perhaps, taking ἕν ἀνθ'ἑνός [*sic*], the most unmixedly painful thing one knows of; and this is (objectively) intensified and (subjectively) destroyed by Catholicism. (L III, 226–27; Hopkins's italics)

whereas he [Christ] would have wished to succeed by success . . . nevertheless he was doomed to succeed by failure. (L II, 137–38)[2]

Speaking of the semantic operation globally subtending Hopkins's poetic communication, I have already defined it as a *sense/counter-sense* argumentative strategy. Hopkins, in other words, in

1. See, for a comprehensive treatment of antithesis in both theory and poetic practice, Lichtmann 1989, 100–128.

2. For Hopkins's attitude to explain the religious in a way opposite to common sense and to the world's perspective see also S, 100, where Hopkins, speaking of the veneration of the Sacred Heart, writes that "out of the store which Christ left behind him [the Holy Spirit] brings from time to time as need requires some doctrine or some devotion which was indeed known to the Apostles and *is old,* but is unknown or little known at the time and *comes upon the world as new*." The well-known distinction between the "overthought" and the "underthought" (L III, 252) is analogous to that between sense and counter-sense. Elsewhere (L I, 262, for example) the underthought is called "afterthought." For anticipations in the poetry of this search for the authentic sense, see the youthful "Let me be to Thee as the circling bird" ("₁₁other science" versus "₉authentic cadence") and "*Nondum*" (₄₃Oh! till Thou givest that *sense beyond*").

the compositions in which he exploits this technique, generally introduces, as a false start, a *common* and *superficial sense* to be unmasked as a non-sense and to be substituted by a sense counter to the common sense, which, however, is discovered by the author and—proportionally to the efficacy of the poetic word—by the reader, as the *true* and *deep sense*. This substitution on the syntagmatic axis of the sense with the counter-sense (which is nothing but a polarization of a technique well known to the science of argumentation, that of the "dissociation of notions" and in particular of the use of the couple "appearance-reality" and of their inversion)[3] can take place only thanks to that more or less explicit summoning of the *heart* (to whom the discovery of the deep sense is entrusted) and to that deactivation of reason (capable of perceiving only the superficial sense) of which I spoke in the foregoing chapter. That is why the "demonstration" of the deep sense necessitates a series of supplementary "levers" capable of breaking up and conquering the reader's credibility, or, in other words, estranging and disautomatizing shock tactics which, more effectively than subtle or academic disquisitions, can assist or obtain singlehandedly the "victory" of the deep sense. This strategy, as we shall see, has undoubtedly the most prolonged and memorable application in the "Deutschland," though it appears hardly less prominent and distinctive in the sonnets immediately following it, of which "God's Grandeur" is the ideal progenitor. The thesis of "God's Grandeur" is in fact the assertion of nature's essence as a dazzling revelation of God as against its

3. See in Perelman-Tyteca 1971 the whole chapter IV of Part Three, "The Dissociation of Concepts" (411–59), and in particular the paragraph "The 'Appearance-Reality' Pair" (415–19). The latter is "the prototype of all conceptual dissociations because of its widespread use and its basic importance in philosophy" (415). The reversal of such a pair is explicitly mentioned (415). In this argumentative frame both "God's Grandeur" and, above all, the "Deutschland" participate. Furthermore, if, on the one hand, religious experience in Hopkins is connoted through oxymoron and paradox, on the other, his poetry is as a whole eminently dissociative: "Paradoxical expressions always call for an effort at dissociation. Every time an adjective or verb which seems incompatible is attached to a noun (learned ignorance, happy misfortune, bitter joy, thinking the unthinkable, expressing the inexpressible, the conditions of unconditional surrender), only a dissociation makes it possible to understand the expression" (443).

seeming extinction and as against, therefore, God's seeming absence. The sonnet, however, constitutes a slight complication of the sense/counter-sense paradigm,[4] as it puts immediately at the outset and then at the close (the first quatrain and the two tercets) the deep sense to be brought to light, while encapsulating in the second quatrain the superficial sense to be unmasked as a counter-sense. This oppositional spatialization of sense (surface versus depth) is mimetically reflected by the sonnet when the "$_{10}$freshness *deep down* things" (depth) is contrasted to the "$_7$*soil* . . . / . . .$_8$ bare" (surface). The argumentation develops therefore as follows: extinction (superficial sense: "nature is . . . spent," deducible from line 9) becomes ignition and explosion (deep sense: "$_1$The world is *charged*"; "$_2$It will *flame out*"); the exhausted, dirty, and sterile world (superficial sense: "$_6$seared . . . bleared, smeared with toil"; "$_8$bare") becomes fresh, clean, and fertile (deep sense: "$_{10}$dearest freshness"); so that the descending sunset engulfing everything in its darkness ("$_{11}$last lights off the black West") is fantastically transfigured into a bright dawn, with the supplementary oppositions, reinforced by the sound-texture, "$_{11}$black" / "$_{12}$brown," "$_{11}$went" / "$_{12}$springs" and "$_{11}$West" / "$_{12}$eastward."

Such a "thesis" is obviously undemonstrable and logically indefensible. A paradoxical truth is what the reader—presumably skeptical and anchored to a materialistic and immanentistic perspective, and furthermore torpid and insensitive, like the one whose foot "$_8$can[not] . . . *feel*, being shod"[5]—is asked to accept. And it is therefore a truth whose mystery only a warm and vibrating faith can perceive. For this reason the poetic message necessitates and even demands within each level—under pain of failing to persuade the reader, which would amount to a failure

4. As Boyle 1961 notes, "The darkness . . . *apparently* has mastered the light. . . . But the sun is only *apparently* gone. . . . There is first the small reflection of God's infinite grandeur, then a huge and growing evil and destruction, and finally a far huger and burgeoning good and rebirth" (38, 41). Boyle devotes to the sonnet the whole chapter II of his book, carrying out an analysis rich in useful and pertinent observations on the scriptural and theological links and associations of its images.

5. For the biblical allusion of this image (Exod. 3:5) see Cotter 1972, 171.

of the entire poetic operation—a range of intensifying and estranging strategies as against the merely straightforward sense.
Here as elsewhere, even "in advance" of the rhetorical organization of the poem, oversemantization is set in motion and established by rhythm, that is, by means of that voiced, declaimed
reading Hopkins often recommended. Obviously, this is something we cannot here submit to direct verification, as it pertains
more properly to the sphere of the *pronuntiatio*. Rhythm, particularly sprung rhythm, is among the principal and primary instruments of semantic and emotional intensification: not just a gratuitous accessory of poetry[6] but an indispensable element for the
transmission of that supplementary or paradoxical sense that
Hopkins's poetry aims to communicate.[7] Rhythm in Hopkins
collaborates with and supports the denotative meaning, or more
often creates subterranean connotative countercurrents. In a passage in his jottings on rhetoric (J, 274) we find the sketch of an a
priori rhythmic typology and suggestions of precise correspondences between rhythm and sense or nuances of sense: iambics
for excited actions, dactyls for narrations, spondees for solemn
moments, anapaests for expressions of gravity or rapid movements, etc. Rhythm accompanies or precedes, like a sensitive
thermometer, the progress of sense and the development of the
argumentative thread: "You will see that as the feeling rises the
rhythm becomes freer and more sprung" (L I, 212); rhythm is,
more explicitly, a "calculated effect which tells in the general success" (L I, 45)—a pivotal element of the rhetorical planning of the
poetic composition:

Why do I employ sprung rhythm at all? Because it is the nearest to the
rhythm of prose, that is the native and natural rhythm of speech, the least
forced, *the most rhetorical and emphatic of all possible rhythms*, combining,
as it seems to me, opposite and, one wd. have thought, incompatible
excellences, markedness of rhythm—that is rhythm's self—and natural-

6. "You will allow there must always be a reason and a call for the reversed
rhythm" (L I, 37).
7. See Ong 1949 for useful elaborations on Hopkins's "sense-stress rhythm."

ness of expression. . . . My verse is less to be read than heard, as I have told you before; *it is oratorical, that is the rhythm is so.* (L I, 46)

"God's Grandeur" is not indeed among the most rhythmically audacious and "queerest" sonnets Hopkins wrote. He himself defined its rhythm simply as "standard counterpointed"; sending it to his mother, he presented it as "not so very queer, but [with] a few metrical effects" (L III, 144). Nevertheless, "counterpoint" (also defined as "mounted rhythm," that is to say, superimposed rhythm), generating as it does a scansion alternative to common rhythm, creates a secondary and disautomatizing effect, capable of taking the reader unawares: "The choruses of *Samson Agonistes* are in my judgment counterpointed throughout; that is, each line (or nearly so) has two different coexisting scansions. But when you reach that point the secondary or 'mounted rhythm', which is necessarily a sprung rhythm, overpowers the original or conventional one and then this becomes superfluous and may be got rid of" (L II, 15). While, therefore, the first rhythmic system, predetermined and expected, institutes a sort of equal rhythmic and semantic weight for all its lexemes, the second, unexpected system establishes, within the first, differences and infractions which not only are of a rhythmical nature but also perform a considerable function of semantic emphasis and support.[8] This is precisely what happens in "God's Grandeur," where within a homoge-

---

8. For a thorough investigation of the semantic functions of rhythm (equivalence and differentiation) see Lotman 1977, chapter 5, "Structural Principles of the Text" (78–93), and the sub-chapter "Rhythmic Repetitions" (112–19). See in particular, as relevant here, the following observations: "In those cases where the possibility of rhythmic 'figures' arises, against the background of a metrical constant, rhythmic division may fulfil a dual function: the assimilation of semantically dissimilar segments of the text (division into equivalent parts), and the dissimilation of these segments (division into rhythmic variants). The possibility of resorting to various rhythmical subsystems within the limits of one metrical system and the varying probability that any one of them will be used, create the possibility of supplementary orderings which in concrete textual constructions are semantized in a way or another. As a result of the multiplicity and mutual intersection of these orderings, that which is regular and predictable on one level represents the violation of regularity and the lowering of predictability on another level. So on the rhythmic level too, a kind of 'play' of orderings arises, thus creating the possibility of high semantic saturation" (156–57).

neous iambic structure[9] the counterpointed inversions and the other rhythmic "figures" put into relief and bring to the fore particular lexemes or syntagmas that the reader—if only for the surprise and the embarrassment he feels in scanning the lines—is compelled not to let pass up unnoticed, but on the contrary to oversemanticize. Common and counterpointed rhythm appear therefore involved in the same oppositional relation existing between superficial and deep sense, or, to be more precise, appear to be their functions. We find a clear example of such a strategy in the rhythmic structure of the opening line, where a regular iambic beginning is followed by an abrupt trochaic-dactylic inversion, so that the stress of "$_1$grandeur" does not fall on the second syllable but on the first, thus giving prominence to the word "$_1$God" in the very moment in which the sonnet pronounces its own eponymous words.[10] This happens in the sonnet not only

9. My estimation of stress distribution is the following:

$_1$The wórld is chárged wíth the grándeur of Gód. / $_2$Ít will fláme out, like shíning from shóok fóil; / $_3$It gáthers to a gréatness, líke the óoze of óil / $_4$Crúshed. Whý do mén then nów not réck his ród? / $_5$Génerátions have tród, have tród, have tród; / $_6$And áll is séared with tráde; bléared, sméared with toíl; / $_7$And wéars man's smúdge, and sháres man's sméll: the sóil / $_8$Is báre now, nor can fóot féel, béing shód. $_9$And, for all thís, náture is néver spént; / $_{10}$There líves the déarest fréshness déep dówn thíngs; / $_{11}$And thóugh the lást lights off the bláck Wést wént / $_{12}$Oh, mórning, at the brówn brínk éastward, spríngs— / $_{13}$Because the Hóly Ghóst óver the bént / $_{14}$Wórld bróods with wárm bréast and with ah! bríght wíngs.

Cf. the reproduction of the autograph in L III, between pages 144 and 145, and MacKenzie's useful remarks on Hopkins's metrical signs in P III, lv–lvii. See also, for a thorough, exhaustive investigation of the whole sonnet in a rhythmical perspective, Schneider 1968, 95, and A. L. Johnson 1991.

10. "In various poems, Hopkins manages to throw an important word into focus by suggesting some detachment from its sentence relations" (Milroy 1978, 218). See also what Boyle 1961 writes: "The rhythm of the Hopkins sonnet is designed to build up to the great smooth flow of the end, expressive of the bursting of the sun over the horizon and the gradual wide-spreading of its rays. The phrases of the octet are short; pauses abound. In the sestet *the rhythm picks up speed* to the dash after 'springs,' which I think is expressive of the moment of apparent pause before the rim of the sun bursts over the horizon. And the last two lines, which flow on without pause, build and lengthen in the vowels and alliteration of 'world broods,' 'warm breast,' 'bright wings,' with the last greatly lengthened by being alliteratively reversed and by the long 'ah!' which expresses not only the poet's emotion but the physical act of the spreading rays" (42).

with words that have a high semantic weight but also frequently with those placed at the opening or at the close of the line (besides "₁God" cf. "₄Crushed," "₆bleared," "₆toil," "₁₄wings"), while the outriding feet (feet in which there may be a superabundance of weak syllables that do not count in the scansion: "₃to a great-ness," "₁₄ and with ah! bright") mime the anxious and dizzy race toward the yearned-for divine goal. But if the world "₁is charged with the grandeur of God," such an explosion is set off and again magnified by the "explosion" of sounds, which are instrumental in the creation of a kind of tensional and emotional platform on which the sense of the overwhelming greatness of God may more easily take root. Hence the prevalence in the first four lines of the sonnet of plosives such as [tʃ], [ʃ], [gr], [k], [kr] that phono-symbolically mime the semantics of the words they initiate or close, or again the frequency of the fricatives in "₂flame," "₂from," and "₂foil," or the hammering repetition of [br] in lines 12–14. And it is in this atmosphere of high emotional tension, skillfully prepared by rhythm and sound, that—if it is legitimate to separate two processes that in the reader's reception occur si-multaneously—the "explosion" of sense, as performed by the rhetorical organization of language at the level of the *elocutio,* takes place. Of the characteristics of "judicial speech," "God's Grandeur" shares the necessity of piercing the probable incredu-lity of the reader-listener with a series of discursive variations. These variations stem from a demand for "ornate" not just with "aesthetic" ends but with an estranging function.[11] I will not here insist on an aspect that is directly relevant in the "Deutschland" and that as such will presently be investigated; I will show only how certain linguistic and stylistic strategies, in the verbal and syntactic *dispositio* and in the "figures of speech" and "of thought"

11. The contextualizing of Hopkins's "ornate" prevents the formulation of any verdict of *audacia* or *mala affectatio,* that is, of any rhetorical exaggeration or gratu-itousness. Cf. the following, crystalline observation on paradox contained in a letter to Patmore: "The use of a paradox is to *awake the hearer's attention;* then, when it has served that end, if, as mostly happens, it is not only unexpected but properly speaking untrue, it can be, expressly or silently, waived or dropped. . . . I cannot follow you in your passion for paradox: more than a little of it tortures . . . paradox persisted in is not the plain truth and ought not to satisfy a reader" (L III, 388–89).

employed, collaborate in conveying the sense in its various phases and nuances. The demonstrative and argumentative character never abates in this sonnet, as can be seen in the vigorous succession of hypotaxis to parataxis, of the secondary to the principal clauses, of the exclamative and the interrogative to the assertive clauses. It is no chance that *and* occurs no fewer than six times in the sonnet, four of them in anaphoric position, not to mention the occurrences of the argumentative conjunctions "$_4$Why," "$_8$nor," "$_9$for," "$_{11}$though," and "$_{13}$Because" and the tendential obedience of the periods to the "law of growing members" $[(1+3+1+)+4+6]$,[12] which gives the sonnet, especially in the sestet, a typical seventeenth-century flavor of "impassioned dialectic." All the single figures can be traced to *amplificatio* with an estranging function. For example, purely semantic and at the same time estranging amplifications are the two similes of lines 2 and 4 and the explosion metaphor of line 1, which are not employed as a precious addition of an ornamental character but perform a strategic action of support, reinforcement, and surprise. They collaborate in making the sense they bear "explode" in the reader with a violence that may even upset logical distinctions and phenomenological correctness, since what constitutes the object of communication is not a logical sense but a truth of faith. This justifies the noted impropriety of "$_2$foil" and of "$_3$oil," in whose place one would have expected *olive*. Yet this synecdoche is also interpretable as a most efficacious *hysteron proteron* and therefore justifiable as a demand for immediacy, "$_3$oil" anticipating the effect of the pressing of olives. In the field of the *verba propria* and *impropria,* we have the Gallicism "$_1$grandeur," which Hopkins employs—with the same expedient used in "The Windhover"—to connote God's kingliness and majesty, as opposed to the simple and hierarchically inferior "$_3$greatness," a *verbum humile.* The other figures also carry out the same function of emotional *amplificatio* of sense. The anastrophe "$_3$oil / $_4$Crushed," for example, on the one hand oversemanticizes the attribution

12. Lausberg 1982, 30 and *passim.* On the hypotactic construction ("argumentative . . . par excellence" [158]) and the argumentative conjunctions, see Perelman-Tyteca 1971, 156–63.

crushed with an enjambment; on the other hand it provides a chiasmus with "$_2$shook foil" in the otherwise syntactically and coordinated isocolon of lines 2, 3, and 4. The isosyntactic and circular framing ("$_1$The *world* is charged *with* the grándeur of God" ~ "$_{13}$the Holy Ghost óver the bent / $_{14}$*World* broods *with* warm breast and with ah! bright wings")[13] and the frequent, phonologically reinforced isocolons (parallelisms) within the sonnet, until the repetition of line 5, create a hammering effect apt to engrave the concepts communicated on the reader's sensibility. The maximum production of emotional sense occurs in lines 5-7, where we have, in a complex but perfect parallelistic figure, a threefold repetition ("$_5$have trod, have trod, have trod"), which flows into the phonologically reinforced *enumeratio* "$_6$seared with trade; bleared, smeared with toil" and closes in the couple "$_7$wears man's smudge and shares man's smell." As Lotman has observed,[14] repetition in poetry is never a mere reduplication of a concept but the source of an emotional enrichment of it. Here the threefold repetition and the following parallellisms function as an emotional climax, simulating the steady decline of humanity and strengthening the feeling of expectation for the "vision" of faith, which indeed in the sestet transcends the sunset with the first light of dawn.

A rhetorical analysis of "The Wreck of the Deutschland" will further verify our hypotheses and confirm what has been observed in "God's Grandeur." The "Deutschland," besides being the pivot of Hopkins's whole poetic output, is of course too semiotically rich and concentrated for anyone to presume to "exhaust" it with sectorial and partial decodings, let alone with the one (although in-depth with reference to the chosen objective) I shall attempt in this chapter. Nevertheless, while I defer to Part Two of this work the investigation of further aspects that have not been sufficiently studied, a rigorous and systematic "rhetorical" interpretation of the poem seems to me, in the exegetic flood with which it has been inundated—Downes's and Pick's Ignatian

13. "The world reflecting the sun opened the poem. The sun returns to close the poem" (Boyle 1961, 37).

14. See Lotman 1977, the sub-chapter "Repetition and Meaning," 119–36.

reading, Heuser's and Boyle's theological reading, Bender's Pindaric reading, Sulloway's apocalyptic reading, Cotter's Gnostic reading, Sprinker's metalinguistic reading and finally Ong's comparatistic and Miltonic reading—one of the few not yet, or not polemically, carried out.

As is well known, the "Deutschland" is the poem with which in 1875 Hopkins broke the seven-year long poetic silence he initiated on his entrance into the Society of Jesus (1868) with the graphic "burning" of all his poetry written until then. If we except a few pieces of a mainly religious or pious character (indeed, composed only because requested by his superiors), his resolution to be "silent" was kept; yet the urgency of the poetic vocation, which could not so easily be extinguished, found diversion, during those seven long years, in the assiduous study of the technique of verse, ancient literatures, Aristotelian rhetoric (of which, in the years 1873–74, he was also a teacher), and, during the period he spent at St. Beuno's (1874–77), ancient Welsh poetry. It is easy then to guess how potentially great—though probably untrained—were his technical, formal and metrical capacities when he set out to write the "Deutschland," especially if we think of the already-prodigious skill of the young Hopkins. A perfect master of rhetorical instruments and rhythm and, thanks to the fresh study of Welsh *cynghanedd*,[15] sound-artifices, Hopkins could draw on this technical and formal wealth in the long poem expressly requested of him by his superiors to commemorate the wreck of the *Deutschland*, a German ship foundered a few miles distant from the Kentish coast in December 1875 during a tempestuous night in which, because of the delay of the rescuers, the majority of passengers were drowned, among them five Catholic nuns exiled from their country.

The argumentative nucleus of the "Deutschland" appears of a nature even more paradoxical than that of "God's Grandeur." What Hopkins now attempts to "prove" is something that is, in the eyes of the materialistic or faithless world or in those of the

15. An in-depth study of the *cynghanedd* influences in Hopkins's poetry is made by Gardner 1949, II, 144–58.

believers themselves—shaken and upset by an event to which the contemporary press gave great prominence[16]—even more destitute of sense, or more contrary to sense, than the "freshness deep down things" of "God's Grandeur." The poem attempts to prove, in other words, an oxymoron, that the *tempest* is *fair weather,* that its *inclemency* is *fruitful,* that the *ruin* of the harvest is its *sowing.* It is, beyond metaphor or allegory, the central and original paradox of Christian faith: that life is death and death is life, that God is a mysterious and unfathomable synthesis of mercy and seeming wickedness.[17] And if this crucial paradox of Christian faith justly demands the thirty–five stanzas of Hopkins's longest poem—inducing him momentarily to postpone the adoption of the "measure" that will prove ideal for its "corollaries," the sonnet—one can easily imagine the quality and quantity of the emotional and intellectual supports indispensable to convey a message so irremediably contrary to common sense and to favor the total acceptance of the reader. What I set out to prove is that the frequently blamed richness of figures, the even inflationary rhetoric of the poem, perform the precious and irreplaceable function of conveying and intensifying the deep sense, breaking a path into the sclerotized sensibility of the reader and providing the emotional and intellectual stimuli necessary to appropriate that sense.

If one surveys the global structure of the poem as a persuasive message it is immediately possible to point out how the "Deutschland" follows, or in any case comes close to, the canonical typology of judicial discourse. The poem shares the three main characteristics of judicial discourse as they have been extensively described by Perelman-Tyteca (1971) ("The Framework of Argumentation," 11–62), and, more concisely, by Lausberg (1982, 15–17):

16. Some significant excerpts are reproduced in L III, Appendix, 439–43.
17. Such a paradox stems of course from Christ's teaching in the Gospel. Let it suffice to quote Matt. 5: 1–12 (from the Sermon on the Mount); 10: 39 ("He that findeth his life shall lose it: and he that loseth his life for my sake shall find it"); 18: 4 ("Whosoever therefore shall humble himself as this little child, the same is greatest in the kingdom of heaven"); 19: 30 ("But many *that are* first shall be last; and the last *shall be* first"). The operations of Divine Providence and its seeming "ambiguity" also form the object of a sermon (S, 89–93).

1. persuasive effect on the addressee;
2. intention to modify the given situation;
3. presupposition of a judge (or referee) of the situation.

As is well known, any judicial discourse is a speech pronounced with the precise aim of influencing (and thus modifying) the opinion of the judge. If so, the "Deutschland" can be seen as a judicial speech that disturbs even the sense of truth of the judge, that is to say, a speech with a very feeble rate of credibility; in our case the judge is to be identified with Hopkins's addressee, that is, with a prejudiced, religiously disbelieving or lukewarm public (cf. the Gospel's "little faith") whose incredulity must become faith. The situation to be modified—that is, according to our previous classification, the superficial sense—is, in its archisemic form, DEATH or CHANCE (DESTINY), while the modification of the situation—that is, the discovery of the deep sense—consists in the process DEATH (CHANCE, DESTINY)→ LIFE (GOD). With its micro-occurrences, such a generative paradox gradually pervades the whole poem: "The intellectual paradox does not present itself merely as *materia,* but also as an estranging phenomenon or as a figure of thought and word traceable in the *inventio.* The paradoxical phenomena of the elaboration are summed up in the *acutum dicendi genus.* To it belong, for instance, irony, emphasis, litotes, hyperbole, some periphrases, oxymoron, the semantically complicated zeugma, chiasmus and such-like phenomena of the *ordo artificialis*" (Lausberg 1982, 23).

Even a cursory analysis of the poem is sufficient to discover the existence of certain partitions and principles of organization considerably similar to those of judicial rhetoric. We can for example detect a *tractatio* (ibid., 24–26) that can be canonically subdivided into its five phases:

1. *Inventio.* Being the "summoning of the ideas . . . serving as emotional and intellectual instruments to achieve the success of the faction with the judge's persuasion" (ibid., 24), it is constituted in our poem by the use of the heroic and exemplary behavior of the nun as religiously persuasive.

2. *Dispositio,* in its turn consisting of

a. *exordium*, or proem, aiming to "direct the judge's attention, his favorite attitude and his benevolence toward the cause of the party represented in the speech" (ibid., 25). In our case the proem may be identified with Part The First of the poem, of which it establishes the isotopy and the nature of reflection-meditation of faith, paving the way to the following

b. *propositio*, that is, the initial communication of the thesis to be demonstrated: the wreck (death) is a sign of God and a source of life. Cf. stanza 9: "₆Thou art lightning and love, I found it, a winter and warm; / ₇Father and fondler of heart thou hast wrung: / ₈Hast thy dark descending and most art merciful then";

c. *argumentatio*, that is, the series of "ethic" and "pathetic" proofs (see below), which is followed by the *peroratio* and by the *conclusio* (sts. 30–35), with the acknowledging of the coincidence of the latter with the *propositio:* "₇Kínd, but róyally reclaíming his ówn; / ₈A releaséd shówer, let flásh to the shíre, not a líghtning of fíre hard húrled" (st. 34).

The remaining three parts of judicial speech, the *elocutio*, the *memoria*, and the *pronuntiatio*, obviously pertain to any poetic text that is conceived, written, read, or declaimed, and as such do not characterize the "Deutschland" in a specific way. Once again, however, it must be noted that the *pronuntiatio* is in no way incidental or secondary compared with the *elocutio* (that is, the creation of the so-called "figures"). Hopkins significantly never tired of repeating that this poem should be declaimed to be fully understood; hence I will hereafter imply the identification of reader and hearer.

I think I have already sufficiently proved, by means of epistolary statements and remarks, the full awareness of a rhetorical planning of the poetic discourse in Hopkins—his precise and unfailing willingness never to lose sight of his reader: it is indeed an objective in which he founds and from which he derives the *raison d'être* of his poetry. It is, however, necessary to recall the concepts of *credibility* and of *shock*, previously mentioned, to point out how they are absolutely crucial in the foundation of the communicative model governing the poem. This will enable us, at the same time, to move a step further in the sounding of its range of objectives and of its rhetorical plan.

Hopkins sets out, in the "Deutschland," to rouse in the reader or hearer a fuller and firmer faith (in an unbelieving audience, simply faith as such) and the certainty that even misfortunes, and the greatest of misfortunes—death—are decreed by God, and ultimately though inscrutably decreed for the good and salvation of man. Yet such a proposed strengthening of faith is not to be obtained by means of a widening of the theological notions and therefore, solely and immediately, through a *mental process,* but through a *sense process,* that is, by stimulating and upsetting sensibility in such a way as to favor the reader's integral acceptance of the mystery of faith. The essence of faith as the acceptance of an incredible mystery, through prevalently emotional proofs rather than through proper demonstrations,[18] is illustrated in a long passage of a letter to Bridges that here and there echoes words and phrases of the poem. Hopkins implicitly advocates the use of "shocking" and traumatizing figures.

A Catholic by mystery means *an incomprehensible certainty:* without certainty, without formulation there is no interest . . . the clearer the formulation the greater the interest. At bottom the source of interest is the same in both cases, in your mind and in ours; it is the *unknown, the reserve of truth beyond what the mind reaches and still feels to be behind.* But the interest a Catholic feels is, if I may say so, of a far finer kind than yours. Yours turns out to be a curiosity only; curiosity satisfied, the trick found out (to be a little profane), the answer heard, it vanishes at once. But you know there are some solutions to, say, chess problems so beautifully ingenious, some resolutions of suspensions so lovely in music that even the feeling of interest is keenest when they are known and over, and for some time survives the discovery. *How must it then be when the very answer is the most tantalising statement of the problem and the truth you are to rest in the*

18. Lichtmann (1989, 131) remarks that "Hopkins meant his poetry to be read . . . not only with the 'transitional energy' of reasoning, deliberation, and criticism, but above all with the mind's 'abiding energy,' that is, with contemplation." In the light of what I have being arguing above in chapter 2 about Hopkins's "perlocutory impetus" and the "paroxistic" assent he aimed to produce, *contemplation* hardly appears Hopkins's objective.

most pointed putting of the difficulty! For if the Trinity, as Francis Newman[19] *somewhere says, is to be explained by grammar and by tropes, why then he could furnish explanations for himself; but then where wd. be the mystery? the true mystery, the incomprehensible one. At that pass one should point blank believe or disbelieve: he disbelieved; his brother, at the same pass, believed.* There are three persons, each God and each the same, the one, the only God: to some people this is a "dogma" . . . to others it is news of their dearest friend or friends, leaving them all their lives balancing whether they have three heavenly friends or one—not that they have any doubt on the subject, but that their knowledge leaves their minds swinging; poised, but on the quiver. And this might be the ecstasy of interest, one would think. So too of the Incarnation, a mystery less incomprehensible, it is true: to you it comes to: Christ is in some sense God, in some sense he is not God—and your interest is in the uncertainty; to the Catholic it is: *Christ is in every sense God and in every sense man, and the interest is in the locked and inseparable combination,*[20] *or rather it is in the person in whom the combination has its place.* Therefore we speak of the events of Christ's life as the mystery of the Nativity, the mystery of the Crucifixion and so on of a host; the mystery being always the same, *that the child in the manger is God, the culprit on the gallows God,* and so on. *Otherwise birth and death are not mysteries,* nor is it any great mystery that a just man should be crucified, but that God should fascinates—with the interest of awe, of pity, of shame, of every harrowing feeling. (L I, 187–88)

Hopkins's purpose—his "will to persuade"—is to fire successful sparks against the hearer's sensibility and interiority, rather than to present a theoretical and scientific contribution (if that were possible) on the mystery of faith. In the three persons of the "Deutschland" who share the same sudden "flash" of insight (the poet, the nun, and, in the pious wish of the poet, the shipwrecked), that flash occurs as a clash and a "$_7$touch" (st. 1), as a sharp and "$_4$smart" (st. 19) "$_8$préssure" (st. 4) on the sense organs, in such a way as to provoke a new and more intense awareness of faith.[21] In the rhetorical plan of the poem the analogous "flash" in the reader—although he is never directly apostrophized—ought

19. Cardinal Newman's brother, as the continuation of the letter clarifies.
20. The "interest" is in the oxymoron "human God" or "divine man."
21. Let us recall the terms with which Hopkins connotes, in his youthful theory of styles, the "language of inspiration" (L III, 215–23; and see above, chapter 2).

to take place as a sort of imitation or "infection."[22] The poet, in stanza 1, is for example "₇touch[ed] . . . afresh" by the metaphorical tempest with which God is made manifest, and "₈feel[s]" his "₈finger and find[s]" him. This touch wrings from his "₃tongue" in stanza 2 a clear and full "₁yes" and makes it "₃confess" the terrible majesty of God. The same spark and the same verbal eruption of assent occur in the poet at the mention of the heroic rising against the tempest of the dauntless nun, in whom an analogous "eruption" of the word of faith ("₈a virginal tongue told," st. 17) is about to occur:

18.1   Ah, *touched* in your bower of bone,
2   Are you! turned, for an exquisite *smart,*
3   Have you! *make words break* from me here all alone,
4   Do you!—mother of being in me, heart.

The assent to faith, and the intensified and strengthened awareness of it, become utterance of the Word, that is, of Christ, the only and true founding word of history:

29.5   *Wording* it how but by him that present and past,
6   Heaven and earth are *word* of, *worded* by?—

30.7   But here was heart-throe, birth of a brain,
8   *Word,* that heard and kept thee and uttered thee outright.

If the "touch" of Providence is much softer and more caressing, so that it resembles the tickling of a feather (st. 31, "₆Finger of a tender of, O of a feathery delicacy," an image that refers back to st. 12, where the shipwrecked are temporarily sighted "₅O Father, not under thy *feathers*"), God's touch remains something rough and violent: "₈a pressure" (st. 4), a "₅Stroke and a stress" (st. 6), a "₆shock" (st. 14 and again st. 29, l. 3). The receivers, the "victims," of these touches, clashes, pressures, blows, etc., are evidently, as already said, the sense organs rather than the intel-

22. What we have here is an argument "by resort to the particular case" (Perelman-Tyteca 1971, 350–71), a case that can serve several purposes: "As an example, it makes generalization possible; as an illustration, it provides support for an already established regularity; *as a model, it encourages imitation*" (350). In the nun's heroic behavior one can see all the three uses. Also strictly pertinent to the poem is the remark that illustration strengthens the "adherence to a known and accepted rule, by providing particular instances which clarify the general statement" (357).

lect. I hinted above at the heart's central role in Hopkins's cognitive system: the heart is mentioned or apostrophized no less than eighteen times in the "Deutschland," and its most significant appearances include its "fainting" before God's terribleness (st. 2, l. 6), its "resurrection" thanks to his love (st. 3, l. 5),[23] its becoming inundated by joy and its bursting into tears (st. 6, "₆flushed" and "₆melt"), its "intellection" (the only organ to do so, "₈only the heart," st. 7) of the mystery of Christ (sts. 7 and 8), the already-seen commotion of stanza 18 and finally, most important, its immediate appropriation and transmission of Truth: "₁thére was a héart right!" (st. 29); "₅unteachably after evil, but uttering truth" (st. 18). As to the senses, it is no surprise that the visual character of the Pauline flash of intuition should be emphasized: "shé that wéather *sees* óne thing, óne" (st. 19, l. 5); "There was single *eye!*" (st. 29, l. 2); "in thý *síght* / Storm flákes were scróll-leaved flówers" (st. 21, ll. 7–8).

If what I have said really applies to the poem—if the transmission of the truths of faith (and truths bordering on what is contrary to sense) programmatically and prevalently relies on the audience's sensibility—there will be no difficulty in admitting the extensive employment of the wide-ranging rhetorical strategy here active, or in seeing as indispensable and perfectly motivated, at each level of the poetic language, the recourse to a series of "distortions" and "deviations" from the stylistic norm.[24] In the terms of classical rhetoric, therefore, the persuasive purpose founding and inspiriting the "Deutschland" acts, at least at the first stage, on the ground of the *movere* rather than the *docere* or the *probare,* that is, it uses *emotional* means rather than an *intel-*

23. Contrast the pre-"Deutschland" Hopkins: "₅I cannot buoy my heart above; / ₆Above I cannot entrance win" ("My prayers must meet a brazen heaven").

24. See the following illuminating observation by Hopkins himself, absolutely prophetic of the structuralist theory of verse: "An emphasis of structure stronger than the common construction of sentences gives asks for *an emphasis of expression stronger than that of common speech or writing,* and that for an emphasis of thought stronger than that of common thought. . . . [In the diction of prose] the great abundance of metaphor or antithesis is displeasing *because it is not called for* by, and interferes with, the continuousness of its flow" (J, 85). For "structure," as is clear from the context, Hopkins means "the artificial part of poetry" (J, 84), that is, meter, rhythm, the syntactic parallelisms, etc.

lectual type of influence, and, within the *movere,* of the most violent degrees (*pathos*) as opposed to the moderate ones (*ethos*).[25] If
on the one hand this leads to the a priori exclusion of demonstrative strategies and processes of a syllogistic or enthymematic
type, on the other it requires the adoption of an estranging semantics. Owing to the thin credibility of its theses, this semantics
will need to employ a great number of preventive measures, *pre*-
semantic and so to speak *pro*-semantic: those operations at the
level of the form of expression which, even before the form of
content comes into play, contribute to give it the desired orientation.[26] Sound and rhythm are predictably, in the "Deutschland,"
among the very first instruments endowed with such a propaedeutic and auxiliary function. They awaken in the hearer, and
correctly point him to, the truths of faith. Even more than in
"God's Grandeur" (in proportion to the greater freshness of the
"discovery") sprung rhythm and sound pave the way to sense,
accompanying and facilitating its penetration. The sound-texture, in particular, creates and keeps, thanks to its coagulations in
frequent iterative figures, the high articulatory tension and constant auditive concentration necessary for the non-dispersion
and, above all, the augmented penetrative capacity of the purely
semantic enunciation.[27] The alliterative couple is the prevailing

25. Lausberg 1982, 34–35, and Barthes 1970, 211–13. The distinction between
pathos and *ethos* seems to me reflected or at least suggested by that made by Hopkins between diatonism and chromatism. As will be remembered (see above,
chapter 1 note 21), diatonic is the expression that avails itself of parallelistic processes of an "abrupt" type, while chromatic is the expression availing itself of parallelistic processes of a gradual type.

26. "Effective presentation that impresses itself on the hearers' consciousness
is essential not only in all argumentation aiming at immediate action, *but also in
that which aspires to give the mind a certain orientation,* to make certain schemes of
interpretation prevail, to insert the elements of agreement into a framework that
will give them significance and confer upon them the rank they deserve" (Perelman-Tyteca 1971, 142). Among the "forms of expression" contributing to this
"presentation," Perelman-Tyteca mention "harmony," "rhythm," and "other
purely formal qualities" (ibid.).

27. It is a phenomenon Hopkins notices, though with different manifestations,
in everyday language. See for example the following observation about Christ's
blood: "*Men bring it* [Christ's blood] *into their oaths,* quite senselessly. But it makes
the things they talk of seem important, more worth your listening about than if
they did not call them by its name. It is because they feel it is important, precious,
and its very name seems to communicate importance to other things" (S, 13;
Hopkins's italics).

sound figure, with symptomatic cases of intensification in the form of triple and quadruple alliterations in the crucial "demonstrative" and narrative phases, generally situated at the close of stanzas, where it is not rare to find a marked isocolic structuring:

4.7   . . . a vein
  8   Of the góspel próffer [pr], a préssure [pr], a prínciple [pr], Chríst's gíft.

5.7   His mýstery [st] múst [st] be instréssed [st, twice], stressed [st, twice]

22.7   Stigma [s], signal [s], cinquefoil [s] token
  8   For [f] léttering [l] of [v] the lámb's [l] fléece [fl], rúddying [r] of [v] the róse [r]-fláke [fl].

23.8   To bathe in his fall-gold mercies, to breathe in his all-fire glances

Apropos of isocolon one cannot but recall *en passant* the natural relevance of the parallelistic method (that Hopkins rightly pointed out as the constitutional foundation of poetic discourse) to the "scansion" of the concepts transmitted, both on the page and in the reader's mind. The "repetition of the same sound-figure"—for Hopkins the essence of verse—tends in the poem to create a continuous correspondence between sense and sound, between semantic and phonological level: "₅to a póise, to a páne" (st. 4), "₃Warm-laid grave of a womb-life grey" (st. 7), "₃lush-kept plush-capped sloe" (st. 8), "₃Take settler and seamen, tell men with women" (st. 12), "₂down-dugged ground-hugged grey" (st. 26). At the purely syntagmatic level—without reckoning the supports offered by sound—the parallelistic tension functioning as a conceptual scansion is evidenced by the perfect balancing of stanza 6 (see figure 1).

There is a further addition of the distant, here unframable, parallelisms "₃(and few know this)" ~ "₈(And here the faithful)" and "₆and melt" ~ "₈and miss").[28]

28. See again what Hopkins writes in the Journal: "The force of this recurrence [Hopkins is here referring to rhythm] is to beget a recurrence or parallelism answering to it in the words or thought and, speaking roughly and rather for the tendency than the invariable result, the more marked parallelism in structure

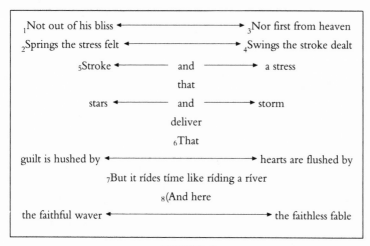

$_1$Not out of his bliss ⟷ $_3$Nor first from heaven
$_2$Springs the stress felt ⟷ $_4$Swings the stroke dealt
$_5$Stroke ⟷ and ⟶ a stress
that
stars ⟷ and ⟶ storm
deliver
$_6$That
guilt is hushed by ⟷ hearts are flushed by
$_7$But it rídes tíme like ríding a ríver
$_8$(And here
the faithful waver ⟷ the faithless fable

FIGURE I

A similarly auxiliary and in a certain sense phatic function is carried out by the occasional puns, paronomasias,[29] and neologisms, and by archaisms and dialect words. All these are not only the tangible result of a search for precision and truthfulness and of an effort at contextualization carried as far as the violation of the norm, but once again signals through which the reader-hearer is kept well awake and involved—or, with the puns, astonished.[30] But certainly the most relevant contribution toward the production in the reader-hearer of a gripping emotional tension is provided by the dramatic—not to say melodramatic—isotopy. Both parts of the poems are characterized by a most evident search for chiaroscuro effects, for violent and grim tones, for insisted con-

whether of elaboration or of emphasis begets more marked parallelism in the words and sense. And moreover parallelism in expression tends to beget or passes into parallelism in thought" (J, 84–85). For a comprehensive analysis of the poem's parallelistic structure see Lichtmann 1989, 61–99.

29. Some examples: "$_1$I am sóft síft" (st. 4), "$_6$she réars [iəz] hersélf to divíne / $_7$Éars [iəz]" (st. 19), "$_5$ócean [ou/n] of a mótionable [ou/n] mínd" (st. 32), "$_7$Never [evə] -eldering [eldər] revel [revəl] and river [drivə] of youth" (st. 18). On the exploitation of puns with a similar argumentative function see Perelman-Tyteca 1971, 145, and chapter 2 note 19 above.

30. Cf. for example the dialectal "$_7$voel" (st. 4), the metaplasm "$_3$hawling" (st. 19), the barbarism "$_5$Ipse" (st. 28), the neologism "$_7$instressed" (st. 5). The same may be said of the numerous solecisms, hyperbatons, and anastrophes.

trasts and plastic effects—once again, vividness and palpability pushed to the utmost. All this is the symptom of a precise strategy to intensify in the reader the pathos of the wreck, to make him more pliant to the conceptual metamorphosis that will follow.[31] Such a melodramatic character, translated into the figures realizing and signaling it, avails itself in the first place of hyperbole, aposiopesis,[32] and parenthesis (the typical "aside" or whispered sentence of drama and melodrama). Apropos of hyperboles and melodramatic straining, here are some of the descriptive connotations and qualifications of the wreck and of the stormy night: "₄the *infinite* air is unkind" and "₆Sitting . . . in *cursed* quarter, the wind" (st. 13); the skillfully alliterated climax "₇Wíry and white-fíery and whírlwind-swivelléd snów" (st. 13); "₆ruinous shock" (st. 14); "₈hurling and horrible airs" (st. 15); the further climax "₄rash smart sloggering brine" (st. 19), "₈wínd's búrly and béat of *endrágonéd* séas" (st. 27). That Hopkins presupposed a naïve and easily impressionable reader is also proved by the quantity of prosopopoeias, among which we find the representation of Death preceded by a pageant of trumpets and drums (st. 11) or that of Hope metamorphosed into a gray-haired widow (st. 15). And no less revelatory are the discreet sallies of the "narrator"—in the form of parenthetic clauses, digressions, "asides"—which retroactively illuminate the otherwise concealed and misunderstandable meaning of the events:

17.1   They fought with God's cold—
   2   And they could not, and fell to the deck
   3   (Crushed them) or water (and drowned them) or rolled
   4   With the searomp over the wreck.

31. Perelman-Tyteca (1971) observe that the function of "hyperboles using concrete expressions" (291) is that of "provid[ing] a reference which draws the mind in a certain direction only to force it later to retreat a little, to the extreme limit of what seems compatible with its idea of the human, the possible, the probable, with all the other things it admits" (291).

32. A celebrated series of aposiopeses occurs in stanza 28, when the nun "sees" Christ coming to her. An analysis of the melodramatic isotopy with an apocalyptic function is carried out by Sulloway (1972, 187ff). See especially her observations on the atmosphere, the adjectival scheme, the lexical level, the "colour scheme" (red, white, gold), etc. See also Ritz 1963, 336–37, and Bump 1982, 67, 95–96, 109–10.

8.6   . . . Híther then, lást or fírst,
7   To hero of Calvary, Christ,'s feet—
8   Never ask if méaning it, wánting it, wárned of it—mén gó.

All of these are strategies employed to maintain the emotional vibration, since they provide a paradoxical semantic (informative)
support despite their nature of properly non-semantic means.
This is confirmed by the abundant employment of repetition,
pleonasm, and redundancy. In poetry, such figures, as Lausberg
has rightly said, "arrest the current of information," yet at the
same time give the opportunity to " 'taste' emotionally the content of information, which is indeed emphasized and highlighted
for the importance it must take."[33] We find on the one hand repetitions that serve to pin down fundamental though hardly credible concepts:

9.5   Beyónd sáying swéet, past télling of tóngue [the referent is
       God]

10.7   Make mercy in all of us, out of us all
8   Mástery, bút be adóred, bút be adóred Kíng.

19.1   Sister, a sister calling
       A master, her master and mine!—

More often we find purely emotional intensification, a function
also performed by anaphora:

33. Lausberg 1982, 81. Similarly, for Perelman-Tyteca 1971: "The simplest
figures for increasing the feeling of presence are those depending on *repetition*.
Repetition is important in argumentation, whereas it is of no use in demonstration or in scientific reasoning in general" (174–75; Perelman-Tyteca's italics).
That the figures of repetition are only apparently interruptions of the informative
flux and in reality emotional and semantic intensifications is again proved by the
use of *distinctio* (Lausberg 1982 [93–94], also defined as "antimétabole" by Groupe
μ 1970 [121–22] and "oratorical syllepsis" by Perelman-Tyteca 1971 [217], that is
the repetition of the same word but with different nuances of meaning) in stanza
3: "₆My heart, but you were dovewinged, I can tell, / ₇Carrier-witted, I am bold
to boast, / ₈To flash from the flame to the flame then, tower from the grace to the
grace." "₈flame" is, in the first occurrence, the metaphorical internal fire accompanying the terrifying manifestation of God, in the second, the purifying flame of
grace. The second hemistich, with the double recurrence of "₈grace," refers to
two different levels of grace. See also Lichtmann 1989, 98: "No repetition is really
pure, for, while it 'afters' the instress of the first, it also instresses or intensifies
it." The source of such a concept and use of repetition is biblical parallelism (ibid.,
43–44).

3.1   The frown of his face
2   Before me, the hurtle of hell
3   Behind, *where, where was a, where was a place?*

10.1   With an anvil-ding
2   And with fire in him forge thy will
3   Or *rather, rather then*, stealing as Spring

19.5   . . . shé [the nun] that wéather sees óne thing, óne [Christ];

15.1   Hope had grown grey hairs,
2   Hope had mourning on,
        . . .
4   Hope was twelve hours gone;

as well as by enumeration with climax and by the *mixtura ver-borum*, evoking an even more frantic and wild upsetting:

2.5   Thou knówest the wálls, áltar and hóur and níght:

28.4   . . . There then! the Master,
5   Ípse, the ónly one, Chríst, Kíng, Héad:

8.3   . . . How a lush-kept plush-capped sloe
4   Will, mouthed to flesh-burst,
5   Gush!—flush the man, the being with it, sour or sweet
6   Brim, in a flásh, fúll! . . .

The useful fiction of the diachronic resolution of a text into its "phases" of reading (whereas they are simultaneous and synchronized)[34] allows one to say that the reader-hearer of "The Wreck of the Deutschland" would be at this point—if only his mere sensibility and receptive capacity were at play—sufficiently warmed up and oriented for the success of the semantic therapy. The intellective centers are activated; but sense, because of its previously explained incredibility, asks again for the employment of auxiliary figures capable of guaranteeing its acceptance, that is, of performing what a scientifically correct, figureless demonstration would be incapable of doing. We are evidently in the traditional ambit of tropes. On their plane, the form of content, they super-

34. Milroy 1978, 114.

impose themselves on figures of speech and pre-semantic effects
in order to assert their constant estranging and amplifying activity on the superficial sense (DEATH, to be unmasked and subverted) and on the deep sense (GOD, LIFE, to be confirmed).[35] If,
therefore, there is in the "Deutschland" a close cooperation between sign and sense, the two key figures in the tropic superabundance of the poem (since its "genotext"[36] is therein materially reflected) are oxymoron and metaphor. Their link and their
strict necessity on the semantic plane can be explained as follows.
If the poem's "genotext" is a problematic oxymoronic statement
("death is life and life is death"; "God is cruelly merciful and mer-
cifully cruel"), the genotextual oxymoron active on the paradigmatic axis will necessitate and invoke, on the syntagmatic
axis, an amplification and confirmation in metaphor, so that a
modelling of the "phenotext" could be the following algorithm:

$$D = n(O \cdot M) \text{ or } D = (O \cdot M)^n$$

(where D is for the "Deutschland", O for oxymoron, and M for
metaphor). On the merely microtextual plane and according to
the synchronic perspective[37] here adopted, the "Deutschland" is

35. One of the techniques Hopkins often exploits to obtain this kind of estrangement is that of the "awakening" of metaphor (Perelman-Tyteca 1971, 405–
10), "brought about . . . by a change in its usual context by using the metaphorical expression under circumstances that give it an unusual character and draw attention to the metaphor contained in it" (ibid., 407).

36. For the distinction between *genotext* and *phenotext* see Kristeva 1969,
"L'engendrement de la formule," 217–310. See also, more briefly, Šaumjan 1966,
169: "Ayant en vue la nécessité de différencier sérieusement les relations syntactiques intérieures des moyens linguistiques qui servent à exprimer ces relations,
j'ai proposé d'introduire dans la grammaire génératrice les notions de génotype
et de phénotype. Les génotypes linguistiques sont des objets syntactiques indépendants des moyens linguistiques qui servent à les exprimer. Les phénotypes linguistiques sont les formes extérieures dont sont revêtus les génotypes."

37. It is however possible to see the "Deutschland" as an amplification even
with reference to the macrotext: with its 35 stanzas and 280 lines, it is the longest
poem by Hopkins and, furthermore, a kind of "summa" of the nuclei of thought
scattered and fragmented in the macrotext. The extent of its amplification is immediately shown for example by the one-line fragment No. 64, (f) (P III, 79)
"They are not dead who die, they are but lost who live," and by "He hath abolish'd the old drouth": "₄He hath . . . / ₆ . . . taught my lips to quote this word /
₇That I shall live, I shall not die, / ₈But I shall when the shooks are stored / ₉See
the salvation of the Lord."

therefore a multiplication and raising to power of its oxymoronic genotext. It is a process of continuous metaphorization of its original polar semes (and therefore a synechdochic process), where metaphors perform the function of varied repetitions/ translations into images of the oxymoronic dimension of both God and the wreck. It is indeed absolutely necessary that such a complex concept of God as that underlying the "Deutschland"— whose essence partakes of the contradictory semes of LIFE and DEATH, of benevolent CREATION and of cruel DESTRUCTION— should avail itself, in order to become a truth of faith in the read-er-hearer, of insisted-upon repetitions and of an incessant meta-phorization confirming this truth while also illustrating it. On the other hand, any margin whatsoever of gratuitousness and mere ornamentation in the oxymoronic uses is out of the question, as they are strictly functional to the work's conceptual plan and ger-minal cell.

Proceeding to an investigation of the rhetorical strategy of the poem at the level of the form of content, these are the assump-tions on which my discussion will revolve: 1) God's oxymoronic nature and the metaphorical propagation of his antithetical semes; 2) GOD as a temporary and superficial disguise of DEATH (and vice versa); until 3) GOD carries off an overwhelming victory over DEATH after a speedy "duel"; 4) the metamorphosis of the tempest, with the ousting of the superficial sense in favor of the deep sense.

If we now take the "Deutschland" only temporarily for a self-enclosed semantic and discursive "universe," and not only as a sum of persuasive strategies, an embryonic modelization ac-cording to some pertinent categories taken from Greimas's *Struc-tural Semantics* can be useful. The poem's Part the Second visibly reduplicates the first according to an interoreceptive/exterorecep-tive[38] bi-isotopy reclaimed by the fact that the latter has a literal TEMPEST (as a nuclear seme) whereas the former has an only meta-phorical "TEMPEST" (as a classeme, a religious crisis, conversion,

38. See Greimas 1983, in particular 120 and 135–36.

	Part the First	Part the Second
sender	GOD	DEATH
receiver	I	NUN
test	"TEMPEST"	TEMPEST

FIGURE 2

mystical ecstasy, etc., that would enable us to speak, in Greimas's terms, of an allegory). We have therefore the correspondences shown in Figure 2.

One of the semic manipulations of the poem consists in making the dramatic "conversion" of Part the First function in terms of a symbolic TEMPEST,[39] which is the bearer of the seeming "DEATH" of the cold and sinning believer and which proves to be a symbolic "LIFE"; and then, by dint of such an identification, in attributing the nonsymbolic TEMPEST of Part the Second—against all appearances—to GOD rather than to DEATH, of which GOD is seen to share—while keeping his own—many of the functions and qualifications. GOD and DEATH are seen to be *temporarily* the two antagonistic senders of the tempest, until GOD finally vanquishes DEATH and locutor and hearer can at last reach Donne's conclusion: "death, thou shalt die" (*Holy Sonnets* 10.4).

Part the First of the poem (sts. 1–10) presents the interoreceptive isotopy, with GOD, I, and "TEMPEST" as, respectively, sender, receiver and test. GOD is at once seen (st. 1) as the origin of life ("₂giver of breath") but also, immediately after, as bearer of death ("₄Lord of living *and dead*"), as a creative but also destructive force:

1.5 Thou hast *bound* bónes and véins in me, *fástened* me flésh,
6   And áfter it álmost *únmade,* what with dréad,
7   Thy *doing* . . .

39. Cf. the sea images and terms: "₃Wórld's stránd, swáy of the séa" (st. 1), "₆roped" (st. 4), "₅stars and storms" (st. 6), "₇in high flood" and "₈at bay" (st. 7), as well as the explicit stanza 9: "₃Wring thy rebel . . . / ₄ . . . with wrecking and storm."

Such an alternation of semically diverging divine attributions continues, on the syntagmatic axis, for the whole extension of the poem, both through the occurrences of sememes (therefore metaphors) of the seme LIFE (CREATION) or of the seme DEATH (DESTRUCTION) and through new antithetic or even oxymoronic manifestations of the type of the above quotation. In the first two stanzas of Part the First, God shares the semes (of DEATH) *rudeness, violence, terribleness, cruelty, insensitivity*:[40] he undoes "₆what with dréad" (st. 1) what he has done, is identified with the "₂líghtning" and lashes his "₂ród" (st. 2), causing the "₄terror" of the speaker who, horrified (l. 7), is "₆trod / ₇Hárd dówn" by his "₆sweep and . . . hurl." Yet an abrupt and radical change in the semic register leads to an altogether inverted metaphorization, and GOD becomes, in stanza 9, "₅Beyónd sáying sweét," "₇Father and fondler," and again "₆sweét" (st. 10). The correct, oxymoronic dimension of GOD is emphasized by stanza 8 and by stanzas 9 and 10: GOD is "₂best or worst / ₃Word last,"[41] "₅sour or sweet,"[42] "₆lást or fírst" (st. 8).[43] Or again:

9.6   Thou art lightning and love, I found it, a winter and warm;

7   Father and fondler of heart thou hast wrung:

8   Hast thy dark descending and most art merciful then.

But a few lines below we meet with a new contradiction of the contradiction ("winter" is now denied by "spring"):[44]

40. Echoes of such a semic characterization are also traceable in the pre-"Deutschland" Hopkins. Cf. for example "₅₄iron rod" ("A Soliloquy of One of the Spies left in the Wilderness"), "₁brazen heaven," "₉My heaven is brass and iron my earth" ("My prayers must meet a brazen heaven").

41. See also Christ's christening by the nun in stanza 24: "₈she . . . christens her wild-*worst Best*."

42. As for the high recurrence of the antithesis-equivalence "sweet"-"bitter" applied to God, cf. "₆Sweet flowers I carry,—*sweets* for *bitter*" ("For a Picture of Saint Dorothea"), "₂God comes all *sweetness* to your Lenten lips" ("Easter Communion"), "₂₀*sweet* Vintage of our Lord" ("Barnfloor and Winepress"), "₁₅can . . . *sweet* . . . / ₁₆ . . . in fasts divine" ("The Habit of Perfection"), "₉sweet, soúr" ("Pied Beauty"), "₄air . . . *sweet-and-soúr*" ("Cheery Beggar"), "₁₀earth's *sweet* being . . . / ₁₁Before it . . . soúr with sinning" ("Spring").

43. Cf. "The Lantern out of doors," where Christ is "₁₄Their ránsom, their rescue, and first, fast, last friend." The same antithesis *first/last* occurs, in a different context, in "The Sea and the Skylark," line 14.

44. Cf. also the opposition "₁cold" (st. 17) versus "₄May" (st. 26).

10.1   With an anvil-ding
  2   And with fire in him forge thy will
  3   Or rather, rather then, stealing as *Spring*

This stanza, specifying the opposition of stanza 9 ("₈dark" versus "₈merciful"), places GOD as an intersection of *mercy* and *mastery* (there also occurs a chiasmus to emphasize the overturning):

10.7   Make mercy in all of us, out of us all
  8   Mástery, but be adóred, but be adóred Kíng.

It is a middle dimension[45] which will be transcoded into a half-light or semi-darkness in stanza 34:

34.6   Not a dóomsday dázzle in his cóming nor dárk as he cáme;
  7   _____Kínd, but róyally recláiming his ówn;
  8   A released shówer, let flásh to the shíre, *not a líghtning of fíre
        hard húrled*.

These are statements that on the one hand contradict the "₂líghtning," the "₆*hurl* of thee," and the trodding "₇Hárd dówn" of stanza 2, and on the other enlarge the range of the oxymoronic descriptions of GOD with the oppositions *dazzle* versus *dark, kind* versus *reclaiming, released shower* versus *lightning*.[46]

Before proceeding, it is useful to show how the dialectic relation of LIFE and DEATH acquires an absolute prominence in the poem, thanks to the high frequency of antithesis, the germinal cell of oxymoron. In this respect especially, Part the First of the poem is a long argument tending to emphasize, by dint of examples, that DEATH and LIFE, given by GOD, are indissolubly united, that DEATH is also partly LIFE and that LIFE is also partly DEATH. After stanza I has affirmed a GOD that *creates* and *destroys,* that *binds* and *unbinds* (ll. 5–7), stanza 4 presents in a marvelous parallelistic structure (4/4: "₁I . . . /₃*Fast*, but *mined* . . ." ~ "₅I stéady

45. Hopkins is even more explicit in "In the Valley of the Elwy," where God is said to be simultaneously "₁₄mighty a master" and "₁₄father and fond."
46. Also in the subsequent nature sonnets Hopkins will constantly emphasize the concept of God as a synthesis of opposites. A transparent and optimistic formulation is in "Pied Beauty," where many of the oppositions we have been examining recur: "₇Áll things counter, origiṇal, spáre, stránge; / ₈Whatever is fickle, freckled (who knows how?) / ₉With swift, slów, sweet, sóur; adázzle, dím; / ₁₀He fathers-forth whose beauty is pást chánge: / ₁₁Práise him."

. . . /₆But *roped* . . .") a reduplication of the antithesis STASIS (of
DEATH) / MOVEMENT (of LIFE), as is suggested by the baroque simile of the hourglass:

4.1   I am sóft síft
2   In an hourglass—at the wall
3   Fast, but mined with a motion, a drift,
4   And it crowds and it combs to the fall;
5   I stéady as a wáter in a wéll, to a póise, to a páne,
6   But roped with, always, all the way down from the tall
7   Fells or flanks of the voel, a vein
8   Of the góspel próffer, a préssure, a prínciple, Chríst's gíft.

In stanza 7, instead, the antithesis-equivalence LIFE/DEATH takes
on the following lexical range: *life* versus *grave, warm* and *womb*
versus *grey, manger* versus *Passion:*

7.1   It dates from day
2   Of his going in Galilee;
3   Warm-laid grave of a womb-life grey;
4   Manger, maiden's knee;
5   The dense and the driven Passion, and frightful sweat:

In Part the Second, antithesis too (which is among the most recurring figures of the poem)[47] emphasizes, amplifying it, the link
LIFE-DEATH. The wrecked, for example, are to all evidence "₅O
Father, not under thy feathers" (st. 12), that is, in the arms of
DEATH, "₇Yet"—it is added immediately after—well protected by
the Father's grace, while the nuns become for their heroism, like
St. Francis, "₂Drawn to the *Life* that *died*" (st. 23). We see the
same antithesis in stanza 25, where, in an effective rhyme contrast, the wreck is the object of a competition between the "₂arch

47. Here is an inventory of the most significant occurrences: "₆únder" / "₇in-
stréssed" (st. 5), "₈faithful" / "₈faithléss" (st. 6), "₄melt" / ₄master" (st. 10), "₅at a
crásh" / "₆língering-óut" (st. 10), "₅Pául" / "₆Áustin" (ibid.), "₅after evil" / "₅ut-
tering truth" (st. 18), "₅Blínds" / "₅sees" (st. 19), "₅lily" / "₆béast" (st. 20) "₅Gertrude" / "₅Luther" (ibid.), "₈Ábel" / "₈Cáin" (ibid.), "₂grey" / "₃blue" (st. 26),
"₂ground" / "₃heavens" (ibid.), "₅present and past" / "₆Heaven and earth" (st. 29),
"₃shóck níght" / "₈béacon of líght" (st. 29), "₃The recúrb and the recóvery" / "₈a
sóvereignty that héeds but hídes, bódes but abídes" (st. 32), "₃lístener" /
"₃língerer" (st. 33), "₇passion-plungéd" / "₇risen" (ibid.), "₂Drówned" / "₃háven"
(st. 35), "₅dáyspring" and "₅east" / "₅dímness" (ibid.).

and original *Breath*" and the "₄body of lovely *Death*"; also in stanza 28, where God is again the synthesis of LIFE and DEATH ("₇lord it with living and dead").

Going back now to the oxymoronic dimension of God (LIFE and/or DEATH, KINDNESS and/or CRUELTY), such a union on the syntagmatic axis of the positive and negative semes referred to God is introduced into the poem with the aim of creating in the reader-hearer first the illusion of the coincidence of GOD and DEATH and then the certainty that the latter is an instrument, though mysterious, used by GOD for the good and the salvation (the LIFE) of man. It is no surprise then that DEATH is temporarily given the same negative semes of GOD, often with the very same lexical characterizations. While GOD has a "₂ród" (st. 2), DEATH boasts of other weapons such as a "₁sword," a "₂flánge," a "₂rail," or a "₈scythe" (st. 11). Itself "₈sóur" (st. 11; cf., for GOD, st. 8. l. 5), but also "₄lovely" (st. 25; contrast "₅lovely-felicitious Providence," st. 31), it provokes, like GOD, "₈hurling and horrible airs" (st. 15; contrast "₆the hurl of thee [God]" and "₇horror of height," st. 2), and is, like GOD, *flame* and *fire*.⁴⁸ But the identification GOD-DEATH is given and then at once taken away, and their antagonism is ephemeral. GOD is the Lord of the universe and, as such, after a speedy duel, eliminates DEATH. One of the concepts—this time *not* oxymoronic!—more firmly ascribed by Hopkins to God is indeed the character of absolute master, judge, and legislator of human things.⁴⁹ The poem opens with the invocation to a "₁mastering me / ₂God" (st. 1) and is circularly sealed by the acknowledgment of "₈oür thoughts' chivalry's throng's Lórd" (st. 35)—a concept often emphasized within the poem, for example, in stanza 10 ("₇Make . . . out of us all / ₈Mástery . . .") and in stanza 28 ("₄the Master"). But GOD is, above all, *Lord,* that is, giver and bestower of another occurrence, of that TEMPEST which might seem the cruel work and the wicked gift of DEATH. GOD is from the start "₃swáy of the séa" (st. 1), and both Parts close

48. Contrast ᶢOD's "₈flame" (st. 3), "₈all-fire glances" (st. 23), "₈fire" (st. 34), and "₈Oür hearts' . . . fire" (st. 35) with DEATH's "₂flame" (st. 11).

49. To this concept Hopkins will also return, outside his poetry, in several sermons. See in particular the two in S, 50–53 and 53–58.

emphasizing this supremacy (st. 10, l. 4 and st. 35, l. 8, whose last word is, as we have seen, *Lord*), thus obliterating the short and seeming hegemony of DEATH beginning with Part the Second (st. 11: "₄And storms bugle his *fáme*"). In stanza 32 we have, in fact, a new and definitive overturning, and GOD is newly worshipped and adored as "₁máster *of the tides*," that is, of the TEMPEST, the inclemencies of which have now become "₈the storm of his strides" (st. 33). The antagonism between GOD and DEATH, for the short time it subsists, could not be more marked and put into greater relief than by their anaphorical "entrances" (both, furthermore, "percussive": Part the First begins [st. 1, ll. 7–8] with GOD's "touch," Part the Second with the bugles and the drums announcing DEATH [st. 11, ll. 1–4]) and by the unmistakably explicit statements of stanza 32:

32.7   Grásp Gód, *thróned behind*
   8   Déath with a sóvereignty that héeds but hídes, bódes but
         abídes;

and by stanza 33:

33.3   . . . a lóve glídes
   4   *Lówer than déath and the dárk;*

The rhetorical purpose may be said at this point to have been achieved. The TEMPEST, which has caused the terrible shipwreck with the sacrifice of so many innocent lives, has been tamed and interpreted; and with the certainty that it is a divine instrument of LIFE and not a wicked gift of DEATH its metamorphosis is complete. The snowflakes are changed into sky-colored lilies:

21.7   Thou mártyr-máster: in thý síght
   8   Storm flákes were scróll-leaved flówers, lily shówers—sweet
         héaven was astréw in them,

rain and blizzard into a golden fall, the rough waters into a balsamic bath:

23.5   . . . and these thy daughters
   6   And five-lìved and leavèd favour and pride,
   7   Are sìsterly séaled in *wíld wáters,*
   8   To bathe in his *fall-gold mércies,* to breathe in his all-fire glances

and the shipwreck into a harvest and the tempest into a grain-
flowering. "₈temp*est*" and "₈harv*est*," therefore, are seen not only
phonically but also semantically to "rhyme":

31 8   . . . is the shípwrack then a hárvest,
        does témpest carry the gráin for thee?

4

❦ FROM THE "DEUTSCHLAND" TO

THE *TERRIBLE SONNETS:*

TOWARD AUTOCOMMUNICATION

After analyzing on the synchronic plane two highly paradigmatic poetic specimens, with the object of proving the functionality of Hopkins's rhetoric, we must now turn to a necessary diachronic verification. Since we have founded the necessity of rhetoric and the functionality of its uses on some precise motivating demands—and in particular on the three main characteristics of judicial discourse (persuasive effect, modification of the situation, presupposition of a referee)—a result different from those so far obtained will be possible in principle (that is, even taking no notice of poetic actualizations) owing to the absence of one or more of the factors. Such a decline in the deep motivations and intentions underlying the rhetorical coding of Hopkins's message is indeed what occurs in varying—and not necessarily increasing—degrees in Hopkins's poetry following the "Deutschland" and the 1877 sonnets, of which "God's Grandeur" inaugurates the series and of which it is a kind of model.[1]

Let us first examine the I-YOU (sender-receiver) relationship,

1. Harris (1982), whom I shall hereafter frequently cite, adopts much the same perspective, although, as I observed in chapter 1, he fails to refer these textual phenomena to a theoretical frame or foundation. More particularly, he sights only two of the three motivating demands of Hopkins's rhetorical planning, neglecting the crucial objective of the modification of the situation.

which so centrally motivates the two poems investigated above. Since the receiver of Hopkins's poems is mentioned again here, it must be stated that I have not attempted in the previous chapters any preliminary, accurate identification and description of the historical and specific addressee of Hopkins's message—in rhetorical terms, its judge and referee—for two precise reasons. First, such an investigation will be carried out in Part Two of this work; furthermore, it would hardly have provided useful and pertinent results, at least with respect to the type of approach I have chosen. Hopkins's receiver is, in fact, a *virtual and potential* receiver, owing to Hopkins's contradictory but firm decision not to publish, which he kept until his death; nevertheless, such a receiver exists, though as a fragile and doubtful alibi, at least in the 1877 sonnets and in the "Deutschland." The presence of a receiver is in this poem, in fact, the veritable germ and motive of the poetic act. It is on the very basis of this important fact that we can indicate in the so-called *terrible sonnets* the only moment of a certain syntagmatic breadth in Hopkins's poetic parabola where the alibi of the—even only—virtual receiver crashes, and where therefore the functionality of rhetoric can be said to decrease or even to become superficial.[2] Concomitantly, the other two components motivating and founding Hopkins's message, as it is structured and realized for example in the "Deutschland," here also disappear. The transformation of the poem into an act of mere "autocommunication,"[3] no longer addressing itself to a re-

2. "None of these poems postulates, as part of its rhetorical form, an individual human audience, much less a society or congregation" or an "implied audience" (Harris 1982, 129). Harris also notices that "the vocative mode nearly vanishes" (77) in the *terrible sonnets,* though he means principally the "colloquy with God" of the Ignatian exercise. A diachronic perspective is essential to an investigation of Hopkins's rhetorical strategies and uses. Thus, Harris justly argues that the *terrible sonnets* "contrast in the sharpest manner possible with Hopkins's earlier poetry" (129), that they represent "a radical shift in imaginative procedure" (xiii) and the crisis of a poetry written in praise of God (xiv). In this specific sense he speaks of them as "failures" (xiii).

3. Ong (1986) says that "the 'I' . . . has no interlocutor other than itself" (146); Harris 1982 sees these sonnets as a "self-debate" and a "self-referential colloquy" (94), where the "speaker" has no other "audience but himself" and "must wrestle in his own vacuum" (80). On "autocommunication" see Lotman's "Autocommunication: 'I' and 'Other' as Addressees," in Lotman 1990, 20–35.

ceiver, even if virtual, is accompanied by the disappearance of any modification of the situation to be effected. Any persuasive action becomes, strictly speaking, unnecessary. No more receivers to convert to faith, no superficial sense to be euphorically overturned into a deep and concealed counter-sense; we even witness a progressive closing up of depth to surface and vice versa, culminating in their flattest and almost total coincidence. The result is that the surviving rhetoric is diverted to the superficial sense, with the aim of deepening it and, in so doing, emphasizing and hyperbolizing it.

I have used the term "surviving rhetoric" because one must immediately make it clear—as the majority of hostile critics have admitted—that, but for the abrupt and conclusive upsurge of the *terrible sonnets,* Hopkins's rhetorical figures after the "Deutschland" and the 1877 sonnets undergo a drastic reduction, in direct proportion to the gradual exhaustion of the motivating foundations of persuasive discourse. It may be useful to tabulate diachronically the breakup and dissolution of the conative function—the gradual disappearance of the interlocutor—from the nature sonnets to the situation of pure autocommunication in the *terrible sonnets.*

PHASE 1: I-YOU, ca. 1875–78. The conative function is correct and functional, since the "you" and occasionally the "we" are in every respect an absolutely real receiver who is the legitimate object of the rhetorical strategy. This is the case for the most famous and typical of the nature sonnets, such as "God's Grandeur," "The Starlight Night" (see, above all, the sestet), "Pied Beauty" (l. 11), and "The Sea and the Skylark" (cf., for the use of "we," ll. 9–14).[4]

PHASE 2: I-YOU(?), 1879–85. This phase begins when it is no longer easy to perceive whether the "you" is real or fictitious (a rhetorical projection of the "I"), which makes one at least suspect that the process of communication is about to taper off. For example, in "The Candle Indoors" the "$_9$you" invited to "$_9$Come . . . indoors" (=inner life) and to "$_{10}$Mend" may well be the

4. Harris 1982, 135.

same interlocutor of the "Deutschland," but it probably is the
"$_1$I" of the octave. This is confirmed by fragment No. 152 (P III,
176), which is discussed below and of which "THE Candle Indoors" is a clear remake. The same ambiguity (conative/autoco-
native function) can be perceived in "Morning, Midday, and
Evening Sacrifice" and in "Spelt from Sibyl's Leaves," where, if
the addressee of the long chain of imperatives of lines 10–14 is
identified by the occurrences of *us* and *our* in lines 1–10, the final
line ("$_{14}$Where, selfwrung, selfstrung, sheathe- and shelterless,
I thoughts against thoughts in groans grind") unquestionably
pushes the sonnet toward the *terrible sonnets* and their situation of
jarring inward torment.[5]

PHASE 3: I-I, 1885–89. We witness here the complete disappearance of the *real* "you." "You" stands now for God or more often
for the subject of the enunciation or its synecdoches. Hopkins an-
thropomorphizes his "self-projections" and the body becomes "a
false interlocutor" (Harris 1982, 58):

a. "[Carrion Comfort]": the interlocutors are Despair ("$_1$thee")
and then God (ll. 5ff.; "$_5$thou");

b. "No worst . . .": the receiver is the same poetic "I" changed
into a "you":

12   . . . Here! *creep*,
13   *Wretch*, under a comfort serves in a whirlwind: all
14   Life death does end and each day dies with sleep.

c. "I wake . . .": this sonnet fully reveals the emptiness and superfluity of the rhetorical function as it searches for a persuasive
testimony ("$_5$*With witness* I speak this") which is not asked for,
insofar as there is no other receiver but the subject of the enunciation;

d. "My own heart . . .": the poetic "I" is once again fractured,
and the "$_{13}$Wretch" of "No worst . . ." becomes a "$_9$poor
Jackself":

5. "[In 'Spelt from Sibyl's Leaves'] the situation is not as it was in 'God's Grandeur.' There the last lights off the black west go and night descends, but one can
look forward to the dawn. Thus in 'Carrion Comfort' . . . the wrestling and desolation take place in a year of night which ends in a consoling dawn. But here

9 ⎧ Soul, self; *come,* poor Jackself, I do advise
10 ⎪ *You,* jaded, *let* be; *call off* thoughts awhile
11 ⎩ Elsewhere; leave comfort root-room . . .

e. "Thou art indeed just . . .": God is here the receiver, against his will, of a message that is, however, "jammed" (ll. 1–4);

f. "The times are nightfall . . .": as in "The Candle Indoors," of which it is a first draft, the "you" of lines 9–11 is nothing but a fictitious interlocutor, that is, the "I" of lines 1–8:

9   . . . There is *your* world within.
10   There *rid* the dragons, *root out* there the sin.
11   *Your* will is law in that small commonweal.

g. "To his Watch": the receiver is the watch, compared, as in "I wake . . . ," to the heart.

The second and parallel operation concurring to limit and normalize the rhetorical function in Hopkins's poetry is the decline of the phenomenological dynamics (superficial) sense to (deep) counter-sense, or, in rhetorical terms, the disappearance of the situation to be modified. After the "Deutschland" and the enthusiastic nature sonnets, Hopkins was no longer capable of finding in himself (or, more probably, of offering to a receiver who had proved cold and indifferent)[6] the emotional stimuli necessary to bring to light the "miraculous" supplies of sense, counter-sense, and supra-sense given off (*charged*)—by nature and the world.[7] My reference to "God's Grandeur" (l. 1) is not casual; together with the sonnets composed in its wake, it is the emblem of a joy that will soon be extinguished and changed into dejection; it is also, above all, a model of semantic, literal, and symbolic content, one that will be significantly repudiated and overturned, in

there is no suggestion that a dawn will come if the night overwhelms" (Boyle 1961, 141–42).

6. Hopkins received refusals in the only two cases when he sought to break the virtuality of the destination of his poems (when he submitted the "Deutschland" and "The Loss of the Eurydice" to the Jesuits' magazine, *The Month,* for publication). On the whole, not even the impressions and the judgments provoked by his poetry in Dixon and above all in Patmore and Bridges can be interpreted (on the basis of Hopkins's reactions to their letters) as unconditional encouragement.

7. For Harris, Hopkins gradually came to lose his "sacramental vision of the world" and fell prey to the Ruskinian "pathetic fallacy" (Harris 1982, 26ff.).

that there will be no passage whatsoever from the superficial sense to the deep counter-sense.[8] Let us recall the conceptual plan underlying "God's Grandeur": the entropy, that is, the consumption of energy ("$_9$spent") of the earth, compared to a sterile ("$_8$bare") sunset, is turned, by God's intervention, into a paradoxical increase of energy ("$_9$never spent," "$_{10}$lives") or, on the metaphorical plane, into a bright and promising dawn ("$_{14}$broods").[9] While several sonnets substantially repeat the argumentative model of "God's Grandeur"—with, in some cases, the minimal variation of the substitution of the *counter*-sense with a *supra*-sense (as happens in "The Starlight Night," "Spring," and "Pied Beauty")—we notice at the same time the progressive gaining of ground of a disphoric vein, which leads to the suppression of any counter- or supra-sense. Such a proceeding, which implies a parallel reduction of the rhetorical vein, becomes particularly evident in a number of poems which, while they do not repeat the argument of "God's Grandeur" (or just because of this), use nevertheless the same lexical, figurative and metaphorical material.

The euphoric moment ends in Hopkins—apart from sporadic and even triumphal revivals (for which, see the "Echoes" and the "Heraclitean Fire")—with "Hurrahing in Harvest" (1877), but already within this unrepeatable moment, disharmonies and dissonances are not lacking. One of the first jarring notes resounds in the sonnet "Spring," where, after an octave proclaiming unreservedly the beauty (l. 1), the music (ll. 4–5) and the "richness" (l. 8) of nature, there occurs undoubtedly the activation of the supra-sense, with the identification of nature itself with the significant triad "$_{11}$Eden"–"$_{10}$sweet"–"$_{10}$beginning"; but at the same time we sense, faraway, lying in wait, its corruption and "sun-

8. "In the early days of Hopkins's vocation nature was a legitimate object of man's affection, and man only was to be suspected (Poem 34, 1877 ["In the Valley of the Elwy"]). Now all nature, both human and botanical, is indicted, for both may draw the mind away from eternal things. . . . Sometimes nature herself and all her fluctuations [become] models for human decay and death and these, in turn, prefigurations for the end of time" (Sulloway 1972, 150, 180).

9. "Entropy contradicted the idea of a divine order" but "divine energy . . . added to, did not subtract from, the amount of energy in a given system" (Ellsberg 1987, 57).

set," in the parallel triad "$_{11}$cloy"–"$_{12}$cloud"–"$_{12}$sour." We are already, in practice, at the antipodes of "God's Grandeur"; there the succession was (dawn)-sunset-dawn (that is, [purity]-corruption-purity), here it is purity-faraway corruption. The margins of survival for the supra-sense, in other words, have already become slimmer. But let us look at what disphoric chords, though still in a homogeneously serene phase, Hopkins's poetry can touch in "The Sea and the Skylark." In this phonologically and structurally over-elaborated sonnet we have at the outset the same situation of "God's Grandeur" (the corruption of history, the twilight of civilization) without the end situation—without, in other words, the overturning of the metaphorical sunset into the dawn of the Holy Spirit. On the one side there is the perennial inexhaustible ("$_1$too old to end"), "$_{11}$pure" dynamism of the sea and of the skylark, and on the other, emphasized by highly negative adjectives, the usual, soiled, stagnating, urban scenery ("$_9$shallow and frail town," "$_{10}$sordid turbid time"). It is therefore here, at the superficial sense, that, unlike "God's Grandeur," the hermeneutic operation stops in "The Sea and the Skylark," as is confirmed by its quite explicit ending. The "$_{12}$past prime" (that is, the "$_{11}$Eden" of "Spring" and, earlier on, the "$_{10}$dearest freshness" of "God's Grandeur") "$_{13}$break, are breaking," and man's destiny appears now, almost materialistically and in the complete collapse of any deep sense, an absurd journey toward the nothingness of death and the pulverization of the body:

13   Our make and making break, are breaking, down
14   To man's last dust, drain fast towards man's first slime.

For its part, "Spring and Fall," though not reaching in its quality of "children's poem" the disphoric abysses of "The Sea and the Skylark," represents a kind of acceptable compromise between the two discordant tensions active in Hopkins's post-"Deutschland" poetry. On the one hand we have the descending line of rhetoric, which here touches a minimum of simplicity and essentiality. (The poem has just two metaphors, or more exactly, catachreses: "$_8$*worlds* of wanwood" and "$_{11}$Sorrow's *springs*.") On the other hand we observe a sad and disconsolate surrender to the superficial sense, any impulse to force it having ceased. Conceptually, the situation is the same as in "God's Grandeur" without the sestet: the lyric is framed within the two semantically equivalent syntagmas ("₁áre you gríeving" and "₁₅you mourn for"). This stresses how inescapable is the "₁₄blíght mán was bórn for." Man's ruin is the conclusion once again reached following a phenomenologial perception: the undoing, the breaking up of nature (recall the "₇soil / . . . ₈bare" and "₉nature . . . spent" of "God's Grandeur"), exemplified by the autumnal falling of leaves, which are "₃líke the thíngs of mán."

"God's Grandeur" is, finally, the model, or antimodel, of the grandiose sonnet that constitutes in all probability the demarcation between the I-YOU and the I-I phases: "Spelt from Sibyl's Leaves" (1885). I have said antimodel because its exceptional rhetorical upsurge, which paves the way to the *terrible sonnets,* is at the service of a semantization opposite to that of "God's Grandeur": there the extinguishing of light ("sunset") was overturned into a "lighting up," at both a literal ("dawn") and an anagogical ("strengthening of faith") register; in "Spelt from Sibyl's Leaves," the actual extinguishing ("evening," "sunset") is amplified on both the literal ("night") and the explicitly anagogical plane ("*our* night"). The dominant rhetorical figure is once again a semantic and emotional *amplificatio* taking the form of an embryonic allegory. This allegory, however, no longer supports a hardly credible (because scientifically and/or empirically unacceptable) and yet euphorical deep sense. On the contrary, it disphorically supports and vehicles a sense that is supplementary but not contrary to the superficial sense. Moreover, if we add that, though superficial and deep sense are at this stage sufficiently contrasted, the receiver begins to fade, the analogy with the *terrible sonnets* becomes strikingly evident. As in the latter, Hopkins proceeds to overemphasize a superficial sense practically indistinguishable from the deep sense (which is in fact suppressed). He thus reduces the "informative" character and the necessary and peculiar estranging function that rhetoric previously had had. It is therefore in the *terrible sonnets* that we may detect more than elsewhere cases of *audacia* or *mala affectatio*—a drying up or an impoverishment of the motives of the rhetorical message.

As I have said, with the *terrible sonnets* the ambiguities concerning the receiver, already present in many poems of the 1877–85 period, are suddenly and explicitly removed. The virtuality itself of the receiver—a motivation so fragile and ingenuous but so solid and deep-seated—is now sorrowfully let fall:

> "*To seem* . . ."
>
> 5 England, whose honour O all my heart woos, wife
> 6 To my creating thought, *would neither hear*
> 7 *Me,* were I pleading, *plead nor do I* . . .

Nor does the meager compensation that his poems are addressed to God—although ardently invoked—last for long:

> "*I wake* . . ."
>
> 6   . . . And my lament
> 7 Is cries countless, cries *like dead letters* sent
> 8 To dearest him *that lives alas! away.*[10]

In such a condition of substantially pure autocommunication, rhetoric performs the anomalous and paradoxical function of pure self-persuasion, the more anomalous and paradoxical in that here there is no longer any change of situation, but on the contrary a repeated and strengthened confirmation of the given situation.[11] Hopkins magnifies to himself[12] and to us his own spiritual depression and his intense and rending torment with such a sumptuous and superabundant rhetoric that one cannot but doubt the authenticity of his alleged plight. The signifier—that is, the rhetorical "effects"—proves but a contradiction of the signified.[13] It is by now clear that, if the widespread rhetorical strat-

10. In this sonnet, for Harris (1982, 109), Hopkins's "description of his unanswered communications reveals a progressive deterioration in both force and rhetorical effect."

11. Natural images become "decorations," and instance Hopkins's "solipsistic and uncontrolled self-projection upon things" (Harris 1982, 19).

12. Figures become "imaginative fictions whose true referent is the speaker's mind" (Harris 1982, 48).

13. Cf. what Sulloway (1972) writes on "Thou art indeed just, Lord, if I contend": "It is often said that the burden of this sonnet is spiritual impotence; and

egy is not only justified but also exalted in Hopkins's poetry proportionally to its tendential analogies with the judicial discourse,
in the *terrible sonnets* the foundations of the judicial discourse definitively disappear, thus enfeebling the very motivations of the
rhetorical framing: the receiver with functions of referee or judge
is absent, any attempt to modify the situation is waived, and
what remains, like the splendid relic of a now empty structure, is
the sole self-persuasive effect.[14]

If the term of reference for the poems belonging to the period
following the three years 1875–77 has been so far "God's Grandeur," the *terrible sonnets* look back and also oppositionally to
"The Wreck of the Deutschland." From it they take, at least at
the level of general metaphorical background, the marine and
nautical imagery, but they overturn the semantic project underlying it and its anagogical lesson. I have no space to enter into an
analysis of this interesting transformational field; I will confine
myself to emphasizing the great difference in results of the two
"battles" fought in the "Deutschland" and in the *terrible sonnets*.
In 1875 the "war" between God and the poetic I, the war of God
with men, ended in a triumphant peace. In the *terrible sonnets* one
must speak, if not of a defeat of the poetic "I," at least of an armi-
stice. The aspect, however, that clearly unites the poem and the

---

impotence there clearly was until the moment the sonnet was undertaken, for the
sonnet itself is a brilliant act of creation, and as such, holds impotence momentarily at bay" (152). Concerning the "desolation" of the *terrible sonnets* and of
"Spelt from Sibyl's Leaves" in particular, Boyle (1961) observes that "the poem
itself, this living and magnificent expression of a Christian's Gethsemane, proves
that Hopkins was wrong in feeling himself a eunuch" (132). Similar conclusions
on the *terrible sonnets* are drawn by Gardner (1969, I, 32), while Heuser (1958, 89–
90) notices tragicomical aspects and "ironic detachment." Ritz (1963, 255) and
Abbott (I, xxxviii), among others, are misled into considering them perfectly sin-
cere and balanced utterances. Harris (1982, 34) strikes the right chord when he
speaks of a "strategy designed to fill, by *inflating the self,* a void produced by the
intuition of an unresponding world."

14. Miller (1963) acutely observes that, in the *terrible sonnets,* words, previously
"the meeting-place of self, nature, and God the Word," "instead of reaching out
to touch things and give them over to man, no longer have strength enough to
leave the self at all. . . . Words become the opaque walls of the poet's interior
prison. . . . Words fall endlessly through a shadowy void and touch neither
things nor the God who made them. Abandoned by God, Hopkins cries out for
grace, but his words have lost their virtue *and cannot reach their destination"* (354–
55).

terrible sonnets is the massive, pervasive, and domineering rhetorical polarization of language, the "sudden and darkly brilliant heightening in . . . linguistic incisiveness" (Harris 1982, xiv). In the "Deutschland," rhetoric had its primary source in the necessity to cover simultaneously two opposite perspectives (sense/counter-sense) and to turn the one into the other; in the *terrible sonnets,* the univocity of sense having taken over, rhetoric loses its dynamic and transformational capacity, since it is at the service of the artificial, fictitious magnifying of the surface sense, which remains totally unmodified. Given this contextual situation the artificiality of rhetoric is particularly revealed, in the *terrible sonnets,* by the multiplication of "meta-logistic" effects, which imply a quantitative and qualitative alteration of the referent and of the "vérité-correspondance."[15] We accordingly notice the occurrence of the following "metaboles":

a. chaos and formlessness at the existential and spiritual level are ordered and put into form (with a relevant play on the signifier) in the poetic actualizations. Hopkins's poetry is never (particularly in the *terrible sonnets*) directly and immediately mimetic of the real;

b. the temporal deception, with the fictitious and misleading (because "untrue") unification and confusion of the time of the described action with the time of writing (time of the énoncé/time of the énonciation);[16]

c. the extraordinary prominence of amplifying figures such as emphasis and hyperbole, whose proper aim is to "falsify" the proportions of reality. On the contrary the generating figures of the "Deutschland," metaphor and oxymoron, which are here abundantly reused, considerably attenuate their crucial informational "explosion";

d. the reappearance and strengthening of the melodramatic function, with frequent instances of climax and of exclamative and interrogative clauses of a "rhetorical type," and of repeated chiaroscuro and plastic effects.

15. Groupe μ 1970, chapter V, "Les métalogismes," 123–44.
16. Harris (1982, 98) speaks of an "odd dislocation in temporal design" and of a "dual time-scheme."

The first of these metaboles is illustrated by almost all the sonnets, but most clearly by "Thou art indeed just, Lord, if I contend," where the confession of the "ruin," dryness, and sterility of poetic inspiration and of religious faith, culminating in the hyperbolic metaphor "$_{13}$Time's eunuch," falls within an admirably formed and organized structure. In this almost testamentary sonnet (Hopkins composed it only a few months before his death) two interesting phenomena concerning Hopkins's poetic involution are also evident: the reaffirmed extinction of any stimulus toward the search for a counter-sense on the part of the observer of nature (ll. 9–14), and, were it still necessary to prove it, the emptying of the conative function ("$_9$See"), long since definitively become self-conative. The involutional aspect of this sonnet is also put into relief by its homology with "The Sea and the Skylark" (nature-man antithesis).

Subtler and more concealed—but as widespread—are the occurrences of the temporal deception. "No worst . . ." for example—itself an "emotion recollected in tranquillity" whose considerable organization associates it with (a)—carries forward to the present of the énonciation a past moment dominated by the sense of spiritual prostration of the poetic "I": "$_1$is," "$_3$is," "$_4$is," "$_5$heave," "$_5$huddle" and so on until lines 12–14, where we have the unmasking of the deception-falsification of deixis:[17]

"No worst . . ."

12   . . . Here! creep,
13   Wretch, under a comfort serves in a whirlwind . . .

"$_{12}$Here," grammatically belonging to the present of the énonciation, must correctly be referred (although metaphorically) to the

17. Harris (1982), who notices in this sonnet "repeated, and apparently uncontrolled . . . synaesthesia," also points out the loss of "all power of spatial signification" of the "final designation of place—Here!—" (53). Concerning the use of deixis and the present tense instead of the past, it must be stressed that it is not simply the absence, in the *terrible sonnets,* of the three motivating conditions of the persuasive argumentation to establish its "mystifying" character. In a correct argumentative context, as Perelman-Tyteca 1971 observe, "The present has the . . . property of conveying most readily what we have called 'the feeling of presence' " (160). Analogously, "unusual use of the demonstrative can create a very vivid impression of presence" (162).

past of the énoncé. The same occurrences are observable in "I wake . . . ," where the *incipit* itself points most clearly to the forced and fictitious coincidence of the time of the énonciation and the time of the énoncé.

Finally, "[Carrion Comfort]" and once again "No worst . . ." and "I wake . . ." jointly illustrate (c) and (d). The first perhaps constitutes the only case among the *terrible sonnets* of temporal orthodoxy. It begins with a future implying present decision ("₁I'll not . . . feast") to switch then to a nonfictitious present ("₃I can") and then to a past ("₅why wouldst") in order to frame the dramatic recollection of the "₁₄now done darkness." For its dramatic effects language avails itself of this clear-cut temporal scansion and, also, copiously, of metaphor, oxymoron ("₁carrion comfort, [that is] Despair"), emphasis, climax, litotes—figures already employed in the "Deutschland." Yet here, as in all the other *terrible sonnets,* any reversal of sense is absent, so that it is an assortment of figures that does not escape an imperceptible stereotype. As for the melodramatization of sense, we may observe lines 5–8, where the characterization of God repeats the semic moduli and the lexical choices of the "Deutschland": ("₅terrible," "₅rude," "₆wring-world," "₆lionlimb," "₇darksome devouring," "₈in turns of tempest"). This melodramatic stereotype is also at work in numerous stylistic micro-occurrences, such as the parentheses, the "asides" ("₂—slack they may be—" and "₁₀(seems)") and the *correctiones:* "₁₀the rod, / ₁₁Hand rather" and (hyperbolic) "₁₃That night, that year." The puns themselves— "₁₀that toil, that coil," "₁₄(My God!) my God"—here belong, unlike the "Deutschland," to (a), being again a case of dissociation and negation of the signified on the part of the signifier.

Entirely based on hyperbole (but a "downward" hyperbole) is "No worst . . . ," where beside that figure (in ll. 1, 5, 10) we find the significant appearance of one of the most classically melodramatic figures of style, prosopopoeia ("₇Fury had shrieked"). Even more rhetorically overelaborated is, to conclude, "I wake. . . ." Further metalogistic figures are here added to the already-mentioned temporal deception active from the *incipit:* the sonnet starts with the paradox "₁I wake and feel the fell of *dark,* not *day*" to re-present the same night of "[Carrion Comfort]" with the same "sensational colors," a task mainly performed by repetitions with the support of a marked isocolic scansion:

"*I wake . . .*"

2 ⌠What *hours,* O what black *hoūrs* we have spent
3 ⌡This night! what sights you, heart, saw, ways you went!

The second quatrain gives the measure of the kind of hyperbolization that informs the *terrible sonnets:* the hours of night have become, with an emphasizing isocolon, years and then the whole life, while, proportionally, laments become "$_7$countless." But the acme of emphasis is in the first tercet, where isocolons, polyptotons ("$_{10}$taste," as verb and noun; "$_{10}$me" and "$_{11}$me"), repetitions, and *gradationes* overheat the melodramatic atmosphere until the eleventh line, a climax with a threefold, masterfully alliterated isocolon:

11   Bones built in me, flesh filled, blood brimmed the curse.

PART TWO

MEDIEVALISM

I

✣ "INTEGRATED" AND "APOCALYPTIC" WRITERS

After examining how rhetoric works in Hopkins's poetry in the light of its precise and peculiar contextual motivations—after performing, that is, a prevalently synchronic operation that has accordingly left out any historical and diachronic focussing—I now intend to re-examine Hopkins's textuality as a confluence of manifold and variously conflicting cultural codes. What I will therefore attempt is a structural and semiotic reading of the relationships linking Hopkins with and opposing him to the cultural models of his time. The posthumous publication and "delayed-action" explosion of Hopkins may well be sufficient to justify this analysis; they are indeed immediately indicative that these relationships are by no means self-evident. Though Victorian by birth, Hopkins and his time graft one onto another not quite perfectly. Robert Bridges—retrospectively the representative, as the Poet Laureate after 1913, of the most orthodox and reliable Victorianism—well understood this, as is testified by his abstaining from publishing his friend's poetry immediately after his death, and then, when the Victorian Age had already expired, by editing a selection based on those aesthetic criteria expounded in the *Preface to Notes* which I have already amply discussed. After the 1918 edition the prevailing tendency became to identify Hopkins—because of his style, mimetic of the subtlest mental processes—as a forerunner and a guiding force of twentieth-century poetry. In more recent times the discovery and investigation, mainly carried out by the first structuralists, of the extraordinary germs of speculation embedded in Hopkins's writings on poetic language and on the theory of verse and rhythm, have constituted a further index of the modernity and the advance on the times that have been seen (and, to a certain extent, objectively are) in Hopkins's textuality. Yet, if nowadays Hopkins's poetic greatness and "prophetic" thrust are beyond dispute, one must hasten to object that such a modernistic interpretation of Hopkins's relationship with his time rests on a basic misunderstanding. Such an interpretation is decidedly superficial, partial, and simplistic. As Bender has made clear, the misunderstanding of Hopkins's modernity could take root because, to the first authoritative critics of the twenties and thirties who discovered and "launched" him (Richards, Empson, Read, Lewis, Leavis), Hopkins's poetry seemed to anticipate the precepts of their naïve aesthetics, essentially based on the criticism of rationality and on the exaltation of mental association (Bender 1966, 1–4, 60). Though I cannot agree with his paradoxical general thesis—that Hopkins is indeed a forerunner, but precisely because he looks back to ancient tradition—Bender got indeed near the thesis that forms the backbone of my investigation: beside an anti-Victorian, twentieth-century Hopkins, there is also a profoundly and loyally Victorian Hopkins, and, above all, there is a regressive Hopkins, who unearths and adopts "buried" codes, inactive in his time and therefore variously incompatible with it.

Among Jurij Lotman's typological researches and his numerous and seminal theoretic assessments,[1] one particularly relevant to our case is his description of the texts of any single culture (both literary and nonliterary) as an expression of its predominant codes (cultural, ethical, religious, behavioral, etc.), so that each text can be seen as a variant of the text of culture ascribable to a given cultural type or system (Lotman 1969, 311; Lotman

1. See above all Lotman 1969, Lotman 1973, Lotman 1977, and Lotman-Uspenskij 1975. For the problems treated in this chapter see also Foucault 1966, Kristeva 1970, Pagnini 1976, 125–36. On medieval literature and its *topoi* see the classic Curtius 1953 and Lewis 1964.

1973, 40; and Lotman-Uspenskij 1975, 150ff.). This does not exclude that, proportionally to the cultural dynamism characterizing and vivifying cultures, each single text might be variously divergent from the sum total of its normalizing codes, and that, therefore, a certain text—enlarging the previous definition—might be seen as a hierarchized and ordered combination of codes, both pertinent to and extraneous to its own cultural system.[2] This seems to me the case with Hopkins's textuality as "variant of the text of Victorian culture." We detect in it both predominant and alternative or conflictual codes. A quick description of the model of Hopkins's textuality according to its code stratification might be the following: to a pre-existing group of Victorian codes two others are added—non-Victorian codes as inactive codes anticipated and inactive codes restored. As a sum of code acceptations, anticipations, and restorings, Hopkins's textuality represents therefore the not-so-rare case in which, as Lotman has felicitously synthesized, a text constitutes "not the incarnation of a certain code, but the union of different systems," so that "the code of one epoch is not . . . the only cipher book, but the prevalent cipher book. It predominates, and while it deciphers some basic texts it organizes others only partially. Consequently the complementary codes may differ considerably, as far as the principles are concerned, from the predominant code, though they must be compatible with it, and must yield to an analogous regulation."[3] In another important essay—"On the Semiotic Mechanism of Culture" (Lotman-Uspenskij 1978), which

2. An anticipation of this—and one which it is tempting to read as a personal prophecy—is formulated by Hopkins in an essay written in 1865 (?) titled "The Position of Plato to the Greek World" (J, 115–17). Hopkins writes, "There need be no inconsistency on either side in seeing how Plato or other thinkers whose position at any time has given them much prominence both represent and contradict the times in which they live." Hopkins mentions the examples of Shakespeare (in whom he sees representation more than contradiction) and Wordsworth (of whom he emphasizes the "contradiction to the spirit of his times"). But the best example is Plato, whose "philosophy and mind as compared with the Greek contemporary world seem to offer opportunities for endless balancing, antithesis as well as parallel." On the relationships between Hopkins and Plato, see below, chapter 6.

3. Lotman 1969, 313. See also, for further elaborations of these concepts, Lotman 1973, 40, and Lotman-Uspenskij 1975, 30–31.

is even more susceptible of application to the typological situation we find in Hopkins—Lotman adds a series of useful remarks concerning the dynamism ingrained in every culture. He points out that the "opposition 'organized-nonorganized' " can be found even "within the very mechanism of culture," and that, therefore, there may be cases of peripheral systems "allowing various degrees of disorganization," of cultures that "break the various links of such a structure and . . . require continual comparison with the nucleus of the culture" (ibid., 222). Later on, Lotman reformulates this opposition as "unity" versus "multiplicity" (ibid., 226), and he affirms the existence of non-integrated cultural fringes, of "little islands of 'different' organization in the general body of culture," which incidentally help overcome the "entropy of structural automatization" (ibid., 227).

In order to begin an investigation of Hopkins's textuality with reference to the codes organizing its messages—an investigation of the relationship that the text establishes with the macrotext of Victorian culture—it is indispensable first to build up a model of that culture. The model must be capable of functioning as a synthetic but reliable term of comparison, at least for the aspects in which contacts or frictions with our specific text can be sighted. I shall try to do this, freely adopting and adapting the useful four-type grid Lotman has applied to Russian history and literary history (Lotman 1973). Though based on extremely flexible and approximate categories, and more appropriately applicable to the culture for which it was created, and barely touching the historical period in Russian history corresponding to the Victorian Age in England (1837–1901), this grid remains nevertheless highly useful for our purposes. Just because of its extreme flexibility and abstractedness, it probably exhausts all past and future typological possibilities and combinations: Lotman himself, speaking of the fourth type (which is the "contamination" of the two preceding it: "semantico-syntagmatic") seems to imply that this type is situated, as far as forecasts can go, close to the moment of definitive saturation of possible codes:

The gamut of the possibilities of change of the cultural codes was exhausted and the abandoning of a system brought to the restoration of another. . . . It is significant that the systems that arose in Russia toward the middle of the nineteenth century, and that aimed to create more complex models of the world, should rise as a creolization of the cultural codes already in existence. For example, for the Russia of the middle of the nineteenth century the attempts to synthesize types III and IV had an exceptional significance. (Lotman 1973, 61)

On the basis of these remarks, all objections as to undue chronological violations/extensions of Lotman's single types may, I believe, be waived. Secondly, the use I will make of Lotman's grid is instrumental and practical, as it does not aspire to add new insights into the cultural history of the Victorian Age, but only to provide an agile and handy model of comparison (which, I may add, is hardly to be found in the manuals and in the other classic works of reference).[4]

Having established this much, we can now reaffirm some typological principles previously touched on and recall some well-known generalizations of history and literary history, as the basis on which to build the typological image of the Victorian Age which we need. In particular we must consider:

a. the existence within every culture of groups of prevailing codes (Lotman 1969, 314), the extension and proportion of which are variable and certainly hierarchized: that is, in practice, the existence of mixed cultures, with the possibility, therefore, of crossbreeds of heterogeneous codes;

b. the "hybrid," pluralistic and composite character of the Victorian Age, and therefore

c. the absence of a "Victorian type" by definition, absolutely and organically predominating;

d. the inadequacy of Lotman's fourth type, "semantico-symbolic," as a model of the Victorian Age (the inadequacy, that is, of the type that logically and chronologically would be the one most adaptable in our case).

4. Among the history textbooks dealing especially with Victorian ideas, see Briggs 1968 and Briggs 1977. See also Trevelyan 1945, 509–86, which provides a sweeping description of Victorian society, somewhat vitiated, however, by superficiality and triumphalism. *L'Inghilterra vittoriana* by E. Grendi (1975) is one of the few texts that seek to read and interpret critically—and not merely to chronicle—the history of the Victorian Age.

On the basis of these considerations we can formulate the hypothesis that the most acceptable model of the cultural system of the Victorian Age—that from which it is possible to deduce the greatest number of its many and contradictory aspects—is the combination of a syntagmatic (with more or less tenuous semantic compensations, therefore partially semantico-syntagmatic) with an aparadigmatic model.

As to the first of the two models, the similarities between the Victorian Age and what Lotman has called "syntagmatic type" seem to me marked indeed. This type, radically opposed to the "semantico-symbolic" type active in the Middle Ages which it chronologically follows in his grid, is characterized by a strong emphasis on the practical and the useful, and it sets great store by common sense. These are values generally and timelessly Anglo-Saxon, yet polarized in this historical phase, which is in many respects one of full and rampant desemioticization.

If, as Lotman maintains, practical life, and the different value and degree of importance it takes, constitute a particularly revealing test of the cultural tendencies of a given epoch, then in the Victorian Age—compared for instance to the first decades of the nineteenth century or the Middle Ages—practical life appears multiplied and magnified out of all proportion in the whole gamut of its manifestations, to such an extent that it almost absorbs the totality of the speculative and intellectual human energies. It is enough to think of the formidable development of technology and industrialization, stimulated by and stimulating a widespread aspiration to a higher and better standard of living, a demand that went hand in hand with the enormous progress of scientific research.[5] The same inventions constituting the pride of the age (the railway, steam-navigation, the penny-post, the telegram, and photography)[6] are both the cause and the effect of an

5. In the early and middle nineteenth century, England became the leading country in scientific research. I shall only mention the foundation of the Royal Institution by H. Davy; M. Faraday and the first electrochemical experiments; J. P. Joule and the discovery of the first principle of thermodynamics; J. C. Maxwell and differential equations and electro-magnetic fields. On the improvement of the standard of living see Trevelyan 1945, 559–61, and Briggs, 1977.

6. The triumph of Victorian technological development was, as is well known,

embryonic "welfare state," and are therefore perfectly in line with a syntagmatic tendency to improve and gratify practical life.

At the level of outlook and style of life, we accordingly notice consequences that fit in perfectly with Lotman's syntagmatic type. The face of England changes radically; the old image of a sedantary and largely rural society is now replaced (with visible repercussions on town planning and scenery) by that of a new dynamic and industrialized society containing the germs of the modern mass society.[7] In this new context the mercantile bourgeoisie and the working proletariat of the textile, mining, and iron and steel industries have risen extraordinarily in importance, as compared to aristocracy and the landed gentry. The values inspiring and giving life to this social and economic reshuffling are new and unpredictable, though they are actually perfectly consistent with the model: capitalistic accumulation, the corporative and competitive spirit,[8] self-interest and the absence of moral scruples,[9] and along with these a rampant conformism. All this is once again a tangible index of a desemioticization and of a general

---

the Great Exhibition which was held at Crystal Palace in 1851. See Briggs 1977, 43–51.

7. On the Victorian city and the problems facing it (urbanization, property speculation, overpopulation, poor sanitation, etc.) see Briggs 1968, especially the first two chapters. Briggs also devotes some acute pages to the debate between the supporters and the enemies of urbanization in literature (71–76). On these aspects see also, for several anecdotes and examples, Trevelyan 1945, 523–24, and 527–30.

8. Victorian society restores strongly atomistic and Hobbesian features, and this is reflected in the meritocratic criteria and the competition system introduced by the administration. These phenomena are obviously linked with the expansion of education. On social climbing and on the effects it provoked, see Briggs 1977, 27–32, 85–90, 116–21.

9. If we except dissent, the Victorian religious revival was substantially an instrument of social control and (in its philanthropic dimension) a pawn of the system, rather than an autonomous and disruptive phenomenon. In spite of appearances it must be observed that spheres of action that previously had been harmonized with time underwent a sharp separation and became irreconcilable, such as science and religion and science and morals. Even in the ranks of aristocracy and high culture, religion, where it does not yield to agnosticism, refuses to be institutionalized and regimented, and becomes lukewarm, vague, pantheistic. The utilitarian and Benthamite presuppositions of bourgeois ethics left no room for an authentic religious sentiment: philosophical utilitarianism was anti-dogmatic and nominalistic, and implied that many concepts and values of traditional ethics (such as conscience, the moral sense, love, right, etc.) were superfluous. See below for the attitude of the Victorians toward religion in literature.

materialistic and empirical trend that inspires and in turn is inspired by the contemporary political, ideological, philosophical, and pseudo-philosophical theorizings. Positivistic and Benthamite utilitarianism (vulgarized as a eulogy of perseverance and self-help by the Scots physician Samuel Smiles) and J. S. Mill's empiricism, in their common emphasis on the Puritan and Calvinistic components of the *mens britannica* and in their firm opposition to any metaphysical adventure and any solution of a "symbolic" type, become the most direct philosophical mediations of the rising bourgeoisie. The same can be said for the even more radical economic and populationist doctrines of Smith and Malthus that inspire governmental policies, and for Darwin's evolutionism and Spencer's evolutionary and mystically oriented positivism, more palatable to the moderate and conservative currents.

Political power itself, far from opposing this syntagmatic tendency, tolerates and fosters it. A closer inspection of the global model of society it favors and shapes, and of the position the individual occupies within it, reveals a highly hierarchized and stratified society characterized by a "humbling of the individual" that might be taken for, but indeed is not, a "semantic," medieval trait. If in the syntagmatic type "the belonging to a whole becomes a token of cultural significance," in the Middle Ages "the part does not equal the whole and joyfully acknowledges its insignificance before it. The whole is not the *meaning* of the part, but the *sum* of the syntagmatically organized fractions" (Lotman 1973, 52; Lotman's italics). Compared to the Romantic Age, its wild idealism and individualism, Victorian society settles down to narrower and more uniforming horizons. The individual no longer aspires to occupy the higher steps of the value scale but rather tends to be evened out in the whole, in the State, or rather in the Empire, and in the "parts" of which it is the "sum," and in a moment in which forms of associations multiply and the most disparate and minute corporatism asserts itself.[10] But the great

10. "The members of the other classes cease to be individuals to acquire instead uniform group features: habits, behaviors, customs become a uniform. . . . The role of outsiders is almost suffocated by a kind of cultural uniformity scrutinizing behavior and branding those who go against the mainstream" (Grendi 1975, 37–

success of the practical sense and flexibility of the Victorian ruling class was to preserve intact, and even increase, consent and solidarity, through the use of effective control and integration systems as well as reliable channels of diversion and outlets for popular discontent—at the very moment when European monarchies everywhere faced dramatic problems of mass governability.[11] But for other aspects, too, the developmental model and the physiognomy of the Victorian Age verify the requisites of syntagmatic ages: "An essential aspect of the organization of this type of culture was its being a part of the progress of time. . . . This means . . . an improvement of the system of laws or the spreading of science" (Lotman 1973, 53). Of the "spreading of science" and the progressivism characterizing the age I have already spoken; that the Victorian Age is a reformist age, an age of hectic legislative activity, one can realize by simply running

---

38). The most typical pseudo-value, the fetish, of Victorian society is consequently *respectability:* "We can indeed speak of a rising consciousness of stratification and of social hierarchies, and therefore of a growing and widespread attention to appearances at all levels of the social ladder" (ibid., 37). For Briggs, who refers to Bagehot and Trollope, the "secrets" of Victorian stability were deference and dignity (Briggs 1977, 99–104).

11. It is superfluous to remember that the specter of proletarian revolution was strongly felt in England, and that the actual governmental policies were considerably conditioned by it. Among the fundamental instruments of social control, the expansion of education and religious propaganda—not accidentally almost interdependent—must be mentioned: "Schooling . . . was to be isolated from social culture and was to be kept under the influence of local ruling groups, and of philanthropists and churchmen" (Grendi 1975, 15; for a more extensive treatment of this interdependence see the classic Altick 1957). The "Society for the Diffusion of Useful Knowledge," one of the bodies that strenuously contributed to the democratization of culture, actually aimed to forge a population entirely enslaved to machines and to the industrial system. Religious propaganda was itself a mediator in the shaping of the intelligent artisan, that is, the temperate, virtuous and system-integrated worker. As R. K. Webb writes: "To the advocates of education, a literate working class seemed essential not only for the domestic peace of England but for its progress. The new statistical societies eagerly received papers proving the direct connexion between crime and ignorance. . . . A working class on the move might be explosive, but liberal doctrine preached a faith in education which would capture and direct the lower classes into right thinking. That meant schooling, not only in reading and writing but in morals, politics, and political economy" (Webb 1968, 212). On schooling and its function of forming the new Victorian gentleman, and on the figure that exercised the greatest impact on it (Thomas Arnold of Rugby) see also Briggs 1977, 148–75. By "channels of diversion" I mean first of all the symbolic role and important function of social aggregation played by the Crown and the Empire.

through the stages of British democratic development. With Peel and Canning, and after the reaction following the Congress of Vienna and Peterloo, the thirties and forties see the first great reformist wave (the First Reform Bill in 1832, soon followed by the Municipal Corporations Act [1835] and preceded by the abolition of the Test Act [1828]). After the legislative stasis of the period 1846–66, a new reformist impetus under Gladstone (1868–74) and Disraeli (1874–80) brought the opening of universities to dissent (1871), the reform of the school system (1870) and above all the second Reform Bill (1867) which, followed by the third (1884), practically established the universal male franchise.[12]

If, after thus sketching the global syntagmatic model of the Victorian Age, we now turn for confirmation to the body of its actualized cultural texts, both artistic and literary, we notice that the latter undoubtedly reproduce but also variously modify and contradict the image so far constructed. Nor is this surprising, not only owing to the internal dynamism typical of all cultures, but also, and above all, because an artistic text—by its very nature—is never a pure and literal reproduction of contemporary codes (linguistic, ideological, social, ethical, philosophical, etc.). It is rather a reshaping and transformation of them. That being stated, let us attempt to classify typologically the Victorian Age as a sum of its artistic and literary texts. We notice:

1. A section of texts constituting a pure reflection and a full confirmation of the existing syntagmatic codes, or texts in which the possible (minimal) code oppositions are almost insignificant compared to the sum of code coincidences and gratifications. "Integrated" authors correspond to this section.

2. A section of texts that modify the existing syntagmatic codes, either radicalizing them or tempering them, but in both cases with the introduction of Enlightenment codes. This is the section corresponding to a certain standard of Victorian artist

12. As Grendi (1975) reminds us, these extensions of the franchise were shrewd measures of social control, "calculated gestures of party policy, of groups born to be rulers and conscious of the importance of enlarging the area of popular consent" (10).

who distances himself from a considerable number of predominant codes but remains, for the compensation constituted by the acceptance of many others, equally "integrated."

3. A section, finally, of texts that oppose the predominant syntagmatic codes, recovering—and here the distancing from the age becomes more pronounced—semantic and even symbolic codes. The corresponding artists are to be defined "apocalyptic" not simply in a metaphorical sense: in them the refusal of certain predominant codes threatens, qualitatively, to overcome the loyalty to some others.

This model must be accepted with the important addition that all these conflicting or even simply divergent codes, far from involving, in a homogeneous and exclusive way, the corresponding sections of texts, often simultaneously "cross" the very same texts and therefore even single authors.

It is well known that, according to the different emphasis and hierarchic position given in the past to each of these sections—or even to each of these codes organizing single texts or groupings of texts—we have had divergent and often even glaringly incompatible evaluations of the literature and of the art in general of the Victorian Age. Remembering that code relationships and orientations sensibly vary in Victorian literature according to genre (fiction, poetry, essay writing, scientific literature, etc.), hierarchization doubtless constitutes a very arduous and delicate task—one would even say a matter of personal taste. Recent criticism, after justly confuting the prevailing view of an entirely syntagmatic Victorian Age, has wisely preferred to speak of a tendential entropy, rather than hierarchy, of codes: "The outlines of the Victorian era blur beyond recognition *in the confusion of contradictory charges.* . . . Almost every Victorian thesis produced its own antithesis . . . and conflict, indeed, may emerge as the only unity in a great diversity" (Buckley 1966, 2, 6, 9). But, despite such a chaotic mixture of codes, it is possible—as Buckley himself has done, bringing to light the leading ideas of the period—to show that the matrices to which such a dispersion is reducible are just the syntagmatic, the aparadigmatic, and the (syntagmatico-)semantic ones.[13] I shall try to demonstrate that, while such a mosaic of codes and "creolization" of types covers almost the whole of Victorian textual activity, Hopkins's body of writings cannot be framed within them, owing to an eclecticism and entropy of codes absolutely superior to the "exceptions" of the period themselves and, furthermore, owing to a hierarchization that is almost not to be found in any other Victorian writer.

Let us now proceed—according to the order given above, which is also one of inverted pertinence to Hopkins's body of texts—to a functional illustration of Victorian literature and the codes organizing it. In the past many models of the Victorian Age have been based on section 1. They have in fact attempted to provide a global image of the Victorian Age as a conventional, conformist age, fully respondent to contemporary codes and as such syntagmatic.[14] This character, though far from covering the whole body of Victorian literature, is undeniably illustrated by the group of the pseudo-philosophical, religious, sociological, political, economic, journalistic texts to which I have alluded above. But even the more restricted body of texts with a self-declared aesthetic end (fiction and poetry) shares, and proportionally intact, the same mechanisms of substantial reproduction of the predominant codes. It is perhaps useful in this connection to analyze briefly the new role of the artist in Victorian society, along with the emergence of an audience that has itself considerably changed—both quantitatively and qualitatively—and is

13. Buckley speaks of "doctrines . . . recurring with an insistency which suggests the breadth of their influence" (9). Among those he lists and describes, the "doctrine of organic development" (5) or "notion of perfectibility" (8), the "Benthamite philosophy" (9), the "distrust" of the "falsehood of extremes" and the "desire for cultural synthesis" (12) belong to the syntagmatic code; the "idea of progress"—significantly qualified as an "outgrowth of Cartesian philosophy" (7)—the "withering faith" and "materialism" (11) belong to Enlightenment codes; the "Evangelical religion," "moral duty" inducing the "morality of art," that is, a "didactic literature" speaking the "language of universal emotion" (10) belong to semantic codes. As can be seen, code pertinence is not univocal, and this is a further confirmation of the hybrid character of Victorian culture.

14. Let it suffice to remember among many, for these unbalanced views, Mario Praz's *Storia della letteratura inglese* (1968), and G. D. Klingopoulos, "The Literary Scene" (1968).

characterized by new cultural demands. While the Romantic Age is marked by a type of writer who is in various ways alternative to the society in which he produces (from which he feels rejected and by which he feels misunderstood), in the Victorian Age the population increase and above all the educational upsurge, now involving strata of previously semi-illiterate people, provide the writer with an enlarged and culturally almost "immaculate" audience, for whose education he now shares the responsibility.[15] The establishment asks him to become a sort of mediator—government official, "cultural attaché"—for the new bourgeoisie and the acculturizing lower classes, to whom he provides the models of ethical and practical behavior that they need, disoriented as they are while being received into the sphere of respectability. Literature can now become one of the instruments of social participation and consent.

With this new relationship between the artist and society, many writers—whose ideal prototype might be Gissing's Jasper Milvain in *New Grub Street*—and a great deal of literature became so zealous in responding to these social demands—or were otherwise induced to make profits out of the fresh opening up of wide commercial spaces—that they complied almost wholly, in their literary mediations, with the contemporary codes. This is a quite predictable phenomenon, especially if we think of the tendencies of the new utilitarian and pragmatic milieu, which coherently promoted the discredit of Art, aesthetic disengagement, "realism," and "sociological purpose" (Buckley 1966, 19).[16] This explains the loss of personal accent and originality, and the tendency to stereotype the writer and the literary work—two of the most commonly criticized features of Victorian literature.[17]

15. See again Altick 1957.

16. See also Cox 1968, 199–200. Buckley (1966, 16–24) shows how the reading of the Romantics made by the Victorians ("the early Victorians . . . were forced to reject certain romantic values, to repudiate specific attitudes and gestures, in order to secure their own orientation" [17]) was guided by the canons of the "social sense," and the "distrust of literature" and its seduction.

17. The canon of *realism* is also active in the parallel field of Victorian painting. In the late nineteenth century, one observes the tendency "*to copy* a conventional expression of an emotion" and "to take an immediately recognizable likeness of a subject already known to be a reliable stimulus to a certain emotion in its be-

While the popularity of poetry declined, fiction was staggeringly promoted by the extension and stratification of the reading public. The Victorian novel is itself stratified, and in some cases it became so contaminated that it appropriated journalistic and institutionally extra-literary functions such as the edification, the mere entertainment, and the gratification of the most superficial demands of the new public.[18]

Yet the Victorian Age is not only the age of the bestsellers of the circulating libraries, or of the yellow-backs and the chapbooks—conventional, escapist literature. It is also—and with this we pass on to section 2 of texts—the age of dignified and *engagé* works, so designated in proportion to their nonidentification with and even refusal of a certain number of predominant codes. The section undoubtedly includes the majority of the great figures of Victorian literature. Examined in its typological constants, section 2 can provide us with an absolutely reliable image of a considerable part of the literary culture of the period. This section has neo-Enlightenment features, though according to two antithetical tendencies. If the Enlightenment type pushes to its extreme consequences the desemioticizing tendencies of the syntagmatic type (Lotman 1973, 54), it is consistent to qualify as neo-Enlightenment a well-identifiable philosophical trend of Victorian culture that, starting from self-declared eighteenth-century and Benthamite premises, was also pronouncedly aparadigmatic. The names of Mill, Darwin, Huxley, and Stephen im-

---

holder" (Piper 1965, 131). It is a significant coincidence that such a propensity for faithful reproduction should be contemporary to the invention of photography.

18. On serial publication and its repercussions, especially on the novels of Dickens and Thackeray, see the masterly K. Tillotson, *Novels of the Eighteen-Forties* (Tillotson 1954); on the stratification of the novel see the extremely significant chart provided by Webb 1968, 216–17, which shows that no less than 46 percent and 20 percent of the books of the circulating libraries were respectively "novels of the lowest character" and "fashionable novels." Novels, just because they were normally published serially, were strongly affected by the sensational tendencies and the commercial conditionings of the contemporary publishing system. In contrast with this sensationalism, "The Wreck of the Deutschland" is an exception to the rule, since Hopkins subjects an event, which the contemporary press amply exploited, to a simply unthinkable reading (or rather, as I have tried to demonstrate, to a reading just the opposite of the expectations of Victorian public opinion).

mediately come to mind. Periodic waves of rationalism, nominalism, agnosticism, and scientism run through Victorian culture from its dawning and reverberate distinctly in specifically literary texts (for instance, the poetry of Tennyson and Arnold). Yet, ignoring for the moment the parallel idealistic counteroffensives, the neo-Enlightenment Victorian writer was, most typically, not a radical but a moderate writer, intent on making socially and politically useful art and mitigating, tempering, humanizing, reforming, and remaining loyal to a cultural model. But the codes adhered to are still neo-Enlightenment codes. After the mystic, wild, and extremist idealism of the Romantic Age, we witness the return of an eighteenth-century, didactic and sententious moralism that is profoundly alien to any revolutionary exhibitionism and any transgressive tendency. As in the Enlightenment, the artist reactivates the role of critic and corrector of social evils, pointing to injustices, combating the spreading philistinism and breaking up the dominant self-righteousness. If we keep this in mind, together with the new mass configuration of Victorian society, the aesthetic culture of this period shares the character, common to all Enlightenment cultures, of a grammaticalized culture, founded on content and rules (Lotman-Uspenskij 1978, 218–19). Unlike the Romantic Age, in which a textualized culture (one in which rules are implicitly derived from texts) prevails in Europe as well as in England, in the Victorian Age rules directly generate and rigorously bind texts according to expressive, ethical, and aesthetic codes, of which the critics—who often had a life-and-death power over writers, as in the Enlightenment— were the compilers.[19] Hectic is the search, in the age, for "critical standards" and "fixed" patterns, for scientifically founded and unarbitrary aesthetic theories which, once applied, may carry out the most heartfelt aspiration of the period: the suppression of anarchic individualism and romantic indiscipline and subjectivism, and the reduction of art to a "language of universal emotion," capable of discovering and revealing "the eternal principle in the

19. According to Lotman, the "Enlightenment code . . . introduced the concept of norm and its transgression into numerous casual achievements" (Lotman 1973, 56).

transitory human experience" (Buckley 1966, 10, 121).[20] Compared to romantic "excess," the touchstones of Victorian aesthetics become the principles of the "golden mean" and of "balance," of gradualness, of the compromise between opposing tendencies, of the refusal of extremisms and even of their mediation, of "verisimilitude" and "realism." Alexander Pope is the eighteenth-century model of the Victorians, who saw in him the artist capable of synthesizing and fully carrying out these values. They identified him with Tennyson. Victorian culture as a whole—or even *this* Victorian culture—is obviously different from the age of Enlightenment. It did not share, among other things, the Enlightenment's sense of falsehood attached to social relationships (Lotman 1973, 56–57); yet the two ages present undeniable typological concordances and correspondences in their "put[ting] at the base of the whole organization of culture the natural-unnatural opposition." Both are opposed to the "chimerae of the signic world" and to any kind of escape into the reign of imagination and of private sensibility; both set "the essence of things . . . against signs as well as the real against the fantastic" (ibid., 54, 59).

From what I have been saying about Victorian cultural codes and their type pertinence, a more marked opposition to the predominant cultural model will be recognizable at this point only in the activity of codes alternative to the syntagmatic and aparadigmatic ones, that is, in semantico-symbolic codes of a medieval

20. Buckley (1966) devotes some excellent chapters (III, VII, VIII), enriched by abundant quotations, to Victorian aesthetics. For Arnold, he notes, "It was the romantic heresy that expression might weigh more than theme and that the accidental and personal might replace the essential and the universal. But significant modern poetry, he said, could 'only subsist by its *contents;* by becoming a complete magister vitae as the poetry of the ancients did' " (ibid., 26; Buckley's italics). On the other hand Newman complained of "his ignorance of any fixed aesthetic values" and deplored that "all criticism of verse [should] remain personal and so more or less arbitrary and unscientific" (ibid., 132). Buckley also mentions the founding, during the Victorian Age, of numerous Aesthetic Societies (such as the Aesthetic Society founded in Edinburgh in 1851), with the precise aim of investigating the nature of the beautiful and the rules of art (144–48). Hopkins himself, in his youth, was in search of the "lawful objects of Art" (J, 74). The Platonic dialogue on Beauty (1865) stems from a search for the "established laws" of a "judicial . . . criticism" as opposed to a "purely common-sense criticism" (J, 86).

type. The emergence of such unpopular codes is undoubtedly identifiable in the Victorian Age, even if it is exceptional and also substantially counterbalanced by the acceptance of a certain number of predominant codes that reintegrate, or render "tolerable," phenomena to be otherwise considered, from the point of view of the given culture, anticultural. Thus many texts and writers appear to take their place astride this and the preceding section, that is, to alternate syntagmatico-aparadigmatic with semantico-symbolic codes. This phenomenon of contamination and hybridization—normal in a tendentially entropic context such as the Victorian—must make us cautious not to take for semantico-symbolic pertinences what are in reality syntagmatico-aparadigmatic ones. This is truly a risk, if only one thinks how much things medieval notoriously circulate in the Victorian Age. Indeed, against the spreading atomistic and secularizing vision of history and society, an organic and altruistic concept of social relationships flourishes; foiled by arid, rationalistic pragmatism, warm and disinterested feelings of solidarity and *pietas* assert themselves. Medieval traits are discernible in neo-Gothic architecture, in Pre-Raphaelite painting, and in the poets of the "medieval school" inspired by the "medieval" Keats and by the medieval romances of chivalry (recall Morris and also Tennyson), while medieval stylistic elements may be considered the linguistic archaisms, religious symbolism, ritualism, emblematicism and allegory. But, we may ask, to what degree are these scattered symptoms of medievalism really a content—a radical and structural option, an integral adherence to some specific codes and to a whole episteme—rather than a superficial fashion or manner, a fragmentary and metaphorical tendency, an external form? Keeping this in mind, it is possible to extract from the Victorian philosophical, religious, and literary culture a few, minority tendencies that are authentically semantico-symbolic—or are as little as possible contaminated by syntagmatico-aparadigmatic alliances—and that clearly show a process of code inversion and of re-semanticization. The "icebergs" of this process—and they are, not casually, the most exorbitant, the most "diverse," the most original, the most "visionary" figures in an age that put at

the top of the scale of values the principles of moderation, realism, and universality—are essentially the idealistic and anti-posi-
tivistic reaction culminating with T. H. Green and F. H. Bradley
in the seventies and beyond,[21] Carlyle, Ruskin, partially Kingsley, and of course Newman and the Oxford Movement. Buckley
has identified the characteristics (and outlined the typology of
narrative functions, of imagery and style at the textual level) of
what he defines as the "pattern of conversion," that is, the widespread yearning for a palingenesis and purgation, in an age that
to many a visionary and apocalyptic spirit seemed on the eve of
its annihilation.[22] In other words, while the neo-Enlightenment
writers raised objections to contemporary secular, materialistic,
and utilitarian trends from inside the model, which they did not
reject but only sought to reform and correct, the "apocalyptic"
writers shared an urge toward a "revolution," toward a "conversion" of the model in a literal sense, toward an overturning and a
metanoia of values that betray a reactivation of the paradigmatic
and verticalizing tendency that is one of the cornerstones of the
semantico-symbolic culture of the Middle Ages.[23]

21. Such a reaction not accidentally looks back to aprioristic and voluntaristic
philosophies such as Hegel's and Kant's. Green and Bradley are significantly preceded by Newman and his revolt against reason and his emphasis on the fideistic
and emotional "assent." Toward the close of the century, these speculative trends
gave birth to forms of a more marked irrationalism, such as Yeats's occultism.

22. Buckley acutely analyzes some "archetypes"—such as the sea journey, the
desert, water and drought, the phoenix—in Carlyle (1966, 95–97), and some images of sacrifice by combustion and of baptismal purgation in Victorian fiction (C.
Brontë, Dickens, G. Eliot, etc.: ibid., 97–102). "Apocalyptic" and "acrophobic"
images (landslides, unapproachable peaks, mortal perils) have been detected in
several Victorian texts by Sulloway (1972) (see below, chapter 2).

23. Apropos of this widespread "pattern of conversion," Dickens's motif of
the conversion of the wicked man may be exemplarily symptomatic and revelatory of the fragmentariness and nonpertinence within the semantico-symbolic
type of many "medieval" devices of the period.

2

❧ ENTROPY AND HIERARCHY

OF CODES

At the close of this discussion, even a quick comparison of Hopkins's body of writings with the three sections of texts described above would doubtless indicate the third as the fittest to match the greatest number of its code options. A more careful and prolonged inspection shows, however, that not even section 3 can fully contain Hopkins's textuality. The assertion that might now be formulated almost automatically, of Hopkins's absolute and total extraneousness to his time and cultural type, would, however, constitute a critical misconception and an unacceptable hyperbole. This is not the thesis I intend to demonstrate, and I have already pointed out, at the opening of this second part of this book, the conditions, limits, and typological requisites within which one can argue Hopkins's opposition to his time. Furthermore, it will be seen that in Hopkins's case such an opposition is not something static and firmly established from the outset, but rather a process, which therefore determines, diachronically, different ratios between acceptances and rejections. Undeniably, however, from his University years and after he joined the Jesuits, Hopkins gradually came to adopt a range of codes exactly antithetical to the predominant ones. That range is far greater, qualitatively and quantitatively, than in any other Victorian artist, and it brings him vertiginously close to a typological opposition to his time and to his culture. More precisely, the reconstruction and investigation of the codes governing Hopkins's mature textuality shows the subordinateness, more often the inactivity or even the abolition of the Victorian syntagmatic and aparadigmatic codes, and a marked and radical adherence to a group of semantic and symbolic codes of a medieval type. To formulate such a hypothesis means of course to take a stand on a question debated in the past (more insistently in the last few decades) by a rich and discordant bibliography of studies: that of Hopkins's typological placing within his culture.

One can say that criticism concerning this problem has formulated three distinct, and to a certain extent chronologically successive, interpretations. There has been a tendency to see Hopkins as (a) ahead of the times in which he lived; (b) behind his times; or (c) perfectly and fully Victorian. The first of these interpretations—as we saw in Part I, chapter 1—was put forward in the twenties and thirties by certain critics (Riding and Graves, Richards, Empson, above all Leavis) who carried out a modernistic reading of Hopkins's poetry, insisting on its germs of novelty and contemporaneity. One of the first critics to advance doubts about this view, suggestive but partial and undoubtedly simplistic, was Abbott, in the introduction to his edition of Hopkins's correspondence with Bridges (1935). Abbott called it a "glaring . . . misconception" to consider Hopkins "a poet in key with contemporary experiment and disillusion," and concluded that, strange though he may have been, Hopkins was "an Englishman and a Victorian" (L I, xxi). An even more Victorian Hopkins was that presented by most of the essays in *Gerard Manley Hopkins by the Kenyon Critics* (Collections 1945). Among its contributors, Arthur Mizener reduced Hopkins's "oddness" to a "surface phenomenon" (Mizener 1945, 94), and consequently saw him as "the typical 19th Century Englishman," concluding, with an almost literal repetition of Abbott's diagnosis, that Hopkins, far from being "a poet in rebellion against his time, an anachronism out of the 17th or the 20th Century" (96), "is Victorian, in a good many respects obviously Victorian" (113). Mizener's assertion that this interpretation was shared "by all the contributors to the *Kenyon Review*'s symposium" (114) was, however, untrue.

MacLuhan's and Warren's essays, in particular, pointed out modes of looking at reality and ways of thinking and sermonizing hardly homogeneous with Victorian standards. MacLuhan observed that Hopkins "looks at external nature as a Scripture exactly as Philo Judaeus, St. Paul and the Church Fathers had done" (MacLuhan 1945, 19); Warren stated that Hopkins's sermons "would have been better understood by a Jacobean congregation than by a Victorian," while medieval elements were detected in his predilection for Gregorian chant (Warren 1945, 6), in the "medieval and Franciscan joy in God's creation" (75), in the "dominantly 'medieval' " (79) poem "The Habit of Perfection," and above all in Hopkins's yearning for an England not yet transformed by the disruptive event of the Reformation: "Hopkins seems to be reaching back, while he reached forward, to an 'English' poetry. Probably we may add, to an English Catholic poetry; and suppose that his pushing back of the Elizabethans had some incentive in his desire to get back of the Reformation to the day when all England was at once Catholic and English" (86). But it all amounted to elements that, undoubtedly eccentric as they were, were not sufficient to suggest, let alone prove, any systematic opposition to Victorian culture, as Gardner too authoritatively argued in his study, which aimed to harmonize Hopkins's atypical (idiosyncratic) and traditional components.

These contributions had the effect of discouraging further presentations of Hopkins's textuality in terms of pure anticipation and modernity. But from the thirties a different critical trend had begun to show how insufficient any series of Victorian codes prove in functioning as its framework. This trend was unwilling to minimize or easily integrate several extra-systematic components or implications. At the same time it also started to point out—principally at the level of influences and textual echoes—the powerful activity or even the primacy of a certain number of obsolete and variously non-Victorian codes. The first of Christopher Devlin's invaluable contributions devoted to Hopkins's assimilation of Duns Scotus's philosophy dates back to 1935, whereas John Pick's *Gerard Manley Hopkins: Priest and Poet* (Pick 1942) was the first of an abundant harvest of investigations of

Hopkins's manifold and decisive connections with Catholic theology and of the influence of St. Ignatius's *Spiritual Exercises*. In many studies the latter were later forcedly given—as in Downes's *Gerard Manley Hopkins: A Study of His Ignatian Spirit* or, in a more sophisticated way, in Ong's *Hopkins, the Self, and God*—an absolute and exclusive modelling capacity they do not have. The relevance of these connections, and therefore the adherence to a type of Catholicism quite foreign to the age, made J.-G. Ritz write, "dans un monde qui ne favorisait en rien l'envol de l'imagination et qui préparait le nivellement et l'uniformisation de la personnalité humaine" Hopkins occupies "le versant opposé," or goes "*à contrecourante* . . . sur des chemins nouveaux ou abandonnés," and conclude that he is a "*poète à part*," belonging "manifestement à la génération des écrivains victoriens 'non-victoriens'," and that his work is "absolument différente de celle de ses contemporains" (Ritz 1963, 272, 273, 638, 650; Ritz's italics). Along the same line, Joseph Hillis Miller—in a contribution that I consider the most penetrating among the long essays written on Hopkins—maintained that a coincidence of Hopkins with "the situation in poetry and in life which is characteristic of nineteenth-century man . . . is experienced by [him] *before his conversion*," and that the latter represents "a rejection of three hundred and fifty years of the spiritual history of the West." According to Miller, what distinguishes Hopkins is "something like the view of nature on which medieval and Renaissance poetry . . . is based" (Miller 1963, 311, 312, 314). For James Finn Cotter, Hopkins is, by contrast, "a Christian Gnostic as that ideal has been defined by Clement of Alexandria. . . . The author and book which he particularly studied and used as a model of his thought and as a source of fresh poetic inspiration" being, he believes, Clement's *Stromateis* (*Miscellanies*) (Cotter 1972, 244).

The gradual focussing of these hitherto unexplored aspects had in some cases the salutary and complementary effect of discouraging hasty verdicts, whether of Hopkins's absolute opposition to his times or of his perfect harmony with them. Attention was therefore drawn to the necessity of a synchronic and diachronic arrangement of Hopkins's body of texts, and thus the perspective was shifted on its pronounced eclecticism and entropy of codes. Bender, for example, saw Hopkins's poetry as a complex process of combinations and aggregations ("the peculiar confluence of Jesuit, classical, and Victorian learning" [Bender 1966, 4]), while Heuser spoke of Hopkins's achievement in terms of "growth and variation" (Heuser 1958, 7) and accordingly divided his production into four phases, culminating in a "Scotist voluntarism and a Pythagorean Platonism of music, memory, and number" reached through a "naturalistic idealism," a "Pre-Raphaelite art and art-criticism," and finally a "philosophy of inscape and instress" (ibid., 98–99). Heuser argued Hopkins's strong links with his time (95), but also the variety and quantity of the divergences and of the heterogeneous components:

Various schools have been invoked along with his name—Wordsworthian, Miltonic, Keatsian or Pre-Raphaelite, the alliterative school of Middle English, the new metaphysical school of Patmore and Thompson. Each of these influenced Hopkins at some stage in his development; the Pre-Raphaelite school was the most significant. If a distinct label is needed, perhaps "baroque" is almost satisfactory, expressing the vehement and fiery incarnation of idea in word-made-flesh, the word rendered sensational. Jesuit tradition in the baroque style links Hopkins directly to the seventeenth-century poetic experience of controlled violence and surprise, of Christian feeling infusing and commanding classical forms, and thus he recalls the poetry of Donne, Herbert, Crashaw, Quarles, and Benlowes. . . . In Hopkins Pre-Raphaelite symbolism and Jesuit emblem-tradition met in a new baroque, independent and fresh, for Hopkins remained deliberately his own species, unique, as he thought all poets should be. (96–97)

Heuser's diagnosis has been recently resumed and developed, after a long interval, by Motto and above all by Ellsberg. Both see Hopkins's poetry as belonging to the baroque tradition (Ellsberg 1987, 97–120) and as having "strong ties to the work of Donne, Jonson and . . . George Herbert" (Motto 1984, 8). In the late seventies and in the eighties, interpretations of Hopkins's position in the literary tradition have wildly multiplied, often resulting in a disconcerting cacophony of suggested "affiliations." Michael Sprinker's book, written in the wake of the post-structuralist, Derridean, and deconstructionist boom of which he elegantly adopts the jargon and many of the issues, "position[s] Hopkins within [the] melancholy fate of the moderns" and in Harold Bloom's "belatedness" (Sprinker 1981, 18–19), and goes on to study him in depth (31–45) in his relationships with Mallarmé's and Valéry's poetics and more generally with the symbolist movement. In his *Hopkins' Sanctifying Imagination,* Downes (who also pays homage to Bloom) identifies Hopkins, contradicting or correcting his previous book, as "an authentic high Romantic" who develops his own aesthetic philosophy and religion from the " 'higher' tradition of the English Romantics," which is his "artistic heritage," and from Coleridge's " 'stereoscopic' imagination" (Downes 1985, 2, 6). Downes fails to mention and discuss Motto's book, which patently defends the opposite thesis and attributes to Hopkins "an absolute revulsion for the Romantic concept of the imagination" (Motto 1984, 6). Downes has been answered by Lichtmann, who states that Hopkins "was at special pains to distance himself from Wordsworth" and is even "anti-Romantic" in his conception of "genius" (Lichtmann 1989, 33–34, 36).

One thing unquestionably proved by this rapid survey is the presence in Hopkins of many disparate and often incompatible codes: Hopkins, one would say, was chameleon-like in his openness to the cultural suggestions he came across. The task facing the critic is qualitatively and quantitatively to hierarchize such a multiplicity of codes. While I consider extremely flimsy the theses of a "modern," Romantic, or Pre-Raphaelite Hopkins, the thesis of a Victorian Hopkins, of a Hopkins largely and substantially integrated in the culture of his time, which I equally do not share, deserves closer inspection and discussion, especially because, after an incomplete development in the forties, it has been put forward and almost definitively perfected in three remarkable studies by W. S. Johnson (1968), by A. G. Sulloway (1972), and more recently by W. J. Ong (1986).

In his *Gerard Manley Hopkins: The Poet as Victorian,* Johnson documents the thesis suggested in his title on the basis of two precise attitudes Hopkins has in common with Victorian literature:

(1) the "feeling of self-consciousness" (Johnson 1968, 8), the tor-
mented search for identity and therefore the "doubleness of
mind, its anxious mood of introspection and uncertainty" (16);
and (2) the "curiously ambivalent attitude toward the natural,
temporal world" (9). To Johnson, the "Deutschland" shares, for
example, the typical Victorian pattern of a "central figure" first
meditating on himself and on his division and then breaking his
isolation and socializing, and making projects for the future (73),
while Hopkins's attitude to nature, as exemplified by "Spring and
Fall" and "That Nature is a Heraclitean Fire," appears typically
Victorian because of the feelings of joy and delight for nature's
beauty but also of sorrow and dejection for its transitoriness. Further probings serve to maintain that Hopkins treats "soaring
birds" (96) much like the other Victorian poets, as "creature[s]
emblematic of the self" (97), or that the crucial figure of the
young "child" links him with Dickens, Meredith, Arnold, and
Tennyson (124). While no one can deny the originality and per-
spicacity of Johnson's readings, the following observations must
be made on the use and interpretation of his data. An analysis
such as Johnson's of themes, attitudes, problems, and obsessions,
though consistent and well carried out, is risky and far from decisive. Superficial consonances and confluences in themes, images,
and situations may equally cover deep-seated code divergences.
Secondly, Johnson's specific findings are almost always unexceptionable, but the link with Victorian culture is often hastily or
gratuitously announced or declared, or in any case appears debatable and scarcely documented. Finally, the two common the-
matic elements Johnson singles out are categories too general and
unspecific to have a real demonstrative weight. On the other
hand no notice at all is taken of the possibly superior modelling
incidence and capacity of other non-Victorian elements and links.
Johnson himself must often admit the difference a theological
perspective brings to similarity.

The complementary operation of a more articulate and exhaustive investigation of the Victorian cultural assumptions behind
Hopkins's poetic texts (which become in their turn of secondary
importance) was subsequently carried out by A. G. Sulloway in

her *Gerard Manley Hopkins and the Victorian Temper*. The influence
of Victorian culture on Hopkins is for her fourfold: "The effect
upon his poetry of the Tractarian wars, Ruskinian aestheticism,[1]
the Victorian concept of a gentleman and the nineteenth-century
apocalyptic mood" (Sulloway 1972, 9). To these four spheres of
influence Sulloway devotes as many astoundingly dense chapters. Though Victorianism is a "shifting" and "prismatic" term,
it is just this "shifting spirit" that "places Hopkins so firmly in the
centre of the Victorian tradition" (1), and that even makes of him
the "prototype . . . [of] so many vigorous Victorians" (213, note
9). Like Johnson, Sulloway maintains that "[Hopkins's] manner
as well as his matter is more often than not a reflection of self-
conscious Victorian England" and that, apart from style, "his poetry contains the stamp of Victorian England as well as of England's past. Highly idiosyncratic as it is, it transcends private idiosyncrasy to speak of Victorian concerns" (5). Such an
interpretation must be held to despite the repeated attempts "to
lift him" (ibid.) out of his age made by critics, and despite the
presence of some components that are not precisely homogeneous with the Victorian spirit, such as the "gnarled and tense"
style, his "radical" prosody and Jesuitism—just because they are
counterbalanced by as many Victorian propensities (religious
anxiety, the criticism of industrialization, and edification, to
name a few) (6).

In this case, too, one cannot but approve of, and admire, the
exceptional quality and acuteness of Sulloway's analyses. I dis-
agree, however, with the conclusions she draws from them.
Sulloway stresses and, above all, atemporally singles out in Hopkins what appear to her Victorian concerns; yet these, existent
and even markedly active within a certain biographical span,

---

1. Few but extremely perceptive pages are also devoted to the Ruskinian genesis of a certain number of Hopkins's rhetorical and stylistic processes, such as the
opposition between octave and sestet in the sonnets (as the typical fruit of the
Ruskinian dualism between *pure* and *moral* artist: 92–93), his prosody, sprung
rhythm and the sound-strategies, which correspond to the canon of an art mimetic of natural paradoxes. Sulloway also traces to Ruskin the conflict between
compositive rigidity and liberty (93), between eccentricity and control, between
superabundance and sobriety, between sprung rhythm and rigor in rhyme-
schemes (97–99).

cease or are superseded with time; in other cases they are accompanied by others quite foreign or even contrasting with Victorian culture. She appears to realize this undue extension or generalization, and that much in Hopkins clashes or simply does not fit in with Victorian culture, and that the major obstacle is Hopkins's Catholicism and Jesuitism; but instead of perceiving the glaring and drastic fracture represented by this option, she inclines to consider it accessory and irrelevant. She even minimizes the difference between Jesuit and Victorian religion. What she does, in fact, is a systematic Victorianizing of Hopkins's Jesuit and Ignatian components. Significantly, there is for her a "close . . . parallel . . . between the Victorian gentleman and the Jesuit priest" (138) and "the Ignatian spirit has in it far more of the Arnoldian spirit of the whole than is usually assumed, zealously missionary as it may be" (220, note 53). Hopkins is accordingly portrayed as "a Jesuit *and* a Victorian priest" (146), one of those "dazzling young Victorians" spawned by public schools and universities who were not unlike the "dazzling young men" attracted by the Society of Jesus (134–35)—a Hopkins who as a Jesuit still had the same missionary spirit of the "intellectually sophisticated Balliol men [and of] Christ Church men" (36) and who at Oxford was under the spiritual guidance of Liddon, that "admirer of St Ignatius Loyola" (60). Sulloway's argument is further flawed, to me, by two misunderstandings that, once clarified, paradoxically show how close she is to my own position. The first is that her Hopkins is not so Victorian as she would have it: in her last chapter she decidedly brings to the fore Hopkins's "uniqueness," "originality," and "superiority" even over the "most sophisticated Victorians." Thus Hopkins is the most atypical of a group of already atypical Victorians. Curiously, she does not realize that, while she is attempting to demonstrate Hopkins's *Victorianism,* she is actually demonstrating his deep-seated *medievalism.* Throughout her whole second chapter she presents Hopkins as a "prophet" of a future England, different from the contemporary one just because he is capable of restoring values belonging to past ages ("by consulting the lessons of the past" [132])—more exactly, to the Middle Ages. She even unconsciously hints at an opposition between semantico-symbolic codes and syntagmatic codes when she delineates a tendential medievalizing reaction in a certain portion of nineteenth-century English culture (by which Hopkins was evidently affected) having a markedly dogmatic, antisecular, apocalyptic character (18–20). As a result, the Hopkins we get from her book is a medieval man, more profoundly and substantially so than the narrow group of the Victorian "prophets" and well beyond the widespread medievalizing tendencies of the period. Hopkins, she says, "preached *literally* what Ruskin and Carlyle had preached *metaphorically*" (178), and "placed . . . comprehensive dogma before the public," while writers such as Tennyson and Morris "did not take the prospect of the second coming *literally,* although they took England's corruption and the apocalyptic mood seriously enough to embrace the Apocalypse as a vehicle for their anxieties" (194–95). Again, Hopkins rejected, she says, the "sordid present for the more satisfactory past, *the modern for the medieval*" (50), and also modelled on the medieval knight the gentleman of whom he advocated the rebirth: "The new Victorian gentleman was to combine the purity of a saint with the steadfastness of the medieval Knight Templar and the beauty and colour of a Renaissance courtier" (124). And after mentioning other medieval traits uniting Hopkins to the other medievalists, Sulloway justly sees Hopkins as the greatest and most radical. Several poems are said to be modern "morality plays" (150, 173, 221, note 64), but Hopkins's medievalism becomes integral and "explodes" in the "Deutschland." Sulloway provides an archetypal reading of this poem in terms of biblical apocalyptic premonitions, numerical and iconic symbolism, and an "aesthetics of identification"—a reading, as will be seen better and more fully in chapters 7 and 8 below, that casts light onto its radically medieval aesthetic and poetic codes.

Ong's *Hopkins, the Self, and God* cites approvingly both Johnson and Sulloway. In brief, his acrobatic diagnosis is that Hopkins is a "truly" (Ong 1986, 7) and even standard Victorian who, however, had "concerns" that make him "a specialist among specialists": "No other Victorian can quite match Hopkins in the in-

tensity of his passion, his insights, and his theories" (3); at the
same time these concerns were derived "from his lived appropriation of the *Spiritual Exercises* of St Ignatius Loyola" (5); yet, at
the same time, Hopkins "was unmistakably a modern in his un-
compromising confrontation of the nameless self" (131), and just
because of his "constant and compelling confrontation of the
self" (129) he belongs to modernism. Ong concedes that "certain
forces . . . that are somewhat special to him" (5) play on Hopkins's sensibility, but they do not suffice to undermine Hopkins's
supposedly granitic, almost self-satisfied and Biedermeier Victorianism: Hopkins "did not want to return to the Middle Ages. He
had no desire to turn back any clocks . . . [he] was . . . inside his
own epoch in history, at home in his own age" (8, 90). Hopkins's
medievalism is admitted, or better, dismissed, by a significant litotes: "Hopkins was not totally untouched by the medieval revival" (132). In fact, Ong's method hardly differs from Sulloway's radical and systematic Victorianization of Hopkins's non-
Victorian disparate options. The core of the book is an obviously
competent presentation of St. Ignatius's *Spiritual Exercises,*
which, however, serves to show how they "fostered the intensive
particularism and self-consciousness in which [Hopkins] outdid
even other Victorians" (55).

My own thesis is that Hopkins no doubt shares a certain number of Victorian codes (or simply themes, ideas, problems, attitudes, even obsessions); yet a correct diachronic approach proves
that Hopkins is a Victorian *tout court* only for the period preceding
his entrance into the Society of Jesus, and that thereafter a decided
prevalence of anti-Victorian, medieval codes begins to assert itself. Hopkins, in other words, literally absorbs his own Victorian
codes. Then, gradually, he partly repudiates and replaces and
partly elaborates, enriches, and distorts them, by means of existential, religious, epistemological, ethical, philosophical—that is,
cultural—options that are, I repeat once again, of a medieval type.

The only critic who has come near to my thesis is Jerome
Bump. Indeed, he has independently followed a course parallel to
mine. His book *Gerard Manley Hopkins* and his essay "Hopkins'
Imagery and Medievalist Poetics" are fundamental at least for one

discovery, Hopkins's crucial association with the Tractarians (Pusey, Keble, Newman) and, through them, with biblical typology. Hopkins is, for Bump, who adopts a correct diachronic perspective, a "religious medievalist" (Bump 1978, 101), who after 1870 overcame the "Metaphysical and Romantic preoccupation with personality" and transferred his allegiance "from Metaphysical to medieval models" (106). As a result, "Keble's influence tended to merge with, and often displace, Herbert's" and "a number of important medievalist traits become more conspicuous, notably vertical correspondences, sacramentalism, multiple meanings, and less emphasis on the self." Unlike Ong, Bump believes that Hopkins "was seeking to identify with an age which offered a more earnest, more secure faith than Donne's could" (ibid.). In particular, what Hopkins took from Keble and the other Tractarians is explained in this passage:

"type" (*tupos*) or "figure" (*figura*) has a particular meaning of special importance to Hopkins. In biblical interpretation, an Old Testament person, event, or thing which parallels, prefigures, or foreshadows a New Testament person, event, or thing is said to be a "type," and the parallel New Testament person, event, or thing is called the "antitype," a word which means not the opposite of the Old Testament type but a recurrence of it in the same mold. . . . In this way "type" has come to mean the signifier and "antitype" the signified. Thus Job's suffering is a type, and its parallel in the New Testament, Christ's passion, is its antitype. Similarly, Eden is a type of our mental state after Baptism and/or our experience of heaven after death. This set of meanings of the word "type" was specially significant for Hopkins because of its focus on Jesus, for him the "archetype," the ultimate "mold" for all aspects of his life and art. Jesus' example was *the* "form" which had the greatest "hold on the mind," was "always reappearing," was "imperishable," a type which had "in some sense or other an absolute existence." (Bump 1982, 81; Bump's italics)[2]

Bump accordingly provides illuminating typological and archetypal readings of various poems, among them "Rosa Mystica," "Deutschland," and "The Windhover." His investigation ends,

2. For a more extensive treatment of biblical typology, see the classic Landow 1980.

however, by falling into a fragmentary search for "echoes" and "influences," such as that of Dante, whose *Divine Comedy,* which Hopkins knew through Christina Rossetti, forms for him the hidden pattern of the *terrible sonnets* (Bump 1982, 43–55; 183–96; to medieval *acedia* he also traces the "melancholy" and the spiritual "sloth" they display [ibid., 173–79]).

Apart from biblical typology, Bump also fails to work in a contrastive perspective, that is, to pinpoint what marks off a medieval from a non-medieval model. For this we have to turn once again to Lotman.[3] As he has shown, the typological macro-characteristic unmistakably identifying the Middle Ages, and distinguishing it from the subsequent ages, is its high *semiotic* character: it is a characteristic that the successive types, though each differs from the others, have *all* unanimously and, in the case of the Enlightenment, polemically rejected, so that the "autumn" of the Middle Ages represents a sharp and decisive break (if not *the* break)[4] with the three types following it in Lotman's grid, and contrasts with them more than each of the three with the others. More analytically, the medieval type can be said to be based on the three following principles:

1. "semantization (or even symbolization) . . . of all reality surrounding man" (Lotman 1973, 42);
2. bi-planarity of the sign (whether linguistic or not): between the expression (signifier) and the content (signified) there is a "one-to-one correlation (rather than an arbitrary one)" (Lotman-Uspenskij 1978, 217), that is, an iconic rather than conventional relation ("Expression is like an imprint of the content" [Lotman 1973, 49]);

3. My "track" will once again be Lotman 1973, with the additions quoted above in Part Two, chapter 1, note 1, and, below, in notes 4, 5, 6, 9, and 10. It is hardly necessary to point out the two totally different meanings with which the word "typology" will hereafter be used: in Bump's and the Tractarians' acceptation of *biblical* typology as shown above, and in Lotman's sense of *cultural* typology.
4. Lewis (1964, 85) stresses "the radical difference . . . between [all ancient and medieval thinkers'] thought and the developmental or evolutionary concepts of our own period—a difference which perhaps leaves no area and no level of consciousness unaffected."

3. "The worth of objects . . . is not determined by their intrinsic value, but by that of the things they represent" (Lotman 1969, 315), so that man "was to despise things and aspire to signs" (Lotman 1973, 43).

To have an idea of the type of opposition that such semiotic bents represent with respect to modern axiology and the modern conception of the sign, let it suffice to recollect how medieval symbolism and pan-semioticism—"all existing things were perceived as provided with meaning (and, conversely, only what was provided with meaning was considered as existing)" (Lotman 1973, 47)—were superseded, in the Renaissance and then in the Age of Enlightenment, by a conventional and discriminating semantization, or more precisely by a "desemioticizing tendency" evident, for example, in the prevalence of nominalism. In the eighteenth century, men believed that "real things, which cannot be used as signs, were provided with a greater value" (Lotman 1973, 54), and discovered the "conventional, unmotivated character of the signifier-signified relationship," so that the "awareness of the relativity of the sign penetrates deeply into the structure of the cultural system," while in the Middle Ages "the word is perceived as an icon, as a reflection of its content" (ibid., 56). Similarly, within the syntagmatic type, bi-planarity is blurred, since men reject the "symbolic significance of events and phenomena" and the world lives "not out of the relationship between the two planes (essence and expression), but rather on just one plane" (ibid., 51). Just because expression was, in the Middle Ages, insignificant in itself—"The object representing itself (or serving practical ends) occupies, in the structure of the cultural code, the lowest degrees of value" (Lotman 1969, 314); "The sign was important for its function of substitution" (Lotman 1973, 44)—we consequently have it that "the substitute could not have an autonomous value: it received a value according to the hierarchical position of its content in the general model of the world" (ibid.). Conversely, in the Age of Enlightenment, "only the things which are themselves exist; everything 'representing' something else is fantasy. Only immediate *realia* appear therefore provided with values" (Lotman 1969, 316).[5]

Granted these basic principles of semiotic theory, it is easy to bring to light its consequences in every speculative and practical activity of medieval man. One of the spheres on which such a pervasive and absolute semiotic character exerted a clear and highly distinctive influence is that of political thinking and social organization. As we have said, medieval society was highly "semiotic," and medieval man, unlike modern man, was inclined to grant only an instrumental and preparatory value to earthly society, and to see the latter as modelled on heavenly society, and its head, the emperor, as Christ's "typological" Vicar on earth. The Universal Christian Empire, arisen out of the ashes of the Roman Empire and founded on the identification of politics and religion, represented, as it is well known, the utopian cornerstone of the medieval political vision. Through the centuries and after St. Augustine's first theorizing, an endless debate arose, aiming to reconcile in less and less utopian and abstract "formulas" and "theses" the profound dichotomy between the temporal and the spiritual. Such a problem and preoccupation makes itself heard in Hopkins, whose speculations on the origin of political power and of social organization ideally precede, in many aspects, Rousseau's theories and the doctrine of natural law.[6] What however

5. With a different terminology, Julia Kristeva has illustrated the same marked separation between the Middle Ages and post-medieval cultures. For her, the orthodox Middle Ages are firmly anchored to a vertical vision of the real or, in her own terms, to its symbolism, whereas in the late Middle Ages and in the modern era the sign is seen as immanent and horizontally chained with other signs, and its symbolic value wanes. Each phenomenon is not, as it was in the Age of Enlightenment, a thing-in-itself, but vertically looks up to a universal of which the particular is a "restricted copy": "ces éléments (les symboles) renvoient à une (des) transcendance(s) universelle(s). . . . La fonction du symbole est donc, dans sa dimension verticale (universaux-marques) une fonction de RESTRICTION" (Kristeva 1970, 26–27). The dissolution of the Middle Ages begins with the first nominalistic philosophies (such as that of William of Occam) and their rejection of universals: "Toute la réalité donc est singulière, faite de TERMES indépendants . . . le nominalisme ouvre le chemin à une pensée qui opérerait avec des TERMES (des NOMS) en tant que SIGNES (et non plus symboles). Il construit un réel comme une combinatoire de termes" (ibid., 31). For the "vertical correspondences" sought in the Middle Ages see also Bump 1982, 84, and Bump 1977, 105.

6. For a synthetic treatment of these problems see Morghen 1968 (above all, 66–70, 109–27, 156–57) and Lewis 1964 ("The Human Past," 174–85).

more directly interests us, with reference to the typological opposition between the Middle Ages and the modern (and, of
course, Victorian) era, is the repercussion on the sphere of aesthetics and artistic praxis of those speculations. Quite consis-
tently, in the Middle Ages, the iconic and "vertical" character of
the sign is paralleled by the iconic and "vertical" character of the
artistic word. Each single text is the expression of a content that
is there *ab aeterno,* a unique "ideal text of culture" (Lotman 1973,
46); consequently, while modern aesthetics considers as virtues
originality and individuality (and, at the same time, repetitiveness as a defect),[7] medieval aesthetics considered "everything individual as sinful and a manifestation of pride" and demanded
"that the artist be faithful to age-old 'God-inspired' models"
(Lotman 1977, 125).[8] Lotman has synthesized (ibid., 289–92) the
opposition between medieval and modern aesthetics as a difference between an aesthetics of identity and an aesthetics of opposition, or between artistic phenomena whose structure (at the level
of lexis, tropes, plot, etc.) is given a priori and obeys certain
rules, and others whose code is not known before they are aesthetically experienced, and whose rules are generated together
with the text.[9] As a result we have, in the Middle Ages, a conception of the artist that is certainly antipodal to that of modern and
contemporary times: the artist is an "intermediary," an "execu-

7. "Far from feigning originality, as a modern plagiarist would, [the medieval
authors] are apt to conceal it" (Lewis 1964, 210).

8. Similarly, wisdom was not acquired, in the Middle Ages, through a "quantitative accumulation of the texts one has read," but through the "study in depth
of a text, through a constant and repeated penetration into its structure" (Lotman
1973, 45). On the timelessness of the *auctores* in the Middle Ages ("All *auctores* are
of the same value, all are timeless") see Curtius's sharp observations (1953, 48–
61; quotation, 51). According to C. S. Lewis, "It is doubtful whether the sense of
period is much older than the Waverley novels" (Lewis 1964, 183).

9. Lotman has subsequently reformulated this difference as "cultures directed
primarily towards expression" versus "cultures directed mainly towards content," and also as cultures regarding themselves "as an aggregate of normative
texts" versus cultures modelling themselves "as a system of *rules* that determine
the creation of texts" (Lotman-Uspenskij 1978, 218; Lotman-Uspenskij's italics).
As Barthes has written, "Au moyen âge, la 'culture' est une taxinomie, un réseau
fonctionnel d'"arts', c'est-à-dire de langages soumis à des règles . . . " (Barthes
1970, 185). See, for a case of obedience to these criteria, Curtius's reading of the
Divine Comedy in chapter 17 of his book, above all § 5, "The Personnel of the
Commedia" (365–72).

tor," a "copyist or scribe," "whose entire service consisted in faithfully repeating the authoritative text," just because "the creator of the world was simultaneously the creator of those 'inspired texts' (or 'icons not made by human hands')" (Lotman 1977, 267).[10] Semantics and semantization are, in modern aesthetics, as unpredictable and arbitrary[11] as they were invariable, established a priori, mimetically decreed by God in the Middle Ages: "For the medieval man the system of the signifieds had a pre-established character and the entire pyramid of signic subordinations reflected the hierarchy of the divine order" (Lotman 1969, 318).[12] To this was linked the typical phenomenon of "stratified" (or "multigraded" [Lotman-Uspenskij 1975, 175]) semantics, a semantics in which the "changes of meaning are but degrees of depth in a signified, degrees of meaning in the process of getting close to the absolute rather than new meanings" (Lotman 1973, 42). The latter consideration evidently lies at the basis of the "tendency to interpret every text as allegorical or symbolic," as well as of the "principle itself of the anagogical sense thrown into light by the comment to the text" (Lotman 1969, 315).

10. "Quant à l'écrit, il n'est pas soumis [in the Middle Ages], comme aujourd'hui, à une valeur d'originalité; ce que nous appelons l'*auteur* n'existe pas . . . " (Barthes 1970, 184–85). The *author* is now a *scriptor* ("recopie purement et simplement"), now a *compilator,* now a *commentator.* "Ce que par anachronisme nous pourrions appeler l'*écrivain* est donc essentiellement au moyen âge: (1) *un transmetteur:* il reconduit une matière absolue qui est le trésor antique, source d'autorité; (2) un *combinateur:* il a le droit de 'casser' les oeuvres passées, par une analyse sans frein, et de les recomposer . . . " (ibid., Barthes's italics). See also, for similar observations, Lewis 1964, 5; Curtius 1953, 328, and—for examples, a historical reconstruction, and the transgressions of such a rule—his excursus XVII, "Mention of the Author's Name in Medieval Literature," 515–18.

11. For Kristeva the figure of the Sibyl, which asserts itself in Europe from the fifteenth century, represents "la mise en figure de la parole quasi-libérée de sa dépendance symbolique et vivant dans 'l'arbitraire' du signe." Romance is a typically post-medieval creation since it is structured "sur l'imprévisible et la surprise" (Kristeva 1970, 30, 33).

12. "There came thus into existence an immense heritage of equivalences which—unlike those of modern metaphorism—are, so to speak, 'guided' by the Divine Word, and are already *ab ovo* embedded in a meaningful frame structuring the cosmos in a firm and reassuring way" (Pagnini 1976, 126–27). See also Lewis 1964, 10: "Medieval man . . . was an organiser, a codifier, a builder of systems. He wanted 'a place for everything and everything in the right place.' Distinction, definition, tabulation were his delight." His was a "passionately systematic" mind (ibid.).

3

❧ VICTORIAN ECCENTRICITY

The nature of the hypothesis I have formulated above regarding Hopkins's medieval code options obviously exempts me from seeking and pointing out code coincidences, both synchronic and diachronic, between Hopkins and the cultural system of his time. I refer, for this type of research, to the studies of Mizener, Johnson, Sulloway, and Ong discussed in the previous chapter. Here I intend to investigate and decode a few quite recognizable instances, from the period preceding Hopkins's entrance into the Jesuits, of violation of and distancing from the acquired syntagmatic codes.

The first group of texts is made up of some papers and essays of the university period written between 1864 and 1867. They not only reveal—along with many passages in contemporary letters—a nature not easily satisfied by the circulating platitudes, socratically inclined to take nothing for granted, and intent on a personal and original redefinition of cultural phenomena,[1] but also surprise one with a series of criticisms of the dominant ideologies, philosophies, and anthropologies. In particular, they let

1. As Collins rightly observed in his interesting essay on Hopkins and philosophy, "the young student was neither content to receive instruction passively nor afraid to open up new ways of thought and expression. . . . What sets him off most strikingly from his many cloudy-minded literary contemporaries is precisely this disciplined incisiveness which could not tolerate shoddy reasoning or vague cosmic notions or a great flow of words masquerading as deep thought" (Collins 1947, 71, 73).

flash through, though amid many contradictions, the rejection of or reservations about the syntagmatico-aparadigmatic codes active in Victorian culture (characterized for Hopkins by the semes: flux, chromatism,[2] mutability). They also manifest the adoption of some medieval categories of a semantico-symbolic type (such as the "fixed points," diatonism and archetypes). In "The Origin of Our Moral Ideas" (1865?; J, 80–83), for example, though he was still influenced by Paterian aestheticism (as is evinced by the long comparison between the perception of beauty and the moral act), Hopkins distances himself from utilitarianism on the problem of the origin and essence of the moral act. Bentham (whose practical and behavioral instructions were widely followed by the Victorians) had reduced the problem to an almost nominalistic question, making morality a mere question of self-interest. Hopkins confutes the utilitarian formula ("the morally good is what attains the good, that is the advantageous, and that of course the greatest such, and that . . . for the greatest number") just because it is based on incidental and a posteriori considerations and is thus capable of explaining only the "objective part of morality." Indeed, Hopkins corrects himself, utilitarianism "fails to explain morality at all": it "explains neither end or extreme and fails historically both in mankind and in the individual. Or it may be attacked analytically, as not being ultimate." It is precisely the insufficiency and the incompleteness of utilitarianism that Hopkins—advocating a personalized and disinterested concept of morality as an ideal rooted and historically developed in the human mind—for the moment intends to counter. There is a more substantial and harder attack against the dominant ideologies and a more explicit reference to medieval codes in the essay "The Probable Future of Metaphysics" (1867; J, 118–21). While the widespread materialism and utilitarianism might be taken as tokens of an absorption and an "emptying out" of metaphysics, which would become a "mere abstraction," Hopkins reaffirms

2. For the distinction between chromatism and diatonism in Hopkins's acceptation, see Part One, chapter 1 note 21.

the great necessity of metaphysics and its indispensable orientating function: "It will always be possible to shew how science is atomic, not to be grasped and held together, 'scopeless', without metaphysics; this alone gives meaning to laws and sequences and causes and developments." After qualifying the materialism of his time as an "afternoon of thought," marked by superficial and conventional thinking ("we are blunted to the more abstract and elusive speculation"; "the run of thought in the age braces up and carries out what lies in its own way and discourages and minimises what is constitutionally against its set"),[3] Hopkins comes to tackle what is for us the crucial issue, those "ideas of Historical Development . . . of continuity and of time" he correctly and prophetically identifies as the prevailing philosophical code ("the philosophy of the immediate future"), against which he tries to indicate some countermeasures. The forms of opposition he outlines explicitly refer to semantico-paradigmatic codes:

One sees that the ideas so rife now of a continuity without fixed points, not to say *saltus* or breaks, of development in one chain of necessity, of species having no absolute types and only accidentally fixed, *all this is a philosophy of flux opposed to Platonism and can call out nothing but Platonism against it*. And this, or to speak more correctly Realism, is perhaps soon to return.[4]

Such a restraint of the "philosophy of flux" might be carried out, Hopkins significantly observes, in the following three phases:

a. the reintroduction of standards, fixed points, guiding principles or archetypes ("forms which have a great hold on the mind and are always reappearing and *seem imperishable*"), in order to counteract the prevailing concept of nature as "a string all the differences in which are really chromatic but certain places in it have

3. It is significant that in a short note (J, 24) on Villari's *Storia* of Savonarola dating back to 1864, Hopkins should quote a passage saying that the Reformation, promising "to bring the faithful into direct relation with the Almighty," "first saved a large portion of the human race from *scepticism* and *materialism*" and then favored the regeneration and reflourishing of Catholicism.

4. Pater's Marius shares with Hopkins an analogous paradigmatic tension: "His longing defined itself for something to hold by amid the 'perpetual flux' " (*Marius the Epicurean*, 122).

become *accidentally* fixed and the series of fixed points becomes an *arbitrary* scale";[5]

b. the reintroduction of the concept of the propagation of the real from the Idea ("from the whole downwards to the parts") and not from the part(s) to the whole;

c. the reintroduction of "Platonic Ideas" against the new "form of atomism" which "like a stiffness or sprain seems to hang upon and hamper our speculation."

The more transparent documents of this early but already unmistakable recovery of semantico-symbolic codes of a medieval type are the Early Diaries (J, 3–73) and, to an even greater extent, the Journal (J, 131–263), as it stretches out into the first Jesuit years and therefore confirms our suppositions concerning the philosophico-anthropological speculations of the university period. If, remembering what we have been saying above, we accept pan-semioticization—and the vision of the real and the particular as a copy of the universal in which their multiplicity is unified—as a sort of pregnant epigraph of the medieval system, it is easy to inscribe therein Hopkins's diaries, regulated as they are by what Joseph Hillis Miller has termed a "rhyme-principle," a principle so predominant and pervasive that it subtends both the youthful diaries and the poetic "explosion" of the "Deutschland" and the subsequent flourishing of the nature poems.

The evident code modification, subsequently strengthened by Hopkins's conversion, of which the Journal and the Early Diaries provide the first hint, is therefore not so much the passage from a condition of desperate isolation and from a sense of abandonment and lack of confidence—as witnessed by poems such as "A Soliloquy of One of the Spies left in the Wilderness," "The Alchemist in the city," "My prayers must meet a brazen heaven," "*Nondum,*" etc.—to the comfort of faith, as it is the gradual "put-

5. Hopkins is clearly referring to Darwin's doctrines, which "had tremendous impact on the intellectual climate and movements of the nineteenth century. Hopkins mentions 'Darwinism' a couple of times in his letters and notebooks, and although he does not address Darwinian theories formally, he was aware of them and their implications" (Ellsberg 1987, 131 note 4). See also Bump 1982, 36, 80 and contrast Ong 1986, 158, who avers that Hopkins "appears everywhere singularly free of hostility or even uneasiness regarding Darwin."

ting together" of a "world of unrelated particulars" finally grant-
ing a "vision of the whole." It is a reorganization of the "dishar-
mony and dispersion" of the phenomenal world, in which each
detail becomes "another tiny area conquered from chaos and
blankness" (Miller 1963, 276, 277); in which, that is, even dissimilar and, in their specificity, unique entities are laboriously but
systematically "made to rhyme." The setting of Hopkins's pro-
tracted search for "rhymes" from his youth onward has been well
synthesized by Miller in the following terms:

This relation may be found everywhere in the universe: in words which
resemble one another without being identical, in trees or clouds which
have similar but not identical patterns, and so on. The universe, even
though no two things in it are exactly alike, is full of things which
rhyme, and by extending the range of observed rhymings who knows
how many things may ultimately be brought into harmony? (ibid., 277)

Hopkins's effort to reorganize the universe begins from the realm
of words. As Miller has shown, the etymological speculations
scattered in Hopkins's diaries are a "reconstruction of the world
through discovery of rhymes": "Words seem a perfect example
of the disorder of the world. The universe is a collection of unrelated things, and words are a collection of unrelated names for
those things, or for their qualities and actions. The best order that
can be given to words is the arbitrary alphabetical sequence of the
dictionary" (279–80). The long chains of phonologically associated words whose semantic links seen by Hopkins have been frequently judged fanciful and philologically debatable are based on
the fact that "words . . . similar in sound . . . will also be similar
in meaning. Hopkins assumes that a group of words of similar
sound are variations of some *ur*-word and root meaning" (280).
Hopkins is moving on to a medieval "diatonism" when he sees
each word as having an autonomy of its own but also as being
placed at a "fixed interval from other similar words" and being
"therefore able to chime with them, both in sound and in meaning" (ibid.). And if, as we have seen, the profound *iconic* motivation between copy and original is at the basis of the signic function in the Middle Ages—and, conversely, the arbitrariness of the

sign at the basis of that of the Age of Enlightenment and of subsequent epochs—the favor with which Hopkins looked at the onomatopoeic theory—which "has not had a fair chance" (J, 5) and in fact had no followers among the Victorians, who held by Bentham's nominalism—is another hardly mistakable index.[6] Already in his youth Hopkins shows an inclination toward an "aesthetics of identity": "If words are arbitrary labels for things, they give no substantial possession of the things they name, but are only signs pointing in the direction of their meaning. An onomatopoeic word imitates in its substance and inscape the substance and inscape of the thing it names" (Miller 1963, 285).[7] The organization and the "rhyming" of words is naturally the consequence, the mirror of the organization and of the "rhyming" of things. In the early entries of the Journal, Hopkins sees "a distance . . . between one item in the scene and another. . . . The basic principle of the journals is the assumption that each cloud or tree or waterfall is unique, and must therefore be described in an individualized pattern of words. . . . The journals are the record of a long series of isolated encounters with unique inscapes" (ibid., 286–87). If this distance between phenomenal entities were not overcome, "disorder and isolation"—and, we may add, pure juxtaposition—"[would] predominate." Yet "certain motifs recur in the journals; there *are* principles of organization" (ibid.; Miller's italics). Which ones? First of all, certain unvarying "qualities" asserting themselves as "rhyme-elements" in things: solidity, colors, and above all instress, the "energy of being" (ibid., 290). Having strenuously searched for the "inner law or pattern" capable of regulating and unifying the manifold and the particular, Hopkins finally reaches a vision of nature as "a structured whole . . . as contiguous forms repeated, like patterns on a quilt

6. See Sprinker 1981, 55–58, for a discussion of onomatopoeia in the context of European linguistic thinking, and Milroy 1977, 53, 62–69.

7. It must be noticed that the iconic relation between *res* and *verba*, that is, the search for often fanciful and strained "etymologies," was one of the most flourishing speculative fields of the Middle Ages. See for example excursus XIV, "Etymology as a Category of Thought," in Curtius 1953 (495–500). In view of the analogies between Hopkins and Dante I shall find (see below, chapter 7), the final observations on Dante's etymologies are particularly relevant.

. . . as [an image] woven in a crisscross pattern, or in parallel rows like waves," "a vision of the universe as a great multitude of strongly patterned things" (ibid., 291, 292, 293, 294). The provisional conclusion of Hopkins's speculation in the Journal is once again, therefore, a paradox:

What all things share for Hopkins is precisely the fact that they are all different, each one unique in structure, shape, and color. Or, rather, things are alike in two ways: all possess the energy of being, "throughout one with itself" [J, 130], and all are distinctive in pattern. All things have instress and inscape. If instress makes things alike, the fact that all things are full of inscape means that things are alike in being unlike. . . . Rhyming can actually be found everywhere in Hopkins' nature. (Ibid., 290)[8]

Fortified by these premisses, Hopkins will be able to tackle (and solve, as a Jesuit, in his mature poetry and in the commentary to the *Spiritual Exercises* of St. Ignatius) the last and most arduous problem posed by the "rhyme principle," that of reconciling to a unique and unvarying pattern the inscape of the self and the differentiation of selves.

The etymological speculations and the theory of poetic styles (see Part One, chapter 2), the philosophical and aesthetic essays, and above all the nature studies in the Journal are unanimously considered the greatest achievement of the youthful Hopkins. Not only is this textual body of an already astounding originality in the panorama of contemporary literature and criticism, but it also foreshadows a sum of epistemic tendencies of a markedly medieval character. The same conclusions cannot be drawn from

---

8. We owe to Miller the definitive explanation of the distinction and even opposition between *inscape* and *instress,* two terms to which, despite whole decades of critical debate, no adequate semantic definition had until then been given. The current equation between inscape and Scotus's *haecceitas* must be therefore radically corrected: "It might seem . . . that Hopkins means by 'inscape' uniqueness of pattern, what Duns Scotus calls the *haecceitas* of a thing, its ultimate principle of individuality. . . . This is not really the case, nor does inscape here mean anything like Scotus' *haecceitas*. The inscape of a poem, far from being a unique, unrepeatable pattern, is the design which different parts of the poem share, and which detaches itself from the chiming of these parts" (281). The first critic to propose this equation had been Peters (1948). Less drastically than Miller, Christopher Devlin writes that it "is a possible shortcut, but it has pitfalls" (1950, 201). On inscape and instress, as concepts related to the Scotist code, see below, chapter 6.

the remaining part of Hopkins's writings of the same period (diaries, letters, poetry), which show on the whole, despite even more numerous and explicit medieval elements, rather a relation with than a separation from contemporary codes.

The behavioral model followed in this period allows us in fact to speak of an "aesthetic" phase (to use the terms of a thinker, Søren Kierkegaard, who almost simultaneously went through a conversion that has many analogies and points of contact with Hopkins's) as opposed to the subsequent "ethic" phase.[9] If, as we have seen, the contempt of things and the devaluation of practical life—and, simultaneously, the aspiration to signs and the withdrawal from the world—are among the distinctive components of medieval life, Hopkins's aspirations, ambitions, and way of life in his university years point to a decidedly antithetical code. He was in that period "the star of Balliol," and aspired, as is frequently witnessed by his letters to his mother and to his friends, to a career of fame and success:

When I called on Jowett, he advised me to take great pains with this [composition of essays in Latin and English], as on it would depend my success more than on anything else. (L III, 73)

I hope, dear Baillie, you will not think me too egotistical in speaking thus at length and thus freely about myself and my hopes. I have now a more rational hope than before of doing something—in poetry and painting. (L III, 214)

To this "aesthetic" code we must trace his interest in and curiosity about, even a more or less veiled longing for, medieval art, in its historical forms as well as in its social repercussions and in its possibilities of present re-enactment. These are indexed in his diaries, letters, and even in poetic texts: let it suffice to think of the setting and atmosphere of compositions like "The Escorial," "The Nightingale," "The Queen's Crowning," "A Voice from the World," "Floris in Italy." Consider his admiration for Gothic art, born from the ruins of the Romanesque, a "beautiful style"

9. See Kierkegaard's *Either-Or*, first published in 1843. Further biographical and specifically philosophical analogies between Hopkins and Kierkegaard have been brought to light by Collins (1947, 77–78, 83, 87, 99, 104).

that died "only in giving birth to another more beautiful than itself, Gothic" (the Gothic, however, "did not last long," though it appears to Hopkins "to have been more capable of grand development than any other" [J, 13, 14]). Consider also his accurate and competent descriptions of Norman cathedrals and his—unfortunately only planned—essay on "Some aspects of Modern medievalism" (J, 14, 26, 187–88, and *passim*). Hopkins was clearly influenced by Ruskin's studies and by the medievalizing inclinations of the Pre-Raphaelites, whom Hopkins frequently mentions in his diaries and in the Journal, where he also refers to the French and German medievalizing painters (the Nazarenes: J, 32–33). He obviously also mentions medieval literature—the Breton cycle (J, 45, 46)—and in his poetry even vaguely imitates its forms and style ("The Queen's Crowning"). Several quotations from Villari's *Storia* (J, 24, 56; L III, 17–18) confirm the dawning longing for an epoch in which the harmonious relation—the symbiosis—between the artist and society had not yet been shattered. Yet such medievalizing inclinations appear to be but tenuous and scattered indexes of a widespread taste in contemporary art, rather than symptoms of a breach in Hopkins's adherence to the general cultural model. In other words, unlike what will happen in the Jesuit period—when the medieval option will become profound, substantial, and absolute—Hopkins's medievalism is epidermic and outward, merely a fashion, inaugurated by Keats and then taken up by the Pre-Raphaelites and by the "medieval school."[10] Had his medievalism remained without the subsequent and decisive code modifications and additions, but with the "diatonism" shown in his essays and the paradigmatic tension characterizing the Journal, we would merely

10. The medieval "vogue" is typical of European Romanticism and late Romanticism. In chapter 16 ("The Book as Symbol") of his study on the Latin Middle Ages, Curtius maintains that the medievalism of the English and German pre-Romantics and Romantics rested on a "shaky foundation" and merely on "the element of emotional enthusiasm—not the sublimation of historical understanding, not the illumination of consciousness, which constitute the high and enduring value of German Romanticism" (Curtius 1953, 325). On Keats's medievalism, the "medieval school," and Romanticism in general, see Hopkins's penetrating observations in L II, 98–99.

include Hopkins's textuality in our third group of Victorian texts, more eccentric but equally integrated.[11]

Hopkins's early poetic production is absolutely emblematic of this strong link with contemporary art and aesthetic taste and with the post-Romantic trend of Victorian literature. If we exclude the sonnets and the lyrics written after 1865 (although dating is extremely difficult in this period), which show a marked internal division, and "The Habit of Perfection,"[12] Hopkins's youthful poetry appears not only predictably derivative but also markedly "aesthetic," nonmedieval in that it variously contradicts the original (medieval) hints on which we have dwelt above.[13] A follower of Pater and even more of Keats, the young Hopkins—the Hopkins of the college compositions and of the first university years—appears animated by a devout and absolute worship of Art and by a spasmodic search for Beauty.[14] The rejection of the present world and the parallel nostalgia for the past do exist, but, as in other contemporary poetic experiences, they are merely metaphorical phenomena, imaginary escapes, little verifiable and controllable. As far as style and imagery are con-

11. See above, Part Two, chapter 1. Bump (1977, 100) justly speaks of "two varieties of medievalism," a "medieval asceticism" such as that shared by Hopkins and Christina Rossetti, and the "secular religion of courtly love," common to Keats, Dante Rossetti, and Swinburne.

12. For an examination of this poem—which bridges the gap between the young and the mature Hopkins and testifies to the adherence to behavioral codes openly ascetic and "renunciatory"—and for a discussion of the evolution of Hopkins's religion and its poetic transpositions, see Marucci 1977, 31–33.

13. One of the reasons for this may be the fragmentariness or in any case the secondary role of poetry with respect to other professional occupations or speculative areas, in a personality whose eclecticism and richness of cultural interests are well known. At Oxford, Hopkins read Classics, but he was already keen on painting, sculpture, architecture, philology, philosophy, and theology. After his entrance into the Jesuits there was a reawakening of his interest in music, rhetoric, semantics, Egyptology (see his letters to Baillie in L III, 199–294), and natural sciences (see his letters to Nature, in L II, 161–66). On Hopkins's eclecticism, see also Collins 1947, 68–69.

14. A youthful Keats is most probably the kind of poet Hopkins would have become without a genuinely medieval "conversion." One can, for example, read the following excerpt of an evaluation of Keats, very allusive in an autobiographical sense, contained in a letter to Patmore: "His poems, I know, are very sensuous and indeed they are sensual. . . . He was young; his genius intense in its quality; his feeling for beauty, for perfection intense; he had found his way right in his Odes; he would find his way right at last to the true functions of his mind" (L III, 381–82).

cerned, the Keatsian models (the youthful and sensuous, musical, flowing, and miniaturist Keats) are easily identifiable in Hopkins's first compositions, as are the Pre-Raphaelite echoes (the insistence, again of a Keatsian matrix, on flowers, and above all on lilies, and on vegetation).[15] In its themes Hopkins's poetry of this period reveals even better the link connecting it to the first Romantics, whose incipient aestheticism Hopkins absorbs and accentuates, thanks to the mediation of Pater's ideas. Hopkins's main theme is, in fact, that of the escape from the gray and prosaic present toward an imaginary world where all conflicts cease in an enchanted quiet, peace, and ecstasy. Accordingly, one of the most recurring narrative situations is that of the journey, either horizontal and more specifically a sea journey (that is, from a tempestuous sea or coast—emblems of the real—to a haven or isle of peace), or vertical or more specifically aerial (that is, a flight from the earth's squalor to sublime and dizzy altitudes). Suchlike journeys and invocations are (or are to be found in) "A Vision of the Mermaids," "Winter with the Gulf-Stream," "The Alchemist in the city," "Heaven-Haven," "A Voice from the World," "Il Mystico," "A Windy Day in Summer," "The earth and heaven, so little known," etc.[16] Even Hopkins's Catholic inclinations, which begin to be manifest in this period (see in L III, *passim,* the letters of the years 1865–66), are due to the same, substantially "aesthetic" and post-Romantic aspirations to abolish mediocrity and life's prose:[17]

15. For the frequent synaesthesias and for his word-painting, Heuser has rightly spoken of Hopkins's youthful production as the poetic equivalent of Pre-Raphaelitism in painting (Heuser 1958, 11–12). See also Miles 1945 and Bump 1982, 43–55.

16. See, for a more detailed analysis of these poems, Marucci 1982, 149–52.

17. This is a "formalistic" attitude to Catholicism, shared by many English Protestants of the period. For Matthew Arnold, the superiority of the Roman Catholic Church resided "in its charm for the imagination—its poetry. I persist in thinking that Catholicism has, from this superiority, a great future before it. . . . I persist in thinking that the prevailing form for the Christianity of the future will be the form of Catholicism; but a Catholicism purged, opening itself to the light and air, having the consciousness of its own poetry, freed from its sacerdotal despotism and freed from its pseudo-scientific apparatus of supernatural dogma. Its forms will be retained, as symbolizing with the force and charm of poetry, a few cardinal facts and ideals, simple indeed, but indispensable and inexhaustible, and on which our race could lay hold only by materializing them." The passage

You said you know yr. repugnance was to view the issues of eternity as depending on *anything so trivial and inadequate as life is.* I do understand the point of view. But I think the answer wh. I gave then comes at once—that in fact the argument tells the other way, because it is incredible and intolerable if there is nothing wh. is the reverse of trivial and will correct and avenge the triviality of this life. To myself *all this trivialness is one of the strongest reasons for the opposite belief and is always in action more or less. . . . I think that the trivialness of life is, and personally to each one, ought to be seen to be, done away with by the Incarnation.* (L III, 19)

That Hopkins was well integrated in the ranks of Victorianism is finally testified—in contrast, for the moment, with what Hopkins wrote in "The Probable Future of Metaphysics"—by his adherence to the Victorian aesthetic "chromatism" under the form of the criteria of gradualness and moderation. These are the aesthetic touchstones informing the frequent judgments on the literary and artistic personalities and on the cultural events of his times. For all their independence and originality (already scandalous and temerarious for the prudent interlocutors), they are not sufficient to call into doubt Hopkins's initial Victorianism.

The presence of beauty and truth ("the ends of Art" [J, 74])— a pair naturally derived, once again, from Keats—is in fact the binding aesthetic criterion regulating Hopkins's judgments and comments in his letters. In them the admiration for beauty, institutionally pre-eminent to truth ("Truth . . . is reducible probably to the head of Beauty" [ibid.]), is subsequently, as it were in the form of a quick second thought, cut down to size and tempered by the latter. Many of Hopkins's evaluations repeat the pattern of the following comment of 1862 on Aeschylus's *Prometheus Bound* and Shelley's *Prometheus Unbound:* "It [Aeschylus's] is really full of splendid poetry; when you read it, read it with Shelley's *Prometheus Unbound* which is as fine or finer, *perhaps a little too fantastic though*" (L III, 6). This limiting truth-principle becomes with time a moralistic qualm, a sense of proportion and of

---

is quoted by G. D. Klingopoulos 1968, 51–52. Hopkins's observations to his father, who had vainly tried to dissuade him from conversion, may be a symptomatic case of Freudian denial: "I am surprised you shd. say fancy and aesthetic tastes have led me to my present state of mind . . . " (L III, 93).

good taste, of gradualness, of balance, of the absence of extremisms and undue falsifications:

Now I hate one sort of extreme men as much to the full as you do. I assure you it fills me with humiliation, almost with despair, to see the excesses of such men as are represented by *The Church Times.* . . . And when I think this more and more I reverence the balance, the heartiness, the sincerity, the *greatness* [Hopkins's italics], of Addis and men like him wherever they are. I assure you Dr. Newman, the extremest of the extreme, so extreme that he went beyond the extremes of that standard and took a large faction of his side with him, is a MODERATE MAN [*sic*]. So is Dr. Pusey, nay, you think he is, I am sure, yourself. . . . I am coming to think much of taste myself, good taste and moderation, I who have sinned against them so much. But there is a prestige about them which is indescribable. (L III, 220–21)

The question [of morality] however is the practical effect, and is of course one of degree, where no line can be drawn. I mean for instance that it is impossible not personally to form an opinion against the morality of a writer like Swinburne, where the proportion of these subjects to the whole is great and secondly where the things themselves are the extreme cases in their own kind. . . . Then with the work itself the question is how far in point of detail one may safely go—another question of degree. . . . To me then the question with your particular book wd. be just this practical balance. (L III, 228–29)

But besides these clearly Victorian scruples, other symptoms of a rebellious, "anarchic," alternative temperament appear. As early as 1863 Hopkins had for example declared his own dissatisfaction with the rigid Victorian dogmatism in the field of literary criticism: "The most inveterate fault of critics is the tendency to cramp and hedge in by rules the free movements of genius, so that I should say, according to the Demosthenic and Catonic expression, the first requisite for a critic is liberality, and the second liberality, and the third, liberality" (L III, 204). Only slightly later comes the "scandalous" confession of having begun "to *doubt* Tennyson" (L III, 215; Hopkins's italics), followed by the well known, quite personal theory of poetic styles (L III, 215–20), one of which, the Parnassian—corresponding to the absence of inspiration—includes, for Hopkins, Tennyson's and also Spenser's and Pope's and even Milton's poetry, as the poetry of an "artificial school" (see also J, 38).[18]

One can therefore conclude that, in his pre-Jesuit years, Hopkins's style, taste, and aesthetics counterbalance the elements of independence and of contrast to the system (shown above all in his essays and in the Journal). Hopkins's position inside Victorian culture, insofar as the pre-Jesuit period is concerned, is therefore neither of full and unconditional acceptance nor of total refusal. It may in fact be defined as eccentricity to the "nuclear structure of a culture mechanism" (Lotman-Uspenskij 1978, 222).

18. See Noon 1949 for interesting observations on the "three languages of poetry" and some twentieth-century echoes. Pater, who was himself, together with Meredith, one of the writers who radically changed and revitalized the shoddy prose of Victorian fiction, may have transmitted to Hopkins, in the brief period of his tutorial at Oxford, this dissatisfaction with the repetitiveness and predictability of current literature and the idea of the urgency of a thorough renewal of poetic style—which was something that contemporary aestheticians and linguists also felt deeply. Significantly, in *Marius the Epicurean* the two students Marius and Flavian conceive a project of a literary reform, a "rehabilitation of the mother-tongue, then fallen so tarnished and languid." Marius's objective is that of "disentangling the later associations and going back to the original and native sense of each,—restoring to the full significance all its wealth of latent figurative expressions, reviving or replacing its outworn or tarnished images. Latin literature and the Latin tongue were dying of routine and languor; and what was necessary, first of all, was to re-establish the natural relationship between thought and expression, between the sensation and the term, and restore to words their primitive power" (*Marius the Epicurean,* 88, 89). The discussion of the evolution and change of Hopkins's critical canon will be continued in the following chapters.

4

Measured against his substantial or barely eccentric fidelity to the Victorian type in the pre-Jesuit period—of which I have tried to give proofs and examples—Hopkins's conversion and entrance into the Society of Jesus (1868) set in motion the gradual dismissal of many Victorian codes and their replacement by medieval ones. Those medieval leanings that were latent or only superficial ripen and take root; what was contingent and asystematic becomes structural; while, as a collateral effect, codes rise and assert themselves where, before, there was simply no code.

If it is true that the Middle Ages, taken as a sum of behavioral, epistemic, philosophical, political, religious, aesthetic principles, represent, unlike the following epochs, the historical period in which Catholicism embodied itself in the fullest and most plenary way, it is even obvious that Hopkins, on entering the Jesuit order, should appropriate a considerable quantity of medieval codes. What is not obvious and automatic is that, while within Catholicism itself one can notice throughout history a wide difference of epistemic orientations (so that one can speak of "medieval," "Renaissance," "baroque," "Counter-Reformation," "romantic," etc. Catholicisms), or instances of slow absorption into the dominant epistemes, or a certain eclecticism, in Hopkins the recovery of medieval Catholicism (and of its codes and subcodes) is almost total, not open to compromise and contamination, and incompatible with other Catholicisms.[1] I have already hinted at the tangible index of Hopkins's disagreement with the culture of his time, represented by the almost thirty year-long delay with which his work reached the reading public. Yet Hopkins was far from being integrated even in Victorian Catholicism and inside his religious order, which were both to a certain extent noninte-grated and alternative—in a Protestant country such as En-gland—to the dominant cultural model. As is known, Hopkins had almost no success inside the order, as either priest, teacher, preacher, or theologian. The official magazine of the English Je-suits, *The Month,* refused to publish Hopkins's poems in the two cases in which he submitted something of his own.

I shall investigate later the nature and extent of Hopkins's dis-agreement with the official philosophy of the Society of Jesus—scholasticism—which is at the basis, though not the sole cause, of this failure. I want instead to deal first of all with an inversion of signic and behavioral codes that begins with his conversion and is completed with his entrance into the Jesuits. With these acts Hopkins's life undergoes, even from a merely biographical standpoint, a marked "revolution": he leaves a youth spent in self-magnifying, in making himself renowned, in a search for success (hoped for and to a certain extent achieved)—in other words, a life of presence in the world and, in Lotman's terms, of exaltation of practical life—and enters a maturity of concealment, absence from the world, and denial and depreciation of practical life. I do not think it is an exaggeration to maintain, in the light of the parallel inversion of the signic code of which I shall speak in a moment, that the behavioral model underlying these choices (or, better, these renunciations) is precisely medieval monasti-cisms, asceticism, the "amor Dei usque ad contemptum sui" (St. Augustine, *De civitate Dei* 14.28), the refusal of—or, rather, the death to—the earthly world in favor of an integral adherence and

1. We have here the measure of Hopkins's detachment from Pater, since he precisely rejects the "aesthetic," ritualistic, gay, optimistic, pagan Christianity of the Renaissance which Pater juxtaposed to the "austere *ascêsis*" of the Middle Ages in a well-known page of *Marius the Epicurean* (chapter XXII, text's italics).

service to the supernatural world and to God.[2] As early as 1864
Hopkins jokingly inserts in a letter to Baillie a sketch of "Simeon
the Stileite" (L III, 210) which is also a precise personal prophecy.
Immediately after his conversion (23 January 1866) he notes in his
diary this plan of spiritual and corporal penances:

> For Lent. No pudding on Sundays. No tea except if to keep me awake
> and then without sugar. Meat only once a day. No verses in Passion
> Week or on Fridays. No lunch or meat on Fridays. Not to sit in armchair
> except can work in no other way. Ash Wednesday and Good Friday
> bread and water. (J, 72)

The "No verses" prohibition will undergo, on 11 May 1868, a
dramatic and drastic escalation, the burning of his poems (alluded
to as the "Slaughter of the innocents" [J, 165]). Nothing could
however be clearer and more explicit than the following retrospective explanation given by Hopkins to Dixon in 1881 about
his own "position in the Society" and in particular about the "ter-
tianship":

> It is in preparation for these last vows that we make the tertianship;
> which is called a *schola affectus* and is meant to enable us to recover that
> fervour which may have cooled through application to study and contact
> with the world. . . . Besides all which, my mind is here more at peace
> than it has ever been and I *would gladly live all my life, if it were so to be, in
> as great or a greater seclusion from the world and be busied only with God.* But
> in the midst of outward occupations not only the mind is drawn away
> from God, which may be at the call of duty and be God's will, but un-

2. St. Paul, Gal. 5:17, quoted in St. Augustine, *De civitate Dei* 19.4. See also,
St. Augustine, the fundamental chapter 17 of book 19: "But the families which
do not live by faith seek their peace in the earthly advantages of this life; while the
families which live by faith look for those eternal blessings which are promised,
and use as pilgrims such advantages of time and of earth as do not fascinate and
divert them from God, but rather aid them to endure with greater ease, and to
keep down the number of those burdens of the corruptible body which weigh
upon the soul." The heavenly city—i.e., spiritual life—is not only *peregrina* but
also *captiva* in this world, and Augustine adds later on: "It has come to pass that
the two cities could not have common laws of religion, and that the heavenly
city has been compelled in this matter to dissent." See also Cotter 1972, 116–20.
Hopkins might have reached Augustine *via* Savonarola, another true medievalist
(Bump 1982, 55–58). Once again Hopkins rejects Pater, who advocated a faith
enjoining "no forced opposition between the soul and the body, the world and
the spirit" (*Marius the Epicurean*, 241).

happily the will too is entangled, *worldly interests freshen, and worldly ambitions revive. The man who in the world is as dead to the world as if he were buried in the cloister is already a saint.* But this is our ideal. (L II, 75–76)

The rigor and inflexibility with which Hopkins "abolishes" the world (by burning his poems, by his seven-year-long poetic silence and his ensuing unwillingness to publish, his fear of art as "dangerous") are hardly Ignatian. Notably, the Ignatian model must be integrated, in Hopkins's case, by the model of medieval asceticism and by the previously mentioned Pauline and Augustianian strict separation between the spiritual and the temporal.[3] Hopkins contradicts St. Ignatius, for whom practical life and the artistic praxis—that is to say, the forms of an active presence in the world—are not in themselves to be condemned, and even possess, if well used, a (high) instrumental value: "Man was created to praise, honor and obey God, and in so doing save his soul; and the other things on earth were created for man and to help him to attain the end for which he was created."

Hopkins's observations on the Incarnation and on Lucifer's sin

3. Downes, in an interesting article in which he discusses a number of issues not yet sufficiently clarified by biographers, argues, "Hopkins' lifelong melancholia and his precocious, ascetic predispositions were fed by those aspects of Christian mortification that especially typify the first thousand years of Christianity, beginning with St. Paul and extending through the Patristic tradition up to and until St. Anselm. Ignatius came into contact with this tradition through Kempis' *Imitation of Christ,* much of the spirit of which he put into his Exercises. However, I propose that Ignatius considerably modified the assumption in Kempis that perfection demands total rejection of this life. . . . [Hopkins] seems somewhat pre-Ignatian on this count, as if Loyola had not modified Kempis at all" (Downes 1961, 593). See also Devlin: "Hopkins's stress on a naked, anti-natural, non-affective will does not come either from Scotus or from St Ignatius . . . he exaggerated Scotus's distinction between nature and individuality" (S, 120). Downes adds that Hopkins was overhasty and mistaken in his choice of the Jesuit order, and even doubts "his suitability for the Jesuits" (Downes 1961, 581). In the light of the scarce success he enjoyed, of the difficulties and misunderstandings of which he was the victim, and of the philosophical and theological divergences I mentioned above, one cannot but agree with him that Hopkins would have felt much more at home in an order having different rules and a different cultural frame, such as the Franciscans or the Benedictines, rather than in the Jesuits. In this case Cardinal Newman's surmise that "the Benedictines would not have suited" him (L III, 408) might have been absolutely wrong. Ong (1986) plays down the difference between Kempis and Ignatius (58–60), but admits that Ignatius "accept[ed] the external world with less trepidation than some earlier Christian ascetics" (64).

(in Hopkins's commentary on the *Spiritual Exercises* [S, 122–209]) illuminate his attitude to art and to the first of its possible consequences—fame and therefore pride. Hopkins elected Christ as a model and Lucifer as an anti-model: "*Erat subditus illis:* the hidden life at Nazareth is the great help to faith for us who must live more or less *an obscure, constrained, and unsuccessful life.* . . . What was his life there?—One of devotion . . . also one of labour; and of obedience: in every way it looked ordinary, presented *nothing* [Hopkins's italics] *that could attract the world*" (S, 176). Conversely, Lucifer is "a chorister who learns by use in the church itself the strength and beauty of his voice," and who becomes "aware in his very note of adoration of the riches of his nature," and, instead of giving them up in sacrifice, "ravished by his own sweetness and dazzled . . . by his beauty . . . was involved in spiritual sloth . . . and spiritual luxury and vainglory. . . . Remark also the 3 degrees of selfishness—love of our goods, which are wholly outside ourselves: *love of our good name* ('vanus honor mundi'), *which is ourself indeed, but in others' minds;* love of our own excellence, of our very selves, pride. *And therefore intellectual goods, as learning, still more / talents, and moral goods, as virtues, graces, are more dangerous to be attached to and proud of*" (S, 179–80).[4]

As I said above, this medieval mortification of the flesh and escape from the world are the consequence of a far more general inversion of the signic code: rejecting the desemioticization which, as we have seen, predominates in Western culture with the advent of the Enlightenment, and rejecting more specifically the aparadigmatic and syntagmatic tendencies of the Victorian Age (which he had moderately accepted but also already challenged in his pre-Jesuit period), Hopkins recovers, or stresses and deepens in a truly medieval sense, the semiotic and paradigmatic character of the real. This is true not only on a personal plane—so that his life loses its autonomy and its intrinsic and absolute

4. The musical metaphor is resumed in S, 200ff., where the personal allusions are as unmistakable: "This song of Lucifer's was a dwelling on his own beauty, an instressing of his own inscape, and like a performance on the organ and instrument of his own being: it was a sounding, as they say, of his own trumpet and a hymn in his own praise" (S, 200–201).

value and conversely takes on one purely heteronomic, signic, and instrumental—but also for the "other-than-self," for the things and the other entities of the phenomenal world. In this sense, the reorganization and the "rhyming" of the real and the snatching of it from the seeming dominion of chaos (see above, Part Two, chapter 3), are the starting point for the sewing together of this phenomenal world (a world indeed of appearances, expressions, signifiers: a world of copies) with the supernatural world (a world of realities, contents, signifieds: a world of originals), and finally with the Principle and Origin of all existing things, God.[5]

Notwithstanding the Journal, there are traces in Hopkins's pre-Jesuit period of a "monoplanarity" and of a desemioticization of an Enlightenment matrix. In particular Pater's influence on his aesthetics and his youthful religion of a pure and absolute beauty reflected in an assiduous and spasmodic contemplation of nature (approached in a prevalently scientific way, with an interest in its perceptive, psychological, and phenomenological implications) exclude almost systematically any paradigmatic call and any verticalizing impulse. Hopkins's theory of the beautiful, on which the greatest part of his university essays revolve, clearly illustrates this absence: the sphere of the discussion remains one of pure syntagmatic immanence, for beauty is "relation of the parts of a sensuous thing to each other" (J, 80), or between the thing represented and the thing as it really is. This kind of approach also crops up in certain examples of "philosophical poetry":

[Fragments of] "Floris in Italy" (a)

1   Beauty it may be is the meet of lines
2   Or careful-spacèd sequences of sound,
3   These rather are the arc where beauty shines,
4   The temper'd soil where only her flower is found.
5   Allow at least it has one term and part
6   Beyond, and one within the looker's eye;

5. Cf. S, 194–95: "His presence is a reality though invisible . . . these copies of His perfections are the merest shadows, the reality beggars expectation. . . . God rests in man as in a place, a *locus,* bed, vessel, expressly made to receive him as a jewel in a case hollowed to fit it, as the hand in the glove or the milk in the breast."

Poem 24

2   The rainbow shines, but only in the thought
3   Of him that looks. Yet not in that alone,
4   For who makes rainbows by invention?

Poem 58

1   Confirmed beauty will not bear a stress;—

Hopkins's attitude to beauty from his conversion onward shows very well, on the contrary, the rejection of the monoplanar, syntagmatic code and the adoption of a symbolic, bi-planar code.[6] The first reaction, typical of the rashness of conversions (but one that will occasionally occur even later: see J, 190, 249) was the suppression of all aesthetic enjoyment of beauteous forms: "On this day by God's grace I resolved to give up all beauty until I had His leave for it" (J, 71). After 1875 Hopkins, violating this "testamentary" commandment (which was also the cause of his seven years of poetic silence), reached a solution of the problem that lasted practically until the *terrible sonnets:* the admission of beauty on condition of its solely signic use.

Hopkins traces beauty first of all in man and in his purely physical and material form, in his body. His extraordinary admiration for the splendor and bloom of the human body, and his equally extraordinary, non-medieval humanity in lamenting its subjection to the laws of time and decay, become medieval when he (a) identifies corporeality as a sign of spirituality and makes both "rhyme" in God and in Christ;[7] (b) paradoxically postulates the

6. "Pater was surrounded by a world full of beautiful creations with no significance outside themselves; Hopkins was part of a beautiful Creation" (Robinson 1978, 31). For the "divergences" between Hopkins and Pater see ibid., 18–52.

7. "The doctrines of the Incarnation and the Real Presence are more than proof that there was and is some connection between the divine and human worlds. Ultimately, with the help of Scotus and other theologians, Hopkins broadens his theory of the Incarnation until he comes to see all things as created in Christ. . . . To say that all things are created in Christ means seeing the second person of the Trinity as the model on which all things are made, nonhuman things as well as men. . . . Each created thing is a version of Christ, and derives its being from the way it expresses Christ's nature in a unique way. All things rhyme in Christ" (Miller 1963, 312–13). The theological implication underlying this theory, as Devlin in several contributions (see Bibliography) and Miller, following Devlin,

only salvation and preservation of the body in its loss, in the gift, the sacrifice, the giving it up to the Father. The signic correspondence between corporeality and spirituality has its origin in God's creation of man in his image and after his likeness (Gen. 1: 26), since God meant "us to copy His nature and character as well as we can and put on His mind according to our measure" (S, 134).

Predictably, such a signic vision of man is manifestly active in the group of poems nearest to the moment of its discovery (and also of the discovery of the signic nature of the poetic word itself), that is, the poems written in the three or four years after 1875 and the "Deutschland." "Spring" (1877) is one of the first poems to state the harmony of the body ("₁₃Mayday") and of the spirit ("₁₃mind") and their providential and saving divine destination through the Incarnation of the Son:

> *"Spring"*
>
> 11   . . . Have, get, before it cloy,
> 12   Before it cloud, Christ, lord, and sour with sinning,
> 13   Innocent *mind and Mayday* in girl and boy,
> 14   Most, O maid's child, *thy choice and worthy the winning.*

Hopkins will explain a little later in a sermon, and almost with the same words, that "the man or woman, the boy or girl, that in their bloom and heyday, in their strength and health give themselves to God and with the fresh body and joyously beating blood give him glory, how near he will be to them in age and sickness and wall their weakness round in the hour of death!" (S, 19). "Spring" is matched by "Morning, Midday, and Evening Sacrifice" (1879): "₁₃mind and Mayday" become, again with an alliterative couple, "₈thought and thew," with the addition of "₁₀Head, heart, hand, heel, and shoulder." All this corporal beauty, "₅beauty" which is "₆fuming" in the same instant in which it is "₅blooming," all this "₁₂pride of prime's enjoyment" secretly signalizing the "₁₆mind, / . . . ₁₈ripest under rind," is to be taken, Hopkins admonishes, "₁₃as for tool, not toy," and kept

---

have made clear, is the univocity of being, affirmed by Scotus (who refers to Parmenides) and denied by Aquinas. See below, chapter 6.

"₁₄at Christ's employment," this being the note on which the poem closes ("₂₁Your offering, with despatch, of!").[8]

Such a signic vision of man—a vision working in terms of exact counter-sense to common sense and to a non-signic perspective—necessitates and demands repeated support, confirmation, and amplification—in the poet as well as in his audience. The first part of "The Leaden Echo and the Golden Echo" (1882) is at the same time a hymn to the flower of youth and an elegy for its inescapable withering. In the second part, however, the "₂₇flower of beauty" becomes "₂₈fastened with the ténderest truth"; beauty is sublimated into "₂₄beauty-in-the-ghost." One can enjoy physical beauty on the basis of an immanentistic perspective, but knowing that it will fade he "₁₃despair[s]." The medievalizing of beauty not only brings hope and euphoria but also makes its preservation possible ("₁₇Spåre!"):

> *"The Leaden Echo and the Golden Echo"*
>
> 43   When the thing *we freely fórfeit* is kept with fónder a care,
> 44   Fonder a cåre kept than we could have kept it, képt
> 45   Får with fonder a care (and wé, *we should have lost it*), ff'ner,
>   fónder
> 46   A care kept. . . .

Naturally this is possible only by spiritualizing beauty, that is, not here and now ("₁₉not within séeing of the sun"), but above in afterlife ("₄₇Yónder"), that is, losing it, subtracting it from human proprietorship and giving it back to God, its legitimate owner:

> 35   Give beauty back, beauty, beauty, béauty, back to God beauty's
>   self and beauty's giver.[9]

This is also the concept underlying "To what serves Mortal Beauty?" (1885). Physical beauty—whose admirable perfection

---

8. The martyrs, to whom Hopkins devoted many poems (see Marucci 1977, 34–38), perfectly illustrate the body and the spirit's functioning as *copies* of Christ. Cf. for example "[Margaret Clitheroe]": "₁₅The Christ-ed beauty of her mind / ₁₆Her mould of features mated well."

9. On the sacrifice of beauty and its loss to God, which thus becomes gain, see S, 245–46, where there is a sort of prose first draft of the "Echoes."

one could be induced to wish it sealed out of time ("₂the O-seal-
that-so I face")—has the task to keep well awake and vigilant
"₄Men's wits" to the "₄things that are," that is, to the "₁₀love's
worthiest" and to the "₁₁World's loveliest," "₁₁men's selves," for
"₁₁Self I flashes off frame and face."[10] After such a use of "₁mortal
beauty" nothing else remains to be done with it ("₁₃then leave, let
that alone"), for the highest aspiration of man is toward "₁₄God's
better beauty."

The beauty of nature in the multiplicity of its manifestations
(floral, vegetal, animal, atmospheric) is for Hopkins obviously
complementary to human beauty, thus integrating the beauty of
creation. It too undergoes with his conversion a marked change
of function. Several passages in Hopkins's letters, essays, and
poems of his youth point to a vision of nature—as in many other
Victorians, disoriented and alienated by the chaotic expansion of
urban areas—as an oasis of quiet and silence, and as a source of
emotions and consolations:[11]

"Winter with the Gulf Stream"

20 But through black branches, rarely drest
21 In scarves of silky shot and shine,
22 The webbed and the watery west
23 Where yonder crimson fireball sets
24 *Looks laid for feasting and for rest.*

In "The Alchemist in the city" Hopkins yearns to land on a
"₃₅houseless shore," or in a "₃₆wilderness," or near "₃₇ancient
mounds" and "₃₈rocks" dominated by silence:

41 There on a long and squared height

10. Or, as Hopkins will say in "On the Portrait of Two Beautiful Young People," the "₁₅looks" are the "₁₅soul's own letters."
11. But contrast a confession made in 1888: "Like you I love country life and
dislike any town and that especially for its bad and smokefoul air. . . . What I
most dislike in towns and in London in particular is the misery of the poor; the
dirt, the squalor, and the illshapen degraded physical (putting aside moral) type
of so many of the people, with the deeply dejecting, unbearable thought that by
degrees almost all our population will become a town population and a puny un-
healthy and cowardly one" (L III, 292–93). Cf. also "The Sea and the Skylark,"
"₉this shallow and frail tówn."

42   After the sunset I would lie,
43   And pierce the yellow waxen light
44   With free long looking, ere I die.

A different kind of feeling—but always devoid of any signic nature—is confessed by Hopkins in a letter written in 1863:

I think I have told you that I have particular periods of admiration for particular things in Nature; for a certain time I am astonished at the beauty of a tree, shape, effect, etc, then when the passion, so to speak, has subsided, it is consigned to my treasury of explored beauty, and acknowledged with admiration and interest ever after, while something new takes its place in my enthusiasm. (L III, 202)

Later Hopkins makes an important step forward with the discovery of nature as a language and a text, though for the moment it does not reveal, subjected as it is to a purely "horizontal" reading, any "over-sense" or counter-sense, and remains a sort of metalinguistic text or self-reflecting language, or a purely sensory image or memory:

Poem 24
8   The sun on falling waters writes the *text*
9   Which yet is in the eye or in the thought.

If then Hopkins, before entering the Society of Jesus, seems to share the agnostic loss of sight of the transcendental dimension—or at least the deep chasm between the syntagmatic and the paradigmatic planes—typical of the Victorians, from his conversion onward, nature and the phenomenal world break their airtight closure to open up to—and gradually to proclaim—the witnessing of God their Creator. It is at this point and on the basis of this precise vision of nature that Hopkins, as Miller has well said, breaks with Victorian culture and poetry and moves toward "what is, in Victorian poetry, an almost unique sense of the immanence of God in nature and in the human soul. Neither Arnold, nor Tennyson, nor Browning is able to transcend so completely the spiritual condition of his age" (Miller 1963, 323–24).

The opening up of nature—previously a static monad—and its becoming God's immanence means a process of discovery of its inexhaustible *dynamism* consisting of two distinct, contrary and complementary motions, which are ultimately a single circular motion: one, ascending, signically marks nature's continuous and vertical reaching out to God and its anxiety to be reunited to its Origin; the other, descending, is nature's "information" on God's part, his reflex and reverberation. This parallels what happens in man, of whom Christ took the flesh and the likeness, though nature tends to God in a spontaneous and automatic way, whereas in man this is an act of the will.[12] Once he has overcome the admiration for nature's autonomous and absolute beauty, man's wonder before it is the wonder for this double imprint becoming manifest after patiently delving into it. The Journal periodically and ecstatically underlines this symbolic character: "One day when the bluebells were in bloom I wrote the following. I do not think I have ever seen anything more beautiful than the bluebell I have been looking at. I know the beauty of our Lord by it" (J, 199). And again: "As we drove home the stars came out thick: I leant back to look at them and my heart opening more than usual praised our Lord to and in whom all that beauty comes home" (J, 254). In nature, however, man not only finds this symbolic testimony but also discovers a reservoir of supplementary energies—as well as a means, a touchstone, an admonition and an encouragement—for his climbing up to God, were his own capacities weakened. Nature, in other words, collaborates with man in a common ascent to God. We have thus reached that hierarchical vision of creation typical of medieval culture,[13] with God

12. There is in this distinction a clear reference to Scotus's theory of the *affective* and *elective will,* on which see below, chapter 6. Hopkins probably derived this double movement of nature from the French mystic Marie Lataste (1822–47): "L'homme vient de Dieu et doit retourner à Dieu. Il y a deux mouvements en l'homme: de son être créé par Dieu vers l'existence et de son être existant vers Dieu. Ces deux mouvements sont donnés à l'homme par Dieu; et par ces deux mouvements, l'homme, s'il le veut, retournera infailliblement à Dieu" (S, 327). For significant excerpts from Marie Lataste's writings and for biographical information about her and Hopkins's comments, see S, Appendix I (325–37).

13. See above, Part Two, chapter 2. Lewis (1964) reminds us, "In modern, that is, in evolutionary, thought Man stands at the top of a stair whose foot is lost in obscurity; in this [the Medieval Model], he stands at the bottom of a stair whose top is invisible with light. . . . Historically as well as cosmically, medieval man stood at the foot of a stairway; looking up, he felt delight. The backward, like

at the upper vertex of the triangle and man and the world at the lower vertexes. In Hopkins's own words, it is a "scale of natures . . . infinite up towards the divine," inside which, "as there is a scale of natures, ranging from lower to higher . . . so also there is a scale or range of pitch which is also infinite and terminates upward in the directness or uprightness of the 'stem' of the godhead and the procession of the divine persons" (S, 147–48). The signic principle at the basis of such a hermeneutics is that the real is, integrally, an insignificant, material expression, or one which merely functions as a copy or surrogate of the ideal content, according to a network of precise and ramified correspondences. Hopkins resumes the youthful metaphor of a world that is literally God's word and text—a word and a text that must now of course be interpreted in a hierarchical sense: the "higher" the contents, the "higher" the expression. This Hopkins never tires of repeating whenever he speaks of St. Ignatius's "Principium et Fundamentum":

WHY DID GOD CREATE? [Hopkins's capitals]—Not for sport, not for nothing. Every sensible man has a purpose in all he does, every workman has a use for every object he makes. Much more has God a purpose, an end, a meaning in his work. He meant the world to give him praise, reverence, and service; *to give him glory*. It is like a garden, a field he sows; what should it bear him? praise, reverence, and service; it should yield him glory. It is an estate he farms: what should it bring him in? Praise, reverence, and service; it should repay him glory. It is a leasehold he lets out: what should its rent be? Praise, reverence, and service; its rent is its glory. It is a bird he teaches to sing, a pipe, a harp he plays on: what should it sing to him? etc. It is a glass he looks in: what should it shew him? With praise, reverence, and service it should shew him his own glory. It is a book he has written, of the riches of his knowledge, teaching endless truths, full lessons of wisdom, a poem of beauty. . . . The sun and the stars shining glorify God. They stand where he placed them, they move where he bid them. "The heavens declare the glory of God". They glorify God, *but they do not know it*. The birds sing to him, the thunder speaks of his terror, the lion is like his strength, the sea is like his

---

the upward, glance exhilarated him with a majestic spectacle, and humility was rewarded with the pleasures of admiration" (74–75, 185).

greatness, the honey like his sweetness; they are something like him, they make him known, they tell of him, they give him glory, but they do not know they do, they do not know him. . . . But AMIDST THEM ALL IS MAN [Hopkins's capitals], man and the angels: we will speak of man. Man was created. Like the rest then to praise, reverence, and serve God; to give him glory. He does so, even by his being, beyond all visible creatures. . . . But man can know God, *can mean to give him glory*. This then was why he was made, to give God glory and to mean to give it; to praise God freely, willingly to reverence him, gladly to serve him. Man was made to give, and mean to give, God glory. (S, 238–39, Hopkins's italics)

This long passage, with its impassioned search for mirror reflections of the divine image and with its allegorizing tension, is full of hints of Hopkins's poetics and of its expressive and aesthetic codes. Here, as in the two chapters that will follow, the conclusions we shall reach are the same drawn through a different route in Part One. The thesis that rhetoric serves—quite summarily said—to turn the sense into the counter-sense can be reformulated as follows: the poet's task is that of pointing out, or making explicit, the divine content "signed," or rather substituted by nature—to make explicit that it is indeed a language and a text.

Prior to investigating, in chapter 7, Hopkins's aesthetic and expressive codes and thereby tackling the aspect that represents our final objective, it is necessary to cast light upon a further proof of Hopkins's medieval vision of nature. Hopkins believed, as in the Middle Ages, that nature is a book of God; he believed, that is, in the truth of a metaphor whose literalness had been long since waning. The metaphor of nature as a book of God is in fact, as Curtius (1953) has shown in chapter 16 (302–47) of his study on the main *topoi* of Western medieval literature, one of the most specific and typical of the period (and a particular species of one more general and universal, that of the book). Curtius sketches the life of the book-metaphor with a massive display of examples: it was born and had an early apogee in ancient Egypt, then it decayed in the Greek and Roman periods, to be resurrected with the advent of Christianity and reach a second and greater apogee in the Latin Middle Ages of the twelfth and thirteenth centuries and in Dante; it then passed intact to the Renaissance, to Italian baroque poetry as well as to English metaphysical poetry and to the Spanish *siglo de oro,* and afterwards gradually died out. What is of interest to us about this metaphor is above all its cultural origins and its exploitation in a religious sense (nature as book of God) in the medieval period. The use of this metaphor was never from the first generalized: "Not every subject matter . . . can be employed by figurative language, but only such as are value-charged; which, as Goethe puts it, are 'life-relations' or through which the 'interdependent life of earthly things' is discernible" (Curtius 1953, 303). Not accidentally, this metaphor arose in ancient Egypt, where "writing and the book have a sacred character" (304). The religious use of the book metaphor, inaugurated by the Bible and by St. Paul, is resumed in the first centuries of the Middle Ages by Isidore of Seville and by the late Carolingian and Spanish Latin poets. One encounters expressions such as "the Book of the Last Judgment" (in the *Dies Irae*), the "book of the righteous," the "book of the damned," the "book of spiritual life," the "book of the heart." In the High Middle Ages, this metaphor is almost unvaryingly referred to nature. The image of the creature as a mirror and a book of the supernatural order is already in Alain of Lille and it reappears in the mystics and preachers of the following centuries, in the *Imitatio Christi,* in Hugh of St. Victor and in Hugo of Folieto, in the Neoplatonic philosophy of Bernard Silvestris, in the *Policraticus* of John of Salisbury, in St. Bonaventure ("creatura mundi est quasi quidam liber in quo relucet . . . Trinitas fabricatrix") and even in such a philosopher of the waning Middle Ages as Nicholas of Cusa, for whom "the things of sense are . . . to be regarded as 'books' through which God as our teacher declares the truth to us" (ibid., 321). Dante's *Divine Comedy* is rife with even more original metaphors. With the waning of the Middle Ages this metaphor becomes secularized, although orthodox uses are to be found in Paracelsus, Montaigne, and Campanella. It is interesting for us to follow its development in England, where, however, we must keep in mind the time lag with which continental periodizations must be applied. Curtius traces the metaphor of nature as a book, and a book of God, in the Latinist J. Owen, in Thomas Browne (from whom he quotes [323]: "the civilitie of these little citizens [the bees and the ants], more neatly set forth the wisedome of their Maker," and elsewhere, "*two bookes* from whence I collect my divinity; besides that written one of God, another of his servant Nature, the universall and publick Manuscript, that lies expans'd unto the eyes of all"), in Donne, Quarles, Herbert, Vaughan, Crashaw, and in Milton and Shakespeare. Highly relevant is Curtius's explanation of the waning of this metaphor, implying the waning of an episteme and of an epoch: "To be sure, many examples of writing imagery could be found in the succeeding centuries. But it no longer possesses a unique, a felt, a conscious 'life-relationship,' could no longer possess it after the Enlightenment shattered the authority of the book and the Technological Age changed all the relations of life" (347). If we keep in mind this observation we will see confirmed and further supported our thesis of a Hopkins behind his times and intent on recovering codes that were inactive in his time. England received continental cultures with a historical delay, and Curtius on more than one occasion justly inclines to reduce the contrast, often more misleading than useful, between Middle Ages and Renaissance in England. If so, Hopkins's ideal place in English culture is in that long period, certainly manifold but substantially unitary, that extends from its beginnings as a national culture with Chaucer, through its culmination in Shakespeare, Milton, and Donne, and its dying-swan song in the Jacobean period before its definitive expiration with the end of the Stuart dynasty. As Austin Warren penetratingly wrote, Hopkins "seems to be *reaching back . . .* to an English Catholic poetry . . . his *pushing back* of the Elizabethans had some incentive in his desire to *get back of the Reformation to the day when all England was at once Catholic and English*" (Warren 1945, 86).

As I have said above, the view of nature as a book of divine messages timidly appears with Hopkins's conversion, "explodes" with the "Deutschland" and the nature sonnets, consolidates itself with only slight symptoms of enfeeblement in the poems of the early eighties, becomes a desperately dumb chord with the *terrible sonnets*,[14] and reappears, *in extremis,* in the "Heraclitean Fire." "Easter" (probably written in 1866) contains the first occurrence of the book-of-God-metaphor applied to nature. It is therefore in singular contrast with the poem that immediately precedes it, *"Nondum,"* the dominant motive of which is suggested by Isaiah's quotation serving as subtitle (*'Verily Thou art a God that hidest Thyself* [Isa. 45: 15]): God's absence, God's silence ("₁₉unbroken silence"; "₃₁Thou art silent"). In *"Nondum"* *"₂No answering voice* comes from the skies," "₄no forgiving *voice replies,"* and

7   We see the glories of the earth
8   But not the hand that wrought them all:
9   Night to a myriad worlds gives birth,
10   Yet like a lighted empty hall
11   Where stands no host at door or hearth
12   Vacant creation's lamps appal.

The divine word, dumb though invoked ("₄₉Speak! whisper to my watching heart") gushes out instead in "Easter," which literally overturns lines 2 and 4 of *"Nondum":*

"Easter"
13   Gather gladness from the skies;
14   *Take a lesson* from the ground;
15   Flowers do ope their heavenward eyes
16   And a Spring-time joy have found;

This euphoric reading of the divine signs into which creation's text is continually disassembled, reassembled, and renovated is resumed, after a temporary suspension, in the "Deutschland." There it laboriously deciphers a sign thought by everyone to be incomprehensible and meaningless (see below, chapter 8). It then continues in all the nature sonnets, where the transparency of the divine messages embedded in nature (and its character of text) be-

14. As Miller notes, the waning of the one-two relation of man with nature is caused by the sensation that the latter is felt as transitory and "trivial" (1963, 332), and because from a certain moment onwards (and particularly in the *terrible sonnets*) Hopkins feels pushed to seek God without intermediaries, along a "straight path" (333).

comes even overflowing and superabundant. The whole of nature ("$_7$All things"), in the multiform variety of its chiaroscuros, is "$_{10}$father[ed]-forth" by God ("Pied Beauty"),[15] the skies are "$_8$all a purchase, *all . . . a prize*" ("The Starlight Night"), the whole world is "$_1$charged with . . . God" ("God's Grandeur").[16] "Hurrahing in Harvest" reaffirms the incessant, incomparable teaching ("$_8$rounder *replies*") obtainable from the skies, and furthermore the perfect likeness of the creation to its creator, of whom it reproduces and repeats, like a double, the physical traits ("$_9$And the . . . hills *are* his . . . shoulder"). The barely checked leap heavenward ("$_{14}$hurls") of the observer of such a magnificent view contrasts with Poem 24 (see above), where the observer remains cold and detached:

> *"Hurrahing in Harvest"*
> 5   I walk, I lift up, I lift up heart, eyes,
> 6   Down all that glory in the heavens to glean our Saviour;
> 7   And, eyes, heart, what looks, what lips yet gave you a
> 8   Rapturous love's greeting of realer, of rounder replies?
> 9   And the azurous hung hills are his world-wielding shoulder
> 10 Majestic—as a stallion stalwart, very-violet-sweet!—
> 11 These things, these things were here and but the beholder
> 12 Wanting; which two when they once meet,
> 13 The heart rears wings bold and bolder
> 14 And hurls for him, O half hurls earth for him off under his feet.

As repeatedly pointed out by critics, "As kingfishers catch fire . . ." is the most explicit and complete formulation of the medieval signic code presiding over Hopkins's observation of creation. The conception of creation (in its two lower vertexes, man

---

15. "Pied Beauty" is the most exhaustive illustration of the relationship between Creator and creation: "The most inclusive case of the relation of sameness and difference is the relation of God to the universe. The creator and the creation rhyme. . . . The creation must somehow be made in the image of its progenitor" (Miller 1963, 303). Miller further observes that nature is different from and inferior to God as "fickle and freckled . . . differentiated in space" and mutable, though remaining "the best earthly image of God's perfection" (304).

16. An echo of "God's Grandeur" is in S, 195, where the book metaphor is explicit and not, as in the poem, only indirectly present: "All things therefore are charged with love, are charged with God and if we know how to touch them give off sparks and take fire, yield drops and flow, ring and *tell* of him."

and nature) as a copy of the Creator takes on the usual metaphorical expression: as the string, plucked, "₃*tells*," as the bell "₄*finds tongue* to fling out broad its name," so "₅Each mortal thing" proclaims the diversity of its self, "₇*myself* [text's italics] *it speaks and spells.*" But in proclaiming itself, it at the same time proclaims Christ, whose imprint is distinguishable in the diversity of the selves, however extreme and irreducible:

> "*As kingfishers catch fire . . .*"

12   . . . For Christ plays in ten thousand places,
13   Lovely in limbs, and lovely in eyes not his
14   To the Father through the features of men's faces.[17]

From a certain moment onward, however, the reading of the divine text stored in creation begins to gush out less natural and automatic, and the yearning toward heaven to be felt less readily and irrepressibly. "Spring and Fall" is one of the first poems where nature also or only shows a human text: the leaves are "₃líke the thíngs of mán" and "₂Goldengrove unleaving" becomes the symbol of the "₁₄blíght mán was bórn for." In "Spelt from Sibyl's Leaves," more dramatically, the sunset no longer conveys the euphoric divine message (under the form of an imminent dawn), but ambiguously gives forth "₁₀Óur tale . . . óur oracle." And the deciphering, the spelling of this oracle is a "₁world" no longer "₁charged wíth . . . God" ("God's Grandeur"), as some years before, but (and with a new occurrence of the book metaphor) a "₁₃wórld where bút these twó tell, eách off the other; of a ráck / ₁₄Where, self-wrung, selfstrung, sheathe- and shelterless, | thoúghts agaínst thoughts ín groans grínd." Hereafter nature will begin to fully manifest to man that supplementary function of admonition and encouragement, in order to help him to imitate it and thus to break the torpor that has caught him and that nails him to the ground. Nature, on its part (just because it has

---

17. Man, too, mirroring Christ, is a book. Among the many and insistent questions Hopkins asks himself in a late private note we find these: "Are we his pipe or harp? we are out of tune, we grate upon his ear. Are we his glass to look in? we are deep in dust or our silver gone or we are broken or, worst of all, we misshape his face and make God's image hideous. Are we his book? we are blotted, we are scribbled over with foulness and blasphemy" (S, 240).

no choice, no elective will), finds it easy to stretch itself out to the Creator (cf. the "$_{32}$hung-heavenward boughs" of "On the Portrait of Two Beautiful Young People"), who distinctly imprints in it his own image (compare also the "$_{39}$heavenfallen freshness" of "Epithalamion"). In the magnificent fragment "[Ashboughs]" nature not only appears again as a language, but nothing is said "$_2$so sighs deep / $_3$Poetry [to the mind]" as an ash whose boughs stand out in the sky. And what does the sublime "poetry" of these boughs "$_7$touch[ing] heaven" communicate?

"[Ashboughs]"

10 . . . it is old earth's groping towards the steep
11   Heaven *whom she childs us by.*

Nature has a similar function in "Ribblesdale," though man stands there in an ever-worse plight. Nature has not ceased to stretch itself out to heaven, but man is at pains to decipher therein the Creator's message, become dumb:

"Ribblesdale"

1 Earth, sweet Earth, sweet landscape, with leaves throng
2 And louched low grass, heaven that dost appeal
3 To *with no tongue to plead . . .*

The double ascensional-descensional movement vivifying it, however, soon appears:

5 Thou canst but be, but that thou well dost; strong
6 Thy plea with him *who dealt,* nay does now deal,
7 Thy lovely dale *down* thus . . .

In the final lines, as in "[Ashboughs]," nature once again takes on human features. Its frowning face and its stern word are the living reproach to man become temporarily insensitive to the transcendent dimension.

5

❧ THE RECONSTRUCTION OF THE

CIVITAS DEI

Hopkins's vision of the creation is regulated, as we have just seen, by a series of signic and metaphorical codes ("the divine book of nature") of a medieval type. An analysis of his no-less-medieval conceptions of history and social organization (so little studied by criticism) will be the initial stage of a verification of the structural and systematic character of the above-described theory of the sign. At the same time we will get an idea of the profound solidarity and homogeneity of Hopkins's codes and subcodes.

The first and most prominent feature of Hopkins's political attitude is a strong patriotic feeling, a strenuous loyalty. He writes in 1881 in a letter to Bridges: "The state of the country is indeed sad, I might say it is heart-breaking, for I am a very great patriot" (L I, 131). In another to Patmore, written in 1886, he writes, "It is a terrible element of weakness that now we are not well provided with the name and ideal which would recommend and justify our Empire" (L III, 367). Alongside this patriotism we frequently find anxiety and preoccupation over the present state of Britain, occasionally bitterness and indignation about its degeneration, and a widespread conviction "of the hollowness of this century's civilization" (L II, 97). In "The Loss of the Eurydice"— as earlier on in "The Wreck of the Deutschland" (for the aspects touched on in this paragraph, see below, chapter 8)—Hopkins deplores "$_{87}$My people and born own nation / $_{88}$Fast foundering own generation," while in "The Sea and the Skylark" nature's purity and the skylark's lightness are contrasted with "$_{10}$our sordid turbid time."[1] Oftener, however, patriotism takes on its most typical shape of a devotion, a carnal and vital bond, and is duly expressed by sexual metaphors:

> *"To seem . . .*
>
> 5   England, whose honour O all my heart woos, *wife*
> 6   To my creating thought . . .
>
> *"What shall I do . . ."*
>
> 1   What shall I do for the land that *bred* me,
> 2   Her homes and fields that folded and *fed* me?
> 3   Be under her banner and live for her honour:
> 4   Under her banner I'll live for her honour.
>   . . .
> 11   Call me England's fame's fond *lover,*
> 12   Her fame to keep, her fame to recover.

The greatest throb of patriotic pride is however kindled in Hopkins by the sight or the thought of the soldier, especially when young and about to sacrifice his life to his motherland, like the "$_{14}$boldboys soon to be men" and Sidney Fletcher ("$_{75}$Every inch a tar, / $_{76}$Of the best we boast our sailors are") of the "Eurydice," or like the bugler-boy, "$_{16}$bloom of a chastity in mansex fine," of "The Bugler's First Communion," who receives "$_{28}$Christ's royal ration" and whose first steps (or, again with a sea-metaphor, whose journey in perilous seas) are followed with the utmost trepidation ("$_{37}$whose least me quickenings lift"). And if man is made after the image of Christ, so much more Christ, the first and greatest of the fighters for faith (as Hopkins repeatedly con-

---

1. See also the sonnet's close: "$_{13}$Our make and making break, are breaking down / $_{14}$To man's last dust, drain fast towards man's first slime." Such a vision of history as a regression, a descent toward its dissolution, is an "apocalyptic," medieval motif which, though not exclusive of Hopkins (Sulloway 1972, chapter 4), is in contrast with the optimistic and often triumphant progressivism of the Victorians. In explaining the semantico-symbolic type of the Middle Ages, Lotman points out, as typical of its culture, the marking of the beginning and of the end (Lotman 1977, 212, and Lotman 1973, 49).

notes him in the sermons: "our hero, a hero all the world wants
. . . a warrior and a conqueror; of whom it is written he went
forth conquering and to conquer" [S, 34; see also 17, 35, 40, 48,
234]), is the *model* of every soldier. This double signic relation
is clearly shown by "[The Soldier]": the heart blesses the soldier
"₄Since, proud, it calls the calling | manly" and assumes that "₅the
men must be no less," that is, "₆deems; dèars the ártist áfter his
árt" and sees in the red "₈the spírit of war thére expréss." But
there the heart also discovers Christ, the soldier, or better the
mariner, *par excellence*:

> "[The Soldier,]"
>
> 9   Mark Christ our King. He knows war, served this soldiering
>   through;
> 10   He of all can reeve a rope best.

This patriotism is obviously by no means anti-Victorian, nor is
it *tout court* medieval; it is a component of Hopkins that is actually
rather typical of Victorian England, and normal and hereditary
in a member of a middle-class family such as Hopkins was born
into.[2] The deep implications and the frame of reference of this
patriotism become, however, surprisingly clear just when, with
Hopkins's conversion and his entrance into the Jesuit order, it
should have undergone a crisis or should at least have cooled
down (owing, first of all, to Britain's Protestantism). Although
a composition reflecting the atmosphere and the spiritual climate
of conversion—"The Half-way House": "₇My *national* old Egyp-
tian reed gave way"—alludes to a possible waning of his loyalty,
the repudiation of Anglicanism and the adoption of Roman Catholicism do not carry along with them an analogous, drastic re-

2. On the patriotism of the Victorians, and its cultural implications and its
most representative figures, see Sulloway 1972, chapter 3, 115–57. As we have
already seen above in Part Two, chapter 2, Sulloway—one of the few critics to
have tackled extensively the issue of Hopkins's social and political attitude—identifies as one of the age's paradigms the pursuit of the ideal of the gentleman, modelled on the medieval knight as well as on the Renaissance courtier. Sulloway's
argument is exhaustive and convincing, despite the fact that she maintains Hopkins's perfect harmony with the group of the "gentleman prophets" and minimizes the originality of Hopkins's medievalism. Milroy (1977) notes Hopkins's
even "linguistic nationalism" (78).

vision of Hopkins's patriotic feeling. As Austin Warren observed, among the many possible there is "an English way of being Catholic," and Hopkins chose precisely that: he chose to be " 'Gallican' not Ultramontane, British not Italian in his devotional life and rhetoric" (Warren 1945, 73–74).[3] From his conversion onward, Hopkins's patriotism, far from becoming weaker or disappearing, deepened and widened. In so doing, however, it gradually took on aspects that were as decidedly extraneous to the Victorian context as they were typically medieval in the multiplicity of their theocratic implications. More precisely, Hopkins's patriotism proves to be a longing for a Catholic Britain that was then non-existent but that he saw as imminent—a Britain capable of taking on the role of vital part, of veritable life-giver, promoter, and linchpin of a new Christian civilization coinciding with the British Empire.[4] As in the Middle Ages, this new political organism was to be harmonious, organic, and compact, and therefore opposed to what he termed the "atomism" (both of creeds and nations) of the contemporary world.[5] It is then very easy to perceive what differentiates Hopkins from the Victorians. Lotman has argued that the medieval world frame is "built on the denial of the syntagmatic principle," which is on the contrary shared by the Victorians and "was systematically achronic" (and in fact "what had a temporal link was not historically existent" [Lotman 1973, 49]), so that the merely temporal, quantitative "progress" did not imply a parallel qualitative progress. Hopkins undoubtedly adheres to this frame when he, unlike for example

3. Or, as Downes puts it, "Hopkins' conversion to Catholicism had its Protestant side" (Downes 1985, 16).

4. "As the nineteenth century wore on, the new gentleman had to take his stand on the question of England's imperial mission to civilize the non-Christian world. . . . For Hopkins, as for most of the latter-day medievalists, England's imperial mission was taken for granted, and anybody who denied it could not have been among 'the true men' " (Sulloway 1972, 129).

5. Hopkins shared this dream with Novalis, whose essay "Die Christenheit oder Europa" (1799) is a poignant, wistful recollection of the lost medieval unity and of a Christian Europe politically and religiously one. Such a rebirth he advocated and saw as imminent. For Novalis, too, the unity of the Middle Ages was destroyed by Luther and the Enlightenment. In the twentieth century, Evelyn Waugh is, in many respects, another medievalist who saw the Reformation as *the* rupture of the medieval *Gemeinschaft*.

Butler and Morris, envisages improvements and corrections of the present social order not in an advance toward a hypothetical future model, but in a return to a past model that is viewed as already perfect and unimprovable, but from which the world has been inexorably drawing away.[6] I think Hopkins wanted to say something of the kind—the rejection of the syntagmatic principle and conversely the exaltation of those which in his university essays he called "fixed points" (see above, Part Two, chapter 3)—when at the close of his last remaining (and unfinished) sermon he spoke of a "great change" brought about by the Middle Ages:

If then you compare the times before the Sacred Heart was commonly known and worshipped with our times, in other words what are called the Middle Ages with the age we live in, and consider the difference between them and the change that has in the meantime passed upon the world, this difference and this change will be by general agreement very great, though all will not agree in what it lies. And now I wish to put aside the *events* of these centuries, their wars and struggles and revolutions, for all history is full of these and, as our Lord said, "These things must needs be"; nay more, I put aside the great religious changes that have been, the Protestant Reformation and the spread of infidelity; in a word I put out of sight all those things in which men take opposite sides and are divided and I wish to look only at things in which all, roughly speaking, have a common interest, in which all men share alike. Now within the space of time of which I speak the New World has been discovered and peopled from Europe; the means of travelling and the speed of it have increased prodigiously; communication between men, by print, by letter, by telegraph, and by other ways, has been made easy in a still more extraordinary degree; the realm of nature has been laid bare and our knowledge of it widened beyond measure. And these are things shared in by Catholic and Protestant, believer and unbeliever alike. Yet after all these are not the things that make much difference to human nature. *Caelum, non animum mutant qui trans mare currunt,* the Latin proverb says; men may travel, but do not change their minds with change of latitude. We write to one another a hundred times as fast and often as our forefathers could, but we do but say fast and often what we should have said seldom and slowly. And learning, the knowing more or

6. On Hopkins's "nostalgia for the Middle Ages" see also Cotter 1972, 161 and 192–96.

knowing less, leaves us with our characters, our passions, and our appe-
tites much what they were. It is not then in these things that the great
change is. In what then does it lie, that great and profound change which
has within the time of which . . . (S, 104; Hopkins's italics)

It is a pity that the sermon was left unfinished on these words,
but already in this preamble Hopkins was suggesting distinctions
and oppositions on which he would not have failed to draw his
hearers' attention; in particular, I think, he would have certainly
contrasted the political, ideological, and religious division set in
motion with the end of the Middle Ages ("the spread of infidelity"; "men take opposite sides and are divided") with the unity
and compactness of the medieval world ("all men share alike").[7]

The foundation of a neo-medieval *civitas Dei*, of a federation
invigorated and welded by the one Catholic faith, in which all
nations should have identified themselves in getting over existing
divergences, is a motif, or rather an ideal—a utopia—only hinted
at in Hopkins's poetry. It is, however, fully developed and discussed first in a group of sermons and then in Hopkins's last letters of his Dublin years, when he was forced by the Irish troubles
and the first symptoms of the breaking up of the Empire to reas-
sert it. Since his Oxford years Hopkins had been steadily and almost obsessively deploring the division of the world and advocating the necessity to reunite it. The dissatisfaction with the
present state of the world is in the young Hopkins—as we have
seen—a post-Romantic *topos* but also a genuine reaction. It is a
dissatisfaction with the environing urban prosaicness and gray-

7. The union/disunion paradigm acts in Hopkins as an instance of an acontex-
tual medieval code. For example, he frequently speaks of man's spiritual division
("in his personality his freedom lies and this same personality . . . unhappily dis-
unites it [man's nature], rends it, and almost tears it to pieces"). He sees the division subverted by Incarnation, which "bring[s] [men] back to that union with
themselves which they have lost by freedom and even . . . bring[s] them to a
union with God which nothing in their nature gave them" (S, 171–72). Furthermore, Incarnation reunites even a socially divided world, a world "divided and
estranged man from man . . . family from family . . . nation from nation by war;
race from race by colour; and so on" (S, 172), a world dominated by egoism and
hatred. On the world's political division hovers the shadow of Adam and Eve's
rebellion and the secession of Lucifer, who "would set up, as Christ has, an
earthly power and kingdom," were it not that "God is continually . . . dividing
Satan's kingdom against itself" (S, 180).

ness ("The Alchemist in the city"), but also, more generally, an intolerance and a confused rejection of the models of society. We have already seen (Part Two, chapter 3) how Hopkins, while still a promising poet and artist, had turned wistfully to the Middle Ages as to the last age in history in which a fruitful and harmonious relationship had been possible between the artist and society. In 1865 he had contrasted Savonarola with Luther in the following terms: "The one martyred in the Church, the other successful and the admired author of world-wide heresy in schism" (L III, 18). A year later, in "*Nondum*," Hopkins once again sorrowfully reflected on the religious division of the world, relating it to the political division:

31   And Thou art silent, whilst Thy world
32   *Contends about its many creeds*
33   And *Hosts confront with flags unfurled*
34   And zeal is flushed and pity bleeds
35   And truth is heard, with tears impearled,
36   A moaning voice among the reeds.

The answer to the question implicitly raised by these juvenile texts will be found and subsequently elaborated in Hopkins's maturity, notably in the envisaged recomposition of the divided world according to the supranational federation (Hopkins's word is "commonwealth") mentioned above, and modelled on the medieval *civitas Dei*. Hopkins's ideas take first shape in "Tom's Garland" and still better in the long "crib" to it contained in a letter to Bridges (L I, 272–74). In the sonnet, while indirectly diagnosing the contemporary evils (injustice, privileges, abuse of power, political division: "₁₉This, by Despáir, bred Hangdog dull; by Rage, / ₂₀Manwolf, worse; and their packs infest the age"), Hopkins sketches the outlines and the features of this utopian Christian society, of this "₈Commonweal" and "₁₇wide the world's weal" where everybody is content with the place he occupies ("₅lustily he his lów lót . . . / ₈ . . . swíngs though") because he gives in the same measure in which he takes, in a harmonious and fully efficient hierarchical society (ll. 10–12). In the "crib," Hopkins more explicitly speaks of a "commonwealth or well ordered human society" and of a "body with many members and each its function"; some higher, some lower, but all honourable, from the honour which belongs to the whole." In this harmonious machine the small mechanism has the same importance and value as the greatest: "The head is the sovereign. . . . The foot is the daylabourer," but the crown of nails of the latter becomes a garland, because, though he is "the lowest in the commonwealth," the true justice and equality reigning there are such that "this place still shares the common honour, and if it wants one advantage, glory or public fame, makes up for it by another, ease of mind, absence of care" (L I, 272–73).[8] Hopkins's great dream was that the British Empire might acquire the characteristics of the Universal Christian Empire, and that inside this Empire Britain might attain and keep the role of leading member and beacon of civilization. He wrote revealingly to Patmore:

Your poems are a good deed done for the Catholic Church and another for England, for the British Empire, which now trembles in the balance held in the hand of unwisdom. I remark that those Englishmen who wish prosperity to the Empire (which is not all Englishmen or Britons, strange to say) speak of the Empire's mission to extend freedom and civilization in India and elsewhere. . . . "Freedom": it is perfectly true that British freedom is the best, the only successful freedom, but that is because, with whatever drawbacks, those who have developed that freedom have done so with the aid of law and obedience to law. The cry then shd. be Law and Freedom, Freedom and Law. But that does not please: it must be Freedom only. And to that cry there is the telling answer: No freedom you can give us is equal to the freedom of letting us alone: take yourselves out of India, let us first be free of you. Then there is civilization. It shd. have been Catholic truth. That is the great end of Empires before God, to be Catholic and draw nations into their Catholi-

8. This is also emphasized by Scotus's distinction of the various types of justice: "Men need to exchange natural goods, and this is called commutative justice, and is often justice only insofar as equivalent goods are exchanged." There is also a *iustitia distributiva,* which "considers the dignity of the receiver according to a geometrical proportion, that is, attributing more goods to the more worthy" (*Oxon.,* IV, d. 49, q. 2). Hopkins's political ideas are influenced by Scotus more than is apparent. We can notice echoes of what concerns (a) the political consequences of original sin; (b) the social contract; (c) the superfluity of a princedom in the state of innocence and its necessity owing to human frailty and violence; (d) the communion of goods and the concept of property.

cism. But our Empire is less and less Christian as it grows. There remains that part of civilization which is outside Christianity or which is not essentially Christian. The best is gone, still something worth having is left. (L III, 366–67)

It is not surprising then that Hopkins, on the basis of such a Christian utopia and these medieval leanings, should have scandalized Bridges many years before this letter with his confession of being "in a manner" a communist (L I, 27).[9] Though Hopkins, faced with Bridges's remonstrances, hastened in the following letter to distance himself from communism as an ideology and as a praxis (L I, 28–30), yet he made it clear why he had entertained such a "sympathy": "It is a dreadful thing for the greatest and most necessary part of a very rich nation to live a hard life without dignity, knowledge, comforts, delight, or hopes in the midst of plenty—which plenty they make" (L I, 27–28). Even clearer is the nature and scope of the medieval utopia in the light of Hopkins's attitude toward the Irish question. One would have expected that, in the harsh debate that broke out over the Home Rule Bill, Hopkins, for obvious reasons of religious solidarity, would side with the supporters of Ireland's independence and with the Catholics. The truth is that the Irish question, as has often been noted, was one of the major causes of that feeling of torment and anguish that flowed into the *terrible sonnets;* and not so much because of the bloodshed and the riots, but because the prospect of Home Rule increasingly endangered and threatened the unity and the longed-for "catholicity" of the British Empire, which was already divided by its religious plurality. Between

9. For another "communist" hint see Hopkins's assertion that in the Earthly Paradise God prohibited theft in that it "was against property (if in that Paradise all things were not to be common, as perhaps they were to be)" (S, 61). Scotus too emphasizes the communion of goods in Eden: "In the state of innocence there is not a distinction in the property of goods, decreed either by a divine or by a human law: rather all things are shared. . . . The first reason for this is that the use of things according to right reason must belong to men, as it is proper to a peaceful and harmonious community and to necessary sustenance: in the state of innocence, in fact, the common use, without distinction of property, seconded both these ends more than the distinction of property. . . . That precept of natural law, to share everything, was repealed after the fall" (*Oxon.,* IV, d. 15, q. 2).

1885 and 1889—when the concession of Home Rule seemed imminent or inevitable—Hopkins's declarations of principle on Irish independence and its paladin Gladstone are numerous, embittered, and full of rancor (L III, 181, 194, 274, 281–83, 286–87; L I, 251–52, 257). What is symptomatic in these letters is that, motivated not by a spirit of political reaction but by a medieval-theocratic vision, Hopkins, instead of appreciating the Irish claims to separatism, emphasizes the spirit of rebellion, the impulse toward disintegration, the assault on the universality of the Empire, and the disobedience to authority:

Home Rule of itself is *a blow for England* and will do no good to Ireland. . . . It is, if people would see it, high praise of our constitution that it should enable us to pass through a crisis of which the natural end is war / without war; for now for the first time *the Irish are using the constitution against England.* But the country is in a *peaceful rebellion,* if you can understand what that is, and *the rebellion is becoming more serious. . . . This is what they call Nationhood.* The passion for it is of its nature insatiable and Home Rule will not satisfy it; it will be a disappointment too like the rest; but it will have some good effects and it will deliver England from the strain of an odious and impossible task, the task of attempting to govern *a people who own no principle of civil allegiance (only religious, and that one is now strained), not only to the existing government, in which they share, but to none at all;* and of enforcing a law which the people wish to set at nought and to defeat. For such a complexion of things no constitution was made: absolute monarchy with strong forces at command alone could deal with it, and that miserably. (L III, 281–82)

More dramatically and synthetically Hopkins wrote the following in a letter to Bridges: "You will see, it is the beginning of the end: Home Rule or *separation* is near. Let them come: anything is better than the attempt to rule a people who own no principle of civil obedience at all, not only to the existing government but to none at all" (L I, 252).

Such declarations of principle can hardly be ascribed to bourgeois conservative ideology—or, conversely, for the profession of "communist" faith and for social solidarity, to Victorian philanthropy—and far from being extemporaneous, must be related to a more profound and rooted medievalizing view of history and politics.[10] This is conclusively confirmed by a long and articulated excursus on the origin of human society and of social organization we find in a group of four sermons written in the Liverpool period (1880; S, 50–68). As is often the case in the sermons and even in the poems, a typically theological issue (the justification of the love man owes to God) unexpectedly pushes Hopkins to a series of demonstrations by analogy and allegory, which, while they help to explain or illustrate to his hearers the arduous complexity of dogma by means of references to situations familiar to them,[11] offer the best exposition of that theory, along with the already mentioned "crib" to "Tom's Garland." In particular, the strict and substantial correlation (and the relation of substitution) between the spiritual and the temporal order rule out any doubt about the cultural frame within which such a discussion is to be placed.[12]

10. Both Gardner (1949) (who classes Hopkins as a conservative aristocrat: I, 159) and Sulloway (1972) (who speaks of "political conservatism" and includes Hopkins among the " 'noble conservatives' " of the period [136, 132]) fall into this misunderstanding.

11. "Now, my brethren, what I am going to say may be dark, it may be dry; yet I shall make it as clear as I can" (S, 55). Devlin—who however speaks of a "*trilogy* of sermons"—observes that in them Hopkins "avoided the obscurity inherent in this approach and dealt with the matter in clear-cut terms of political philosophy" (S, 6). Curtius reminds us that "in the Middle Ages *exemplum* can also mean any story 'which serves to illustrate a theological doctrine' " (1953, 61, note 75).

12. Devlin implicitly observed, in the first of his introductions to S, that the absolute novelty of these sermons for the times in which Hopkins was writing was his reference to outdated political codes (in this case, medieval). He writes that Hopkins "overran his time and had to omit all mention of the restoration of the kingdom by spiritual warfare," and at the same time, "In a different century or in a different place—say, in a hypothetically Catholic Jacobean Court—one could imagine solemn and sensitive faces, propped on long delicate fingers, watching him with grave intensity. But under the circumstances one can only wonder at the perverse courage which tried to bridge the three-century-widened gap between poetry and theology" (S, 6–7). A precise and in-depth comparison between Hopkins's political thought and that of the Middle Ages (extremely hard to synthesize as it is) would be out of place here. With respect, however, to two of the best-known formulations, those of St. Augustine and of Dante, observe that Hopkins can claim his share of originality or, in any case, a certain ingenious syncretism. Hopkins would seem to lean toward an Augustinian rejection of the temporal and the mundane and an exclusive exaltation of the spiritual, but actually, following Aristotle and Dante, he revalues human society, though as a means and not as an end in itself. Dante's political vision is organically expounded in his *Monarchia,* but see also *Convivio* 4.4–5; his Epistles 5, 6, and 7; *Purgatorio*

An outline of Hopkins's discussion can be the following. The first of the four sermons (S, 50–53) analyzes in depth the nature of the love man ought to give God, and God's special sovereignty and lordship over the world. This theme is taken up and continued in the second, dealing with the "kingdom of God." The third and fourth sermons deal in detail with Adam's "society" with God, its statute and organization, its short existence, and the causes that brought about its end.

In the first sermon Hopkins poses the terms of the theological question that proves to be the germinating nucleus of the whole discussion: "*what kind of love should we give God?* [Hopkins's italics] what kind of love should he, or reasonably can he, ask of us? who is God that he wishes our love?" (S, 52). Hopkins avoids answering these questions directly, but he introduces an analogy, or more exactly a simile, between divine society—that is, the bond of love uniting man to God—and human society. God, he says, is "a *sovereign,* a lord and master, a *king,* a *sovereign;* he a *sovereign,* we his *subjects*" (ibid.). Hopkins, a master of parallelisms, henceforward untiringly works to identify God with an earthly sovereign and men with his subjects; yet instead of a merely instrumental and illustrative value—that is, a formal one (as in post-medieval ages, when the second term of comparison becomes indifferent)—this analogy gradually acquires a real and substantial value. The correspondence between spiritual and temporal order, between God and an earthly sovereign, between the faithful and the sovereign's subjects, between the kingdom of God and a worldly kingdom comes to be seen and presented in a truly medieval fashion, thus bringing into relief the function of substitution that the latter terms carry out with respect to the former. It is the same function that in the Middle Ages existed between the particular (or the particulars) and the universal, or between the expression (or the expressions) and the content, between matter and spirit.

Just as the subject, Hopkins says in the first sermon, loves his

6.76–151, 16.85–129; *Paradiso* 6.34–111. In Hopkins's political, or politically allusive writings, the great figure not surprisingly missing is the pope.

sovereign with an unconditional and voluntary obedience by performing his duty, "So God as our sovereign has only one will and that will we ought to do and to do it is to love him" (S, 52). In proposing this analogy, Hopkins tends to specify unequivocally the elements of his allegory for his hearers:[13] "*a* sovereign" becomes "*our* sovereign," that is Queen Victoria, while God's kingdom takes on the features and characteristics of the British Empire, optimistically idealized (as in the hints on its outposts) and enriched with typically medieval traits such as unity, harmony, justice:

A sovereign asks his subjects for love, not, mark you, his courtiers, his family, his friends, those who are about him and see him daily, but those who know him least, know him only as their lawful and their just sovereign, the last and least of these he asks for love; and he must mean that sort of love which only / subjects as such can give and so which only / sovereigns as such can ask—*the doing his sovereign will,* willing obedience. (S, 52; Hopkins's italics)

Having thus prepared an analogical basis for his hearers, Hopkins can perform, in the second sermon (S, 53–58), the change of perspective noted above. It is immediately clear, from the very title—"Thy Kingdom come"—that the concept of divine sovereignty, previously used in a metaphorical sense, is now used in an absolutely literal one. The result is that now worldly sovereignty and the subjection to an earthly monarchy have become metaphorical with respect to divine sovereignty and subjection. The medieval primacy of the heavenly over the worldly city— degraded as a copy, a shadow or material ghost of the former[14]— is thus re-established:

13. "As her Majesty is seen at the opening of Parliament, as she drives in her Parks in the sight of her subjects / so God in those days took his delight in some bodily shape to be with man" (S, 59). See also this further analogy: "There are then, as you know, in commonwealths ranks or (as they say) *estates;* for instance in our own are three, the crown, the peers, the commons. In this divine commonwealth, *in this kingdom of God were two* estates—God and man" (ibid.; Hopkins's italics).

14. About the superiority and supranational character of the divine jurisdiction, the Church, as compared to any political organization, see *De civitate Dei* 15–18. It must be remembered that throughout this work, the heavenly city is

God is our King. . . . So then God is a king and men are his people, his subjects, the nation he rules over. . . . God is our owner and master. . . . We are God's subjects; and again we are God's things, his goods and chattels, his property, his slaves . . . whereas it is sometimes said of constitutional sovereigns, that the king or queen reigns but does not govern, meaning that *he of his dignity gives a name and marks a period but does not manage the state by his own mastery, God on the contrary must govern, must direct and master the world* . . . (S, 54, 55)

Here Hopkins spontaneously offers an answer to a question that might be raised about the historical foundation of such a theocratic vision: "Was this always so?—No. Was it so in the beginning?—Yes. It was so at the beginning, then it must have ceased to be, and now it is again" (S, 55). Hopkins therefore localizes the original divine monarchy, directly set up and such as to require no visible representative of God,[15] in the biblical Eden and in the covenant signed by God with Adam ("in the beginning"). The original sin broke this alliance ("then") until ("now") Christ's sacrifice restored God's alliance with man on a different basis. The reconstituted human society (after the Fall and "God's First Kingdom" [S, 62]) is, however, a faithful reproduction of its model, and is therefore—in openly Augustinian terms—"God's second kingdom . . . kingdom of God which Christ brought in . . . *new City of God* and commonwealth of the Catholic Church" (ibid.).[16] The "social contract" and the delegation of power by

qualified—most symptomatically—as "tamquam peregrina" on earth (see above, Part Two, chapter 4, note 2).

15. In the earthly Paradise, "Neither was the king invisible only and his throne hidden in heaven: he let himself be seen, he played his part, as we may say, in the show and pageantry of the country, he was indeed on familiar terms with his subjects" (S, 59).

16. *De civitate Dei* 11–22 and, for Christ's role, 18.44ff. Scotus agrees with St. Augustine when he says that the "lex positiva humana" became a historical necessity as a consequence of Adam's sin (*Oxon.,* IV, d. 15, q. 2). See also *Oxon.,* IV, d. 14, q. 2: "The end of the law . . . is not the legislator himself or his good: it is the common good." The origin of the social contract is described by Scotus as follows: "Formerly there lived in cities, on earth, many foreign and diverse peoples, none of which was bound to obey the other because none had authority over another. Then by mutual consent of all, in order to establish peaceful relations, they decided to elect one of them Prince, and to obey him only, as subjects, as long as he lived."

men to the earthly sovereign, after the end of God's first kingdom, are in fact for Hopkins an almost exact copy of the primitive contract between God and Adam. The social contract may
have a strictly historical record or be lost in the "darkness of the
past" (S, 55), but in both cases, looking back toward creation,
one encounters the original that subsequently shaped all the historical copies:

> Wherever there is a sovereign power, a king, an emperor, any kind of
> prince, ruler, governor, one such or more of them, or even a whole peo-
> ple selfgoverning and selfgoverned, *there must always some understanding*
> *have gone before about the governing and the being governed*—I mean those
> who are governed must have agreed to be governed and those who gov-
> ern, they too must have accepted the task of government. . . . The *agree-*
> *ment,* the *understanding,* the *contract,* must have somehow *come about*
> [Hopkins's italics], and it will always have been brought about for the
> good of both parties, governor and governed, for their common good,
> their *common weal* [Hopkins's italics]; and this is what we call a common-
> wealth. . . . And now, brethren, one more thought and that a surprising
> one far higher, far more glorious, than any I have hitherto entertained.
> . . . What if God were to come to terms with man; make a covenant, a
> contract with him; share with him a common good, a common weal,
> undertaking a task and binding himself to duties; were, I say, to make
> one commonwealth with man, himself the sovereign, the king, man the
> subject; then in this divine commonwealth, in this kingdom of God,
> while man did his duty, for God could not fail in his, both sides would
> be just, equally just—unspeakable stately dignity of man! man as just as
> God, just with God's own justice? What if this were to be?—It was.
> When there was but one man Adam, not only *a* [Hopkins's italics] man
> but man, for Adam was the whole of humanity, he was mankind in one
> person, God entered with man, with that one man and then presently
> with him and his wife, the one woman, into a noble commonwealth,
> which was God's kingdom, and it was held together by justice, that fa-
> mous *original justice* [Hopkins's italics] of which you have all heard,
> which is passed away, except for Christ and Mary, for ever. (S, 55, 55–
> 56, 57)[17]

17. Hopkins will refer again to this theory of the birth and development of
human society (in the same terms though in an abridged form) in his commentary
to the *Spiritual Exercises* (S, 164–66). In the original alliance between God and
Adam ("God first entered into relations . . . with man in Adam and a common-

The conclusion of Hopkins's theorizing, only implicit here, is the divine origin of temporal power and the divine investiture of any earthly sovereign, and this Hopkins clearly states in the "crib" to "Tom's Garland": "The head is the sovereign, who has no superior but God and *from heaven receives his or her authority*" (L I, 273). It is therefore evident that only because divine monarchy and sovereignty—that is, the "divine commonwealth"—are the content and the guarantee of earthly monarchy and sovereignty—the almost genetic expression and continuation through time of that divine commonwealth—this expression and the duties it demands (i.e., obedience and submission) have a meaning. That is why, Hopkins argues, a united, just, and prosperous system of earthly monarchy is the perfect fulfillment of the signic situation (i.e., of the function of representation). With such a slightly utopian image the British Empire is once again identified:

Remark these two words, wellbeing or advantage and duty, for on them the commonwealth turns. The aim of every commonwealth is the wellbeing, the welfare of all, and this welfare of all is secured by a duty binding all. . . . So in the commonwealth: the prince may have more prudence in planning the campaign, the soldier more fortitude in storming the breach, but justice, justice is halved between them or, if you like, whole in each of them, the sovereign on his throne cannot be juster for claiming obedience than the subject for yielding it. (S, 56, 57)

I believe that it is on this correlation between earthly and divine monarchy or, more exactly, on his longing for its implementation, that both Hopkins's monarchical creed and above all his defense of the status quo[18] rest. In an analogous way it is possible to

---

weal arose"), Hopkins emphasizes the distribution of duties, functions, and benefits: "It is equitable that [the common good] should be in proportion to the work done. Besides the common good to be attained by common action there is status, the status of sovereign and the status of subject. To the status belongs duty or functions, in the sovereign to legislate, command; in the subject to obey, but in the sense of consenting." Hopkins, furthermore, emphasizes the primacy of the divine over human jurisdiction (explicitly, the city of God over the city of man): the world is "a commonwealth where God is the sovereign . . . divine commonwealth, City of God, or Kingdom of heaven."

18. See, for example, this statement: "People are born to things and rest content with them much as they are: look at ourselves, we have no two thoughts about the matter; we find the queen on her throne, houses of parliament, judges sitting or going, the army, the police, the postoffice at work; the common good

explain his firm condemnation of any rebellion against the original contract or any historical copy of it:

At any particular time when orderly government is going on there *is* [Hopkins's italics] such an agreement, there exists such an understanding: the subjects obey, at least they are not in rebellion, the rulers govern, at least they have not thrown up the reigns [*sic:* reins?] of power. For if the governed had never, neither at first nor after, submitted to be ruled / all would be riot. (S, 55)

Since exactly the same signic spirit of the Middle Ages is involved, it is not, I think, fanciful—to revert to the Irish question—to find in the foregoing statements a precise reference to contemporary history, and to maintain that in Hopkins's eyes the Irish secession, by splitting the unity of the British Empire, had a power of disintegration almost equal to that of Adam and Eve's disobedience, which irreparably broke up the primordial "divine commonwealth." It is no coincidence that in referring to the two events—the Irish secession and the disobedience of Adam and Eve—Hopkins uses the same term, *rebellion* (see, above, the quotation from L III, 281–82):

she [=Eve] freely yielded herself to the three concupiscences; *she took and eat* [*sic;* Hopkins's italics] of this devil's-sacrament; she *rebelled,* she sinned, she fell . . . for her he [=Adam] took the stolen goods and harboured the forfeit person of the thief, *rebelling* against God, the world's great landlord, owner of earth and man. (S, 66, 67)[19]

---

is being provided for, we share it more or less, we share the common weal, we are part of the commonwealth" (S, 56).

19. There are striking analogies between these conclusions and Dante's *Monarchia,* where he says that "mankind behaves very well indeed when it imitates, as much as human nature allows, Heaven's imprints" (1.9). For Dante, universal monarchy is the only political form capable of implementing justice, liberty, and peace on earth (1.1–4 and 11–12). About the divine investiture of the sovereign, see also St. Augustine, *De civitate Dei* 5.1: "Human kingdoms are established by divine providence." Hopkins frequently refers to the divine investiture of the temporal sovereign in his spiritual writings: "The heart of the king is in the Lord's hand to turn which way he will . . . " (S, 151). See also S, 153: "God can always command if he chooses the free consent of the elective will, at least if by no other way, by shutting out all freedom of field (which no doubt does sometimes take place, as in disposing the heart of princes . . .)"

6

I have often hinted in the foregoing pages at Hopkins's agreements and disagreements both with single thinkers and, in some
cases, with entire philosophical schools, movements, and tendencies. His poetry too—though the poetic discourse is autonomous and regulated by its own intrinsic laws ("all poetry is . . .
speech wholly or partially repeating some kind of figure *which is
over and above meaning, at least the grammatical, historical, and logical
meaning*" [J, 289; see above, Part One, chapter 2])—is often characterized by a high philosophical density. An example is the
"Heraclitean Fire" in which, Hopkins wrote to Bridges with a
suggestive image, "a great deal of early Greek philosophical
thought was *distilled*" (L I, 291).[1] We must, then, proceed to focus
our attention on Hopkins's philosophical code, especially because, in this case too, it is a complex, highly composite, and entropic code, and one subject to successive transformations ("but
the liquor of the distillation did not taste very Greek," Hopkins

---

1. In Hopkins's time, Heraclitus's is a fashionable, tempting philosophy. Pater
in *Marius the Epicurean* speaks of a seeming "mass of lifeless matter . . . in which
things . . . were ever 'coming to be', alternately consumed or renewed" (109).
Hopkins hoped with Marius that flux should not give way to a philosophy of
desperation ("$_{17}$Away . . . dejection," says Hopkins in the sonnet). Marcus Aure-
lius's speech in chapter XII of Pater's novel contains further distinct Heraclitean
echoes of both the "Heraclitean Fire" and "God's Grandeur," such as the following: " 'I find that all things are now as they were in the days of our buried ances-
tors—all things sordid in their elements, trite by long usage, and yet ephemeral.
. . . For the wheel of the world hath ever the same motion, upward and downward, from generation to generation. When, when, shall time give place to
eternity?' " (*Marius the Epicurean,* 151).

added in the letter to Bridges quoted above). Such entropy does not rule out, however, the possibility of a hierarchy: in Hopkins, philosophical code means medieval philosophical code and medieval philosophical code means Scotist philosophical code.

Hopkins's encounter with Scotus dates back to a fairly advanced stage of his cultural history, but one can safely surmise that it was the manifestation of a pre-existent Scotism, an unconscious, latent Scotism mingled with many other superficial leanings but also with some original speculations. Some of these leanings and speculations Hopkins later retained and easily integrated, while others he decidedly rejected. Hopkins's approach march to Scotus can be synthesized as follows. His university essays on philosophy, aesthetics, and ethics already show his definitive detachment from the dominant utilitarian, positivistic, and materialistic ideas (Bentham, Mill, Darwin, etc.)[2] without however substantially distinguishing him—apart from his theory of "fixed points"—from the most "enlightened" and most critical spirits of his time (such as Carlyle, Arnold, Dickens, and Kingsley). In this period, however, it is just the "early Greek philosophical thought" that is the primary source of Hopkins's ideas. As I have shown above, a certain form of Platonic realism was singled out by Hopkins as being among the measures capable of restraining and subverting the widespread "atomism" (J, 120). Platonism was indeed one of the philosophical options of his youth that was not involved in the ups and downs of refusals and acceptations, and that, ingrained with Scotism, became part and parcel of Hopkins's philosophical code (Plato's anamnesis surfaces distinctly in Scotus's theory of knowledge).[3] Even in the Jesuit period Plato remained "the greatest of the Greek philosophers" (S, 37), and in a letter written to Dixon in 1886, Hopkins still granted him the first and most typical quality of the philoso-

2. On Darwin and evolutionism see the excellent essay by Collins 1947, 96–99.

3. Devlin 1950, 125, 191–92. The dialogue "On the Origin of Beauty" and the other essays on aesthetics are modelled on the Platonic theory of ideas. Platonic influences (the charioteer myth) have been noticed in Hopkins's poetic images by Heuser (1958, 60–61). Others, such as Cotter (1972), judge "exaggerated" Hopkins's alleged "dependence on Platonism" (22).

pher-poet, the "spiritual insight into nature" (L II, 141, 147–48). By far the most important documents of the pre-Jesuit years are, however, for us the essay on Parmenides (J, 127–30) and, above all, the so-called essay on words (J, 125–26), where Hopkins sketches a theory of the univocity of being and of the origin of knowledge that shows more than one contact with Scotus's gnoseology. I will deal extensively with these later on; in the year of their composition (1868), a passage in a letter dating back to the period Hopkins spent at Edgbaston at Cardinal Newman's Oratory informs us of a slight change in his philosophical options and at the same time shows a more marked and generalized rejection of nineteenth-century philosophies:[4]

I have not read Ruskin's new book: the title is perhaps vulgar. Ruskin is full of follies but I get more and more sympathetic with "the true men" as agst. the Sophistik (observe I say K—it is not the same thing as sophistical), Philistine, Doctrinaire, Utilitarian, Positive, and on the whole Negative (as Carlyle wd. put it) side, and prefer to err with Plato. This reminds me to say that I find myself in an even prostrate admiration of Aristotle and am of the way of thinking, so far as I know him or know about him, that he is the end-all and be-all of philosophy. (L III, 230–31)

Such a hierarchy will undergo new revisions, as is witnessed by a letter written to Bridges in 1875 when Hopkins was already a Jesuit: here we find Scotus mentioned for the first time. The dissension becomes more explicit and categorical, as it involves the nineteenth-century philosophy *par excellence,* Hegel's: "After all I can, at all events a little, read Duns Scotus and I care for him more even than Aristotle[5] and more *pace tua* than a dozen Hegels"

4. "Judging from the printed sources, Hopkins was not widely read in modern philosophical literature. . . . He never felt at home in German, and could not share Bridges' enthusiasm for the language and the philosophical traditions. . . . Even before his acquaintance with the Hegelian tendency to identify the structure of reality with the articulations of spirit, Hopkins had expressed his deep and typically British distrust of the purely logical mind" (Collins 1947, 76). For a stringent criticism of Hegel's theory of the "universal mind" see S. 125.

5. A. Thomas writes that with time "Hopkins grew away from Aristotle" and that Hopkins's self-definition "we Aristotelian Catholics" (L I, 95) "smacks of convention rather than conviction" (Thomas 1968, 627–28, note 37). Collins (1947), too, notes that Aristotle "seems to have had more an intellectual rather than an affective influence upon Hopkins' outlook" (72). If, as I believe, Scotus is an almost systematic "source" of Hopkins, it seems to me more useful to remem-

(L I, 31). The almost hyperbolic terms with which Hopkins con-
fesses his admiration altogether dissipate the perplexity and almost the incredulity with which he had noted in his diary, on 3
August 1872, his "discovery" of the medieval philosopher: "At
this time I had first begun to get hold of the copy of Scotus on
the Sentences in the Baddely library and was flush with a new
stroke of enthusiasm. It may come to nothing or it may be a
mercy from God" (J, 221).

The complexity of Hopkins's work has been rewarded by its
critics, as I observed in Part One, by a considerable variety of
approaches. Although "the influence of Scotus on Hopkins" has
been and is even now a standard section of any contribution on
our poet,[6] what is surprising in such an eclecticism of decodings
is not so much the absence of a full-length study in a Scotist key
as the way in which the majority of scholars (excepting Heuser
1958 and Miller 1963) have treated this fundamental relationship.
Critics usually do not go farther than refreshing the philosophical
culture of the common reader, which is often defective on the
whole medieval philosophy and handicapped by a case of hom-
onymy (Scotus Eriugena). Indeed, they simply repeat a series of
conventional, extremely evasive statements: the opposition between Scotus and Aquinas, the supposed analogy between Scotus's *haecceitas* and Hopkins's *inscape,* the primacy of the will over
the intellect, the exaltation of individuality. This superficiality is
perhaps due to the outdatedness and cultural distance of a philosophy, such as Scotus's, whose orthodoxy has been proclaimed
only recently by the Catholic church. To this we may add the
difficulty of access to and high hermeneutic arduousness of volu-

---

ber that Aristotle *is* Scotus's philosopher (Devlin 1946, 465) and that the latter's
theory of knowledge is an attempt "to reconcile Augustinian 'exemplarism' with
Aristotelian 'rationalism' " (Devlin 1950, 121). See also Cotter 1972, 22ff.

6. Excepting, of course, the studies that have as their thesis Hopkins's exclusive *Victorianism:* Sulloway's (1972) silence on Scotus, for example, is total.
Highly perplexing is the fact that Bender should judge "overemphasized" Scotus's influence on Hopkins, and even "fortuitously congruent" with those of Scotus Hopkins's ideas (Bender 1966, 38). Ong 1986 surprisingly fails to connect to
Scotus Hopkins's "sense of self" which distinguishes him from so many others
(Nietzsche, Freud, the deconstructionists: 22–28), and sees a substantial harmony
(106–12) between Hopkins's Scotism and his other philosophical options.

minous works that still lack a critical edition and have not been translated in their entirety into any of the main modern languages. Really useful contributions on Hopkins's Scotism can be found, more than in the standard studies in volume, in some fifteen specific essays in journals. Of them, however, only about half are valuable and in-depth investigations, and of these no fewer than five were written by the incontestable pioneer and greatest expert in this field of research, Christopher Devlin.[7] Because of the competence, reliability, and comprehensiveness with which this scholar has pieced out the concordances between Hopkins and Scotus, it is not my intention here to enlarge, let alone improve, on Devlin but only to summarize the terms of this vital relationship. What mostly interests me about Hopkins's Scotism is not primarily its specific and eminently speculative aspect but its mediations, irradiations, and repercussions on different grounds from the purely philosophical, and therefore the functionality and consistence of the Scotist choice within Hopkins's medievalism. The Scotist code will even throw a new and suddenly clarifying light on all code elements hitherto examined, including as well the rhetorical code discussed in Part One.

Hopkins's enthusiasm for Scotus reaches its zenith with the theory of knowledge and perception, as he himself informs us in the Journal entry of 3 August 1872: "But just then when *I took in any inscape* of the sky or sea I thought of Scotus" (J, 221). This statement enables us to assume that Hopkins found in Scotus a confirmation, a clarification, a rigorous philosophical systematization as well as a development of his own insights, then still confused and inchoate, about inscape and instress. It is a well-known fact that in the whole of Hopkins's writings there is no adequate definition or semantic explanation of these two most famous of Hopkins's coinages. The contexts in which they recur allow us to describe their meaning, very synthetically, as follows: *inscape* means the distinctiveness and uniqueness of any phenomenal entity and at the same time the instantaneous intuition of a co-essen-

7. See in particular Devlin 1935, 1946, 1949, 1950 (in two parts), 1959; Thomas 1968; Coogan 1950; Collins 1947; Gérard 1946.

tiality and connaturality between the perceiving subject and the perceived object; *instress* is the special force, even sharp and pungent, with which an *inscape* manifests itself. Before investigating the nature and scope of the clarification about this kind of perception that Scotus's reading could bring to Hopkins in 1872, we must go back to the two essays of 1868, on words and on Parmenides. They are not only the first formulation of the theory of inscape and instress but also an anticipation of some important gnoseological speculations of Scotus, as expounded in the eleven *quaestiones* of the third *distinctio* of the first Book of the *Oxoniense* (the work Hopkins directly consulted in 1872). The similarities are striking—apart, of course, from obvious terminological differences, occasional conceptual discrepancies, and the quantitative disproportion between the three or four pages by Hopkins and Scotus's several hundred.

Hopkins distinguishes, in the first of the two essays, three successive "moments" in a word: (1) "a passion or prepossession or enthusiasm"; (2) "its definition, abstraction"; (3) "its application, 'extension.' " In its turn, "abstraction" is subdivided into two "terms": "the image (of sight or sound or *scapes* of the other senses), which is in fact physical and a refined energy accenting the nerves, a word to oneself, an inchoate word, and secondly the conception" (J, 125; Hopkins's italics). Without explicitly using the terms *inscape* and *instress,* Hopkins is here clearly trying to describe the moment in which the purely sensible perception ("*scapes* of the . . . senses") produces in some special cases ("not always or in everyone") an instantaneous "quasi-" or "pre-knowledge," which is neither of a sensible nature nor already intellectualized, and which afterwards is dissolved and resolved into a pure "conception" through abstraction. Incidentally, it is to this form of "knowledge" that art, for Hopkins, must aim: "Works of art of course like words utter the idea and in representing real things convey the prepossession with more or less success" (J, 126). Of this threefold distinction there is no trace in the essay on Parmenides, in which Hopkins is instead preoccupied with unifying rather than dividing up both the process of knowledge and the subject and object it involves. The unifying element, and at the same time the source and guarantee of any form of knowledge having a claim to universality, is the univocity of being that Hopkins finds in Parmenides and so interprets and reformulates:

His great text . . . is that Being is and Not-being is not—which perhaps one can say, a little over-defining his meaning, means that all things are upheld by instress and are meaningless without it. . . . But indeed I have often felt when I have been in this mood and felt the depth of an instress or how fast the inscape holds a thing that nothing is so pregnant and straightforward to the truth as simple *yes* and *is*. . . . There would be no bridge, no stem of stress between us and things to bear us out and carry the mind over: without stress we might not and could not say / Blood is red / but only / This blood is red / or / The last blood I saw was red / nor even that, for in later language not only universals would not be true but the copula would break down even in particular judgments. (J, 127; Hopkins's italics)

"Felt," "stress," and "instress" are of course echoes of the "prepossession of feeling" and of the "energy . . . accenting the nerves"; yet it is important to recall that the univocity of being is a principle that Scotus, too, postulates.[8] Apart from this, however, one can say that this essay does not contain, on the whole, substantial developments with respect to that on words, despite the introduction and the extensive use of the terms *inscape* and *instress*. Indeed these appear to be, on the basis of the contexts in which they are used, not only almost identical and interchangeable (cf. "all things are upheld by instress" versus "how fast the inscape holds a thing"), but also considerably incomplete: the Journal, and even better and more frequently Hopkins's mature poetry from the "Deutschland" to the *terrible sonnets,* make it clear

8. In 1882 Hopkins wrote, "In shewing there is no universal a true self which is 'fetched' or 'pitched' or 'selved' in every other self, I do not deny that there is a universal really. . . . Neither do I deny that God is so deeply present to everything . . . " (S, 128). Devlin notices in this passage "a possible back-reference" (S, 284–85, note 128.1) to the essay on Parmenides and proves the agreement between the univocity of being of Parmenides and the *universale concretum* of Scotus, which is so real that it objectively asserts itself to the intellect and guarantees the correspondence of ideas to reality. Devlin also comments, "Such a conclusion would have come as a revelation to the man who wrote [the essay on Parmenides]" (S, 285, note 128.1).

that *inscape* simultaneously covers two distinct processes: being as a moment of individuation of each single existing entity and being as a moment of unification of everything existing. Another important addition is that, proportionally to the intensity of instress, God's presence is perceptible in the inscape of the phenomenal world.

Of each of these "moments" analyzed in the essay on words, as well as of *inscape* and *instress,* there exist in Scotus (and therefore Hopkins could find) synonyms, homologues, and also timely corrections. Hopkins, in other words, saw confirmed and oriented by Scotus certain "pushes in a direction that [he] was already, but diffidently, following" (Devlin 1950, 117). With reference to the distinctions made in the essay on words, Scotus ratified that between the "prepossession of feeling" and the "inchoate word" and that between the "conception" and the "abstraction." This ratification comes through Scotus's own distinction between the *confuse cognoscere*—a direct perception of the real, a form of knowledge that makes one immediately enter into contact with it (otherwise termed by Scotus *visio existentis ut existens* and, with a greater analogy with Hopkins's own terms, *passio in anima*)—and the *distincte cognoscere,* while the "image . . . accenting the nerves" can be identified with the *phantasma,* the secondary image to which the intellect recurs in the absence of the object itself (Devlin 1950, 114–19).

We have so far found a certain number of agreements between Scotus's cognitive theory and Hopkins's essay on words. A further investigation of that theory will enable us to see how Scotus paved the way for Hopkins toward a series of conclusions he had hardly guessed in 1868. Indeed Scotus became for Hopkins, from 1872 onward, a kind of bottomless pit: having accepted his gnoseological system, he was then forced to accept also its corollaries and deductions, that is, first of all the marked voluntaristic component, the theophany of reality, ascesis and the "great sacrifice," and even his theological vision, which hinges on a peculiar interpretation of the Incarnation. Through his distinction between *intellectio intuitiva* and *intellectio abstractiva,* Scotus first reminded Hopkins of the Aristotelian principle that each form of knowledge comes from the senses, then made him see the superiority of the pair sensation-intuition over imagination-abstraction, and finally encouraged him "to put more trust in the primitive way of knowing," while suggesting "that sensation is nobler, more spiritual, more akin to the intellect than imagination" (Devlin 1950, 117). If we observe the contents of knowledge at this first level of sensation-intuition, as distinct from imagination-abstraction, we will arrive at a rationalization of Hopkins's inscape and instress.

Each being is constituted for Scotus by a *natura communis* and by a *singularitas* (otherwise and successively called, according to the context, *ultima solitudo, ultima realitas entis, haecceitas*,[9] etc). This is true for man, too, in whom *haecceitas* becomes united to the common nature and in so doing differentiates itself from other *haecceitates* and each being from other beings with which it shares the common nature. While the *distincte cognoscere,* the abstractive knowledge, separates the common nature from individuality, the *confuse cognoscere* simultaneously involves both the senses and the intellect of the knowing subject, and thus helps to capture the *species specialissima* of the object itself. "And I say this, that what is first known in a confused way through experience is the *species specialissima,* the uniqueness of which strikes at once, and in a stronger and more effective way, the senses, either of hearing or sight or touch. . . . Therefore, the knowledge of a *species* of any entity that strikes the senses in a stronger way is first of all a *cognitio confusa*" (*Oxon.*, I, d. 3, qq. 1 and 2). Such an expression—*species specialissima*—is a contradiction in terms, for *species* is a synonym of *natura communis* and *specialissima* a syn-

9. This term, Devlin reminds us (S, 293–94, note 151.3), occurs in Scotus—despite its notoriety—only once, and not in the *Oxoniense* but in the *Reportata Parisiensia* (II. d. 12, q. 5). Hopkins writes *ecceitas* (S, 151) and Devlin conjectures (S, 349) that Hopkins may never have read the *Parisiensia.* Devlin's editing, incidentally, does not appear flawless from a philological point of view. He does not specify the edition of Scotus's works from which he quotes, while some quotations are taken from a certain "Venice edition used by GMH" (S, 283, note 122.2). Such an edition, however, has been identified by A. Thomas (1968, 617–21) as the one published in Venice by Gregorio de Gregoriis in 1514–15. Largely groundless criticisms of a philological kind, apropos the essay "The Image and the Word" (Devlin 1950), have been aimed at Devlin by W. H. Gardner (see Gardner-Devlin 1950).

onym of *individual* to the utmost degree. Besides, it is not clear if it is "the genuine nature of the object (using *species* in the sense of specific nature), or the impression made by it on the mind of the subject (using *species* in the sense of likeness)" (Devlin 1950, 117). If, however, we assume, which is more probable, that it is a purely psychic entity, and that therefore the perception of the *species specialissima* implies "the expression of universal nature in the act of reaching individuality" (ibid., 120), the *species specialissima* and the *confuse cognoscere* represent, as I was saying, the most faithful translations of Hopkins's *inscape* and *instress*.

A second, equally fertile and fundamental field of Scotist irradiation on Hopkins is Scotus's theory of the primacy and central role of the will, starting with the very first phases of the cognitive process. Far from remaining inactive or extraneous to this process, the will in fact accompanies, spans, and orients all the operations of the mind, to the extent that it becomes "a sort of *third* level of consciousness in which the former two, the first and second acts, can be combined" (Devlin 1950, 124; Devlin's italics). In other words, as Devlin more suggestively says in the other essays, "Knowledge ceases on the threshold that Desire may enter in" (Devlin 1935, 113); or: "Scotism is a method of subordinating the intellect *truthfully* to the will" (Devlin 1949, 304; Devlin's italics). And having accepted the voluntaristic implications of Scotus's gnoseology Hopkins could not but embrace its further developments, namely, the theophany implied in any act of knowledge and the transformation of knowledge into a praxis. Yet, while these developments are already contained and perfectly delineated in the first book of the *Oxoniense*, to prove these borrowings our observation will necessarily leave Hopkins's middle phase (to which his theory of inscape and instress is traceable), and focus on the mature writings, on the poetry written after the "Deutschland," and above all on the theological writings.

The level of the sensation–intuition, of *cognitio confusa* or of *visio existentis ut existens,* corresponds for Scotus to a *primus actus;* the *secundus actus* is distinct, abstractive knowledge. The *primus actus* is therefore performed by nature, while the *secundus actus,* ordering and adapting what has been perceived, is performed by individuality. These two acts, in their turn, together form a phase of *cognitio actualis* (in that, with Aristotle, this form of knowledge stems from the object and is obtained through the senses), a knowledge made possible by (and therefore distinguished from) a sort of "innate memory," a *cognitio habitualis* or *virtualis*. Here Scotus is clearly influenced by Platonic idealism and Augustinian exemplarism: ". . . since the object is present to the intellect in such a way that the intellect can at once elicit an act concerning that object" (*Oxon.*, I, d. 3, qq. 1 and 2).[10] The will is intimately present, although with different modalities and manifestations, in all these subsequent phases of the cognitive process. If, again following Augustine, one considers the soul as the synthesis of three distinct faculties—memory, intellect, and will—at the pure level of the *cognitio habitualis* the subject draws from a *memoria* whose source is a *natura communis* that is comprehensive of the forms (bodily, vegetative, sensitive) through which the evolution of humanity has advanced as far as the present rational form. Before the *cognitio actualis* the soul re-lives, so to speak, this evolutionary process and feels drawn toward an even greater perfection, the perfection of the species and, far from any individuation, the infinitization of nature. At this initial stage the will manifests itself in the subject as universal: it is an impulse of the *natura communis* toward its full self-realization. In the *cognitio actualis confusa*, on the contrary—just because it has as its contents the *species specialissima* (common nature individuating itself) and represents the moment in which object and subject are about to dissociate but are not yet dissociated—there occurs the revelation of the universal will of the *cognitio habitualis* (nature tending to its perfection) in the instant in which it is becoming particular. The

10. Devlin 1950, 122–23. According to Devlin, such a distinction between *cognitio actualis* and *cognitio habitualis* is reflected by Hopkins's distinction, in the essay on words, between the "transitional kind . . . of energy" and the "abiding kind" in the human mind (J, 125–26). The distinction between *actus primus, actus secundus,* and *actus tertius* (that is, the will) is also taken from St. Augustine, who distinguishes in the *De Trinitate* the three powers of the soul as *memoria, intellectus, voluntas*. A further Augustinian element is the modelling of the cognitive process of the soul on the Trinity (Devlin 1949, 308; S, 343–44).

contents of the *cognitio habitualis* and of the *cognitio actualis confusa* cannot, however, be transferred intact to the intellect: the apprehension of the *memoria* reaches the intellect under the form of the *phantasma* and the concept. It is then the task of the soul in its "third level of consciousness," that of the free will, to choose the infinite being whom the *memoria* has confusedly guessed and the intellect has intellectually known. In this sense one can say that the soul in its third state sums up and connects the operations of the will in the previous stages.

Such a configuration of the mechanism of knowledge implies first of all a theophany. This refers not simply to the tripartite cognitive process and to the functioning of the human mind as a mirror of the Trinity as postulated by Scotus (*Oxon.*, I, d. 3, q. 9, "Utrum in mente sit imago Trinitatis?" and see Devlin 1950, 124–26 and S, 343–45), but to the actual presence, or rather to the progressive revelation of God in all the phases of the cognitive process. At the level of the first act, God is manifested as the source and the origin of the *cognitio habitualis,* that is, as the mysterious cause the mind wants to retrace starting from the effect ("desiderium naturale est in intellectu cognoscente effectum ad cognoscendam causam" [*Oxon.*, I, d. 3, q. 3]), and as the Infinite, pursued and confusedly perceived but, owing to its transcendence, not expressed. Such an Infinite, as we have already seen, reaches the intellect in the second act only as a concept or *phantasma,* which prevents the distinct and immediate acknowledgment, in that Infinite and that perfection of uncreated nature, of Christ Son of God and of the perfection of created nature. It is the task of the will, in the third act, freely and consciously to tend, thanks to God's grace, to that Infinite Being that had formed the object of a natural attraction in the first act and had been known as an abstract concept by the intellect. Two things must be emphasized: for Scotus, any object falling under our senses is capable of eliciting the theophany, so that any cognitive process is in the last analysis, *ipso facto,* a theophany; the immediate contact with God does not come from on high, through an operation of the intellect, but from below, from the confused "vision" of the most common phenomena of inanimate nature. It is here that the second consequence of Scotist voluntarism comes to the surface, the transformation of knowledge into praxis. Of the three acts, by far the most important and the highest is the act of the free will aided by grace, the being's conscious tending to God. Against Aristotle—this time—Scotus denies that human happiness rests in "speculation" and the intellect: higher still is the *freedom of choice,* which the intellect does not possess. Besides a *cognitio speculativa,* self-enclosed and confined within the sphere of pure abstraction, the intellect is capable of a *cognitio practica,* an intellection causing the intellect to "go out" of itself and to transfer whatever it possesses to the will. Sensation and volition acquire therefore in Scotus's cognitive process a decided pre-eminence over the traditionally primary "moment," the intellection, which is given the role of a mere intermediary. More than the precision of the abstract concept, Scotus emphasizes the tending to God of the whole being, in its twofold dimension of *voluntas ut natura* (the original attraction toward the Infinite in the first act) and of *voluntas ut arbitrium* (the free stretching out of the whole being toward God).

This synthetic exposition[11] of the foundations of Scotist gnoseology has been necessary because the *distinctio formalis a parte rei* and the mechanism of knowledge with its voluntaristic, theophanic, and pragmatic implications are the basis as well as the frame of Hopkins's mature textuality (or, as we indeed can say, intertextuality). Many "sophisticated" interpretations, in the sestets of Hopkins's sonnets, of the natural phenomena perceived and described in the octave, and many "extravagant" images and metaphors, show that "Hopkins was aiming at truth rather than fancy," and are therefore much more and much less than mere "affectation" (Devlin 1935, 116). The "vision of St. Francis" (ibid.) that Scotus tries to express in his philosophy[12] (as an origi-

11. For a more exhaustive and detailed discussion of the problems treated here (voluntarism, theophany, praxis) I refer to Devlin 1946, 463–66; Devlin 1950, 119; S, 344–47.

12. On the "vision of St. Francis" in Hopkins and Scotus, see also Devlin 1950, 191 and 195; Gérard 1946, 37; and Thomas 1968, 622.

nal *consubstantialitas* between man and nature and as an immediate apprehension of God at the bottom of things) is Hopkins's "vision" too: recall Hopkins's wonder at the blooming bluebells and the shining of the stars in the Journal (J, 199, 254) or the revelation of the Creator behind the stars, the "brute beauty" of the windhover, the figures drawn by the clouds, the multicolored landscape, respectively in "The Wreck of the Deutschland," "The Windhover," "Hurrahing in Harvest," and "Pied Beauty." If, while speaking of the signic code of Hopkins's nature poetry, I had traced indexes and manifestations of a medieval spirit in the interpretation of the phenomenal world as a "book of God," this signic attitude and this metaphor receive an even more precise explanation by the Scotist code. In Scotus's philosophy is most probably the secret origin of another singular metaphor (singular, but far from gratuitous and fanciful) used by Hopkins, the attribution to man of natural and vegetal elements—often in the very instant in which the perception of the inscape occurs. The final lines of "Moonrise" are surely the best proof of the equation between the poetic act and the perception of inscape (in the sense of a *consubstantialitas* between man and nature) and between the inscape and the *confuse cognoscere* and *actus primus* of Scotus:

"*Moonrise*"

6   This was the prized, the desirable sight, I unsought, presented so
     easily,
7   Parted me *leaf and leaf,* divided me, Ieyelid and eyelid of slumber.[13]

Hopkins's most Scotist text is however, undoubtedly, the commentary on the *Spiritual Exercises* of St. Ignatius, which he wrote at intervals between 1879 and 1883 (S, 122–209). Here Hopkins not only enucleates, redefines, and elaborates without filters and mediations the salient points of his own Scotism (the distinction between nature and individuality and that between memory, intellect, and will; voluntarism, pragmatism), but ex-

---

13. See also "The Wreck of the Deutschland" ("₅we are rooted in earth" and "₆our flower" [st. 11]); "Peace" ("₂my boughs"); "Patience, hard thing! . . . " ("₆Natural heart's-ivy"); "Thou art indeed just, Lord . . . " ("₁₄Mine, O thou lord of life, send my roots rain)."

ploits it to put forward a series of theological "theses," which are again perfectly in tune with the thought of the medieval philosopher. Just because of the systematic nature of Hopkins's Scotism in this text, the title given to it (by Hopkins himself)—*commentary*—appears doubly inaccurate: the *Spiritual Exercises* are treated too selectively for it to be a commentary. Indeed, they quite often function as a starting point—if not as a pretext—for theological reflections that are as foreign to the Ignatian letter as they are close to Scotus's theology. This "deviation" did not pass unobserved by the censors of his order, who in fact nipped in the bud any hope of publication Hopkins might have entertained and thus were partly responsible for its incompleteness.[14]

Scotus's ontology, summarily expounded above, is the frame of all Hopkins's reflections on the creation inspired by Ignatius's *Principium et Fundamentum*. At the outset one encounters the distinction between *natura communis* and *singularitas* ("human nature" versus "my individuality"):

We may learn that all things are created by consideration of the world without or of ourselves the world within. The former is the consideration commonly dwelt on, but the latter takes on the mind more hold. I find myself both as man and as myself something most determined and distinctive, at pitch, more distinctive and higher pitched than anything else I see. . . . And when I ask where does all this throng and stack of being, so rich, so distinctive, so important, come from / nothing I see

14. "A somewhat obstinate love of Scotist doctrine" was, according to the historian of University College Dublin, at the base of Hopkins's failure or in any case of his modest career inside the Jesuit order: "His idiosyncrasy got him into difficulties with his Jesuit preceptors who followed Aquinas and Aristotle" (quoted in S, xiii by Devlin, who, however, in a note disputes the latter statement: "On the contrary they [the preceptors] followed *Suarez*" [Devlin's italics]). Even with this adjustment, however, the clash between Hopkins and his order remains. One can read for example, on Suárez, the following relevant evaluation contained in a letter to Dixon: "Suarez is our most famous theologian: he is a man of vast volume of mind, but without originality or brilliancy; he treats everything satisfactorily, but you never remember a phrase of his, his manner is nothing" (L II, 95). Cotter (1972) remembers that "Hopkins held a higher opinion of Luis de Molina" (138) but blunders when he makes him the originator of that "controversial theological movement . . . called Molinism." As any reader of Browning's *The Ring and the Book* or Shorthouse's *John Inglesant* knows, the founder of Molinism was Miguel de Molinos. For a more generalized incompatibility between Hopkins and Jesuit spirituality, see Part Two, chapter 4 above, note 3.

can answer me. And this whether I speak of human nature or of my individuality, my selfbeing. (S, 122)

This "selfbeing," this "taste of myself, of *I* and *me* above and in all things," is in its turn "more distinctive than the taste of ale or alum, more distinctive than the smell of walnutleaf or camphor, and is incommunicable by any means to another man" (S, 123; Hopkins's italics). This is how the union of the self to human nature is accomplished for Hopkins, who once again follows Scotus:

In the world, besides natures or essences or 'inscapes' and the selves, supposits, hypostases, or, in the case of rational natures, persons / which wear and 'fetch' or instance them, there is still something else—fact or fate. For let natures be A, B, . . . Y, Z and supposits or selves *a, b, . . . y, z*: then if *a* is capable of A, B, . . . Y, Z (singly or together) and receives, say, A, if *b* capable of the same receives also A, and if *c* capable of the same receives M, so that we have *a*A, *b*A, *c*M, these combinations are three arbitrary or absolute facts not depending on any essential relation between *a* and A, *b* and A, or *c* and M but on the will of the Creator. Further, *a* and *b* are in the same nature A. But *a* uses it well and is saved, *b* ill and is damned: these are two facts, two fates / not depending on the relation between *a* and *b* on the one hand and A on the other. Now as the difference of the facts and fates does not depend on A, which is the same for both, it must depend on *a* and *b*. So that selves are from the first intrinsically different. (S, 146–47)

The whole chapter on the creation (S, 122–30) revolves around the demonstration of the distinctive character and incommunicability of the self and its divine provenance: "to be determined and distinctive is a perfection," yet man remains a finite being, and "to determine is a perfection, greater than and certainly never less than, the perfection of being determined" (S, 124–25). This corresponds to the *carentia entitatis* of Scotus, for whom each being "habet intrinsecum sibi gradum suae perfectionis, in quo est finitum" (*Oxon.*, I, d. 2, q. 2). Having discarded the possibilities of man's provenance from chance and self-determination, Hopkins's conclusion ("The third alternative then follows, that I am due to an extrinsic power [S, 128]) closely echoes Scotus's: "Ra-

tio intima haecceitatis non est quaerenda nisi in Divina voluntate"
(*Rep.*, II, d. 12, q. 5, quoted by Devlin in S, 342).

Scotus's psychology, gnoseology, and voluntarism are the
frame of reference of Hopkins's commentary on St. Ignatius's
first exercise (on the three sins: of Lucifer and the rebel angels; of
Adam and Eve; of an unspecified person) and of the fifth exercise
of the first week, the meditation on hell. As we have seen above,[15]
Hopkins refers repeatedly and almost obsessively throughout
this commentary to the rebellion of Lucifer and to his sin (which
is, preeminently, a sin of the will, "an election of the free will,
arbitrium" [S, 135]). He does so especially in the subsequent series
of notes on the exercises of the second week ("De Regno
Christi," "De Incarnatione," "De duobus Vexillis"—the standards of Christ and of the Devil), where Christ becomes the exact
counterpart of Lucifer precisely owing to an opposite working of
the will. Lucifer's rebellion and Christ's obedience, on which the
entire treatise hinges, also function as a stimulus, along with
other Ignatian meditations of the third and fourth week (on the
Passion, Death and Resurrection of Christ), toward the formulation of some bold theological theses about Christ and Incarnation. At the same time, the opposite results of the acts of will in
Lucifer and Christ push Hopkins to a deeper analysis of the relationships between Divine Grace and free will.

Hopkins, following Scotus, believes that even apart from
Adam's Fall and the necessity of Redemption, Christ would have
become Incarnate:

The first intention then of God outside himself or, as they say, *ad extra,*
outwards, the first outstress of God's power, was Christ; and we must
believe that the next was the Blessed Virgin. Why did the Son of God
go thus forth from the Father not only in the eternal and intrinsic procession of the Trinity but also by an extrinsic and less than eternal, let us
say aeonian one?—To give God glory and that by sacrifice, sacrifice offered in the barren wilderness outside of God, as the children of Israel
were led into the wilderness to offer sacrifice. This sacrifice and this out-

15. Part Two, chapter 4.

ward procession is a consequence and shadow of the procession of the Trinity, from which mystery sacrifice takes its rise; but of this I do not mean to write here. It is as if the blissful agony or stress of selving in God had forced out drops of sweat or blood, which drops were the world, or as if the lights lit at the festival of the "peaceful Trinity" through some little cranny striking out lit up into being one "cleave" out of the world of possible creatures. The sacrifice would be the Eucharist, and that the victim might be truly victim like, like motionless, helpless, or lifeless, it must be in matter. (S, 197)

This dense passage contains practically all the foundations of Hopkins's theology of the Incarnation. Far from being a consequence of creation and its effects, creation is rather the consequence of Incarnation, so that the effect of Adam's sin is just that of having added sufferance and atonement to an act of love on the part of Christ that should have been a joyous and adoring sacrifice.[16] The first manifestation of God's love is therefore Christ "in the eternal and intrinsic procession of the Trinity"; the second is in a procession "extrinsic and less than eternal, let us say aeonian": Hopkins draws once again from Scotus the certainty of a "pre-Incarnation" of Christ at the time of the creation of the angels, and of subsequent theophanies:

I suppose Melchisedech to be a theophany of Christ in human shape out of this pre-human being of his and to differ from other theophanies in that when Christ appeared as an angel he might be "installed" or "steaded" in some real and personal angel, as St Michael or St Gabriel, and this was their dignity to be vessels of Christ, but that there was no man Melchisedech, no such person but in person Christ. Incarnation then, ἐνσάρκωσις, is not the same thing as ἐνανθρώπευσις. (S, 171)

Hopkins even postulates, as we have seen above, what Scotus only "conjectures as possibility" (Devlin, S, 307, note 197.4), that is, the presence of Christ under the sacramental species since the beginning of the creation: "Ex hac secunda conclusione sequi-

16. Devlin (S, 296, note 170.1) quotes the following passage from the *Parisiensia* (III, d. 7, q. 4): "I say however that the fall was not the cause of Christ's predestination; on the contrary, even if Adam had not fallen, or man, Christ would have been predestined, even if none other than Christ were to be created." Devlin's note refers to a passage by Hopkins having the same content as the one I am quoting (S, 170ff.).

tur corollarium quod ante incarnationem potuit ita vere Eucharistia fuisse sicut et nunc, et hoc tamen quantum ad significationem quam quantum ad rem signatam et contentam" (*Oxon.*, IV, d. 10, q. 4, quoted by Devlin, S, 307, note 197.4).

The distinction between the two successive phases of Christ's Incarnation, ἐνσάρκωσις and ἐνανθρώπευσις, rests, finally, on another series of speculations by Scotus: the assumption of a parallelism between Christ's revelation to the angels and his earthly life (or between his conception *outside* time and his birth *in* historical time), and therefore a distinction between *intentional* and *temporal* order:

And here remark that his birth and the Gloria in excelsis, the persecution by Herod, the flight into Egypt, the massacre of the innocents, the return to Nazareth and the life of toil there, all symbolise the manifestation of the eucharistic victim to the angels, Satan's attack on it, its disappearance from his eyes in the world of matter, the ruin of man—which reminds one again of that river that after all did not drown the woman in the vision—and the theophanies and preparation made for Christ's coming. (S, 177)[17]

The aim of Christ's descent to earth and of Incarnation is the sacrifice which the unforeseen Fall of Adam transforms into a "great sacrifice" (S, 137–38). Hopkins draws from Scotus and above all from St. Paul (Phil. 2:5–11) this interpretation of the mission of Christ, as he more diffusely explains in a letter to Bridges:

. . . finding, as in the first instant of his incarnation [Christ] did, his human nature informed by the godhead—he thought it nevertheless no snatching-matter for him to be equal with God, but annihilated himself, taking the form of servant. . . . It is this holding of himself back, and not snatching at the truest and highest good, the good that was his right, nay his possession from a past eternity in his other nature, his own being and self, which seems to me the root of all his holiness and the imitation of this the root of all moral good in other men. (L I, 175)

Christ's voluntary renunciation of equality with God and his obedience to God's plan are thus contrasted with Lucifer's and

17. See also S, 181: "And there are 3 degrees in Christ himself. . . . (1) in the procession of the godhead; (2) in his entrance into creation, his incarnation

the rebel angels' behavior: though they could have kept their own
free will under check even if an image of God even more faithful
than theirs had been offered for their adoration, once before
Christ they as willfully moved away from God and disobeyed
him.

The question that engages Hopkins—who takes his start from
Scotus's psychology and voluntarism—in the central pages of the
commentary is how in every man the freedom of choice can be
possible: how in other words, following the example of Christ
and Lucifer, it is possible to choose the good and obey God but
also to choose the evil and disobey God, though God offers to all
men, in an equal degree, his Grace.[18]

A *compositio loci* (on Christ's nativity) offers Hopkins the opportunity to expound—in his usually most personal but sufficiently recognizable (that is, Scotist) terms—his own theory of
the cognitive process (based on the distinction of the three powers of the soul, on the three "acts," on the theophany, on the "issue" of the intellect from itself, etc.):

On the contemplating Persons, Words and Actions—These three points
belong to the three powers, memory, understanding, and will. Memory
is the name for that faculty which towards present things is Simple Apprehension and, when it is question of the concrete only, γνῶσις,
ἐπίγνωσις, the faculty of Identification; towards past things is Memory
proper; and towards things future or things unknown or imaginary is
Imagination. When continued or kept on the strain the act of this faculty
is attention, advertence, heed, the being *ware,* and its habit, knowledge,
the being *aware.* Towards God it gives rise to *reverence,* it is the sense of
the *presence* of God. The understanding, as the name shows, applies to
words; it is the faculty for grasping not the fact but the meaning of a
thing. When the first faculty just does its office and falls back, barely
naming what it apprehends, it scarcely gives birth to the second but

---

proper; (3) on earth, in the ἐνανθρώπευσιν, the becoming man." For the Scotist
source of this tripartition, see Devlin in S, 300, note 177.2.

18. The whole discussion follows closely Scotus both in its general drift and
in the single details, though Hopkins, in postulating a quasi-opposition between
voluntas ut natura and *voluntas ut arbitrium* and in some other speculations, goes
beyond Scotus. On the extent of Hopkins's distortions of Scotus and for a more
detailed discussion of the question of the freedom of choice in the light of Scotus's
doctrine, see Devlin's essay "Scotus and Hopkins," in S, Appendix II, 338–51.

when it keeps on the strain ("attendere, advertere, et contemplari") it cannot but continuously beget it. This faculty not identifies but verifies; takes the measure of things, brings word of them; is called λόγος and reason. By the will here is meant not so much the practical will as the faculty of fruition, by which we enjoy or dislike etc, to which all the intellectual affections belong. For all three faculties are the mind, the intellect, νοῦς. I ought to have added that the second faculty ends in admiration, which issues in *praise,* and the third in enjoyment, which issues in love, which issues in *service.* (S, 174; Hopkins's italics)

The tending of the being toward God occurs then, and is manifested, according to a progression from a totally unconscious to a totally conscious form:

The memory, understanding and affective will are incapable themselves of an infinite object and do not tend towards it; they are finite powers and can get each an adequate object. But the tendency in the soul towards an infinite object comes from the *arbitrium.* The *arbitrium* is in itself man's personality or individuality and places him on a level of individuality in some sense with God; so that in so far as God is one thing, a self, an individual being, he is an object of apprehension, desire, pursuit to man's *arbitrium.* (S, 138–39)[19]

Yet of the *arbitrium,* a prerogative of the self, one can make—just because it is free and cannot be conditioned, not even by God—a good but also a bad use. The latter is sin, the archetype of which is the rebellion of the angels and the "fall from heaven" (S, 137), when the spontaneous tending of Creation toward God, set in motion by God himself ("strain or tendency towards being, towards good, towards God"), that is, the tending of the universal will—*voluntas ut natura*[20]—was interrupted, broken and inverted through an act of pure *arbitrium:*

19. With reference to the first statement contained in this quotation (which contradicts what is said in the preceding one), Devlin justly comments that "Scotus would not agree with this. It is true that the conscious intellect, if left to itself, cannot conceive the infinite; but in the whole of man's nature, especially in the natural will, there *is* a tendency to the infinite, though grace is needed for this tendency to attain its end" (S, 291, note 138.4; Devlin's italics).

20. As Hopkins makes it clear: "being, that is / their own more or continued being, good / their own good, their natural felicity, and God / *the God at least of nature,* not to speak of grace" (S, 137).

This strain must go on after their fall, because it is the strain of creating action as received in the creature and cannot cease without the creature's ceasing to be. On the other hand the strain or tendency towards God through Christ and the great sacrifice had by their own act been broken, refracted, and turned aside, and it was only through Christ and the great sacrifice that God had meant any being to come to him at all. (S, 137–38)

To the presuppositions and the purely theoretical implications of this twofold use, Hopkins devotes a long and dense discussion, which Devlin published as a separate unit and titled "On Personality, Grace and Free Will" (S, 146–59). Substantially, Hopkins explains the mechanism of Grace as an offer to man by God— through Christ, the original pattern of the creation and the "bridge of reconciliation" between God's intellect and God's will—of a glimpse of his ideal nature. In other words, God lets the creature indistinctly see (and transports it into) a "possible world" where the self, from the "actual pitch at any given moment existing," passes on and is shifted to a different pitch, where the creature sees itself "gracious and consenting; nay more, clothing its old self for the moment with a gracious and consenting self":

This shift is grace. For grace is any action, activity, on God's part by which, in creating or after creating, he carries the creature to or towards the end of its being, which is its selfsacrifice to God and its salvation. It is, I say, any such activity on God's part; so that so far as this action or activity is God's it is divine stress, holy spirit, and, as all is done through Christ, Christ's spirit; so far as it is action, correspondence, on the creature's it is *actio salutaris;* so far as it is looked at *in esse quieto* it is Christ in his member on the one side, his member in Christ on the other. It is as if a man said: That is Christ playing at me and me playing at Christ, only that it is no play but truth; That is Christ *being me* and me being Christ. (S, 154; Hopkins's italics)[21]

What can then be, if God is apparently the main actor of man's choice, the space left to his freedom? His freedom consists in his "sigh of correspondence" (S, 156) to divine grace:

21. The self therefore expresses itself (in opposition to any other self, as we have seen above) and, through the operation of grace, also expresses Christ. There are echoes and elaborations of this twofold reflection (and of the last sentence of the quotation to which this note refers) in several contemporary poems,

For there must be something which shall be truly the creature's in the work of corresponding with grace: this is the *arbitrium,* the verdict on God's side, the saying Yes, the "doing-agree" (to speak barbarously), and looked at in itself, such a nothing is the creature before its creator, it is found to be no more than the mere wish, discernible by God's eyes, that he might do as he wishes, might correspond, might say Yes to him; correspondence itself is on man's side not so much corresponding as the wish to correspond, and this least sigh of desire, this one aspiration, is the life and spirit of man. (S, 154–55)

Scotus's *gradus,* in which the creature possesses and does not possess the perfection of its nature, becomes Hopkins's pitch: "As there is a scale of natures, ranging from lower to higher . . . so also there is a scale or range of pitch which is also infinite and terminates upwards in the directness or uprightness of the 'stem' of the godhead and the procession of the divine persons" (S, 147–48). Not even God, as already said, can determine or change the pitch of a creature, "so that God makes pitch no pitch, determination no determination, and difference indifference" (S, 148); he can, however, second the correct choice with a "change or access of circumstance" (S, 149), that is, with his grace. God therefore can, without touching or conditioning human freedom, "instress[ing] the affective will . . . towards the good which he proposes . . . strengthen[ed] the motive for consent" (ibid.) by means of a "grace accompanying" and a "consequent grace or grace of execution" (S, 150, also defined [S, 158] as "quickening, stimulating," "corrective," "elevating"). The latter, the "grace of execution," is comprehensibly the most decisive, the one thanks to which God "can shift the self that lies in one [pitch] to a higher, that is / better, pitch of itself" (S, 148). In this emphasis on the *doing* ("*pitch* is ultimately simple positiveness . . . and it is with precision expressed by the English *do* . . . might be expressed, if it were good English, *the doing* be, *the doing* choose, *the doing* so-and-so . . ." [S, 151; Hopkins's italics]) one can once again trace one of the most marked and crucial contacts between Hop-

---

namely, in "As kingfishers catch fire . . . " (ll. 6–14) and in "Henry Purcell," above all in the epigraph (Purcell "has . . . uttered in notes the very make and species of man as created both in him and in all men generally").

kins and Scotus. The will does not simply take note, as we have seen, of the acquisitons of sensation and intellect, but accepts, adapts, and orients them in an operative sense, projects the whole being toward that Infinite of which memory and intellect have grasped the presence—the former as a confused perception, the latter as a mere concept. The final page of Hopkins's commentary reaffirms the distinction between pure speculation and *praxis,* thus relating Scotus to St. Ignatius:

And as the Spiritual Exercises though called exercises only become really πρᾶξις proper or a course of conduct when made; for in them the exercitant reforms his life, listens to Christ's call, and so on; / so with this first way of praying (which St. Ignatius says can scarcely be called a "method of prayer"): it is practice for prayer, practice in praying, but it is also meant to give rise to penitence, acts of contrition, and amendment of life, and will thus be the most efficacious prayer. (S, 209)

Having investigated the contacts of a specifically theological and philosophical nature between Hopkins and Scotus, I will try to see the conscious adaptations and even the purely involuntary repercussions Hopkins's Scotism brought about. I will start from the following question: Do there exist reasons other than purely philosophical, but equally decisive, for which Hopkins should have been further encouraged to "choose" Scotus rather than another thinker or theologian? From what I have been saying, not only is the answer affirmative, but these very supplementary reasons offer us new confirmation of a medieval Hopkins in the sense spoken of in the foregoing chapters.

The first in order of importance of these motivations is of an aesthetic nature. In 1872 Hopkins found in Scotus a philosopher who met his strong aesthetic demands, a philosopher who did not condemn, and on the contrary justified and in a certain sense even exalted, them, suggesting—that is the important thing—the possibility of a cohabitation—even of a symbiosis—of art and faith. Critics have been unanimous in remarking how Scotus, better than Aquinas and St. Ignatius, offered Hopkins a theological system "in which it might seem easier to be both a priest and a poet" (Downes 1961, 582; Devlin has in his turn spoken of "fateful connection, or confusion, between prayer and poetry, which was to be the making, or the marring, of his art" [Devlin 1950, 124]). In particular Aquinas's philosophy, which Hopkins studied at Stonyhurst, could not but appear to him, in comparison with Scotus's, as what it is: a philosophy in which the aesthetic problem is barely touched on, and then merely to decree the superiority of philosophy over poetry and even to sharply declass and explicitly condemn the latter, branded as *infima scientia*.[22] The philosophical justification of art offered by Scotus to Hopkins is not simply, however, a generic form of aesthetic sanction, but appears to be a more precise and deeper kind of influence.

The results of our investigation (see above, Part One) of the main characteristics of Hopkins's poetic language in the light of its "context" are confirmed, supported, and developed by the most peculiar cognitive function Scotus attributes to art, which Hopkins spasmodically pursued. The poetic message, we said, is first of all a translation into words of a mysterious and miraculous experience, of a form of intuitive knowledge that for an instant, and with an even painful pungency, lets one recognize things in all their reality and uniqueness, as if one saw them for the first time. We also noticed that the effort of reproducing—and therefore reviving—this experience in the addressee transforms the poetic message into a both poetic and rhetorical message. If we keep this in mind, where could Hopkins find a better philosophi-

22. About Aquinas and art, see more in detail, Lewis 1964, 214, and Curtius 1953, chapter 12, "Poetry and Theology," 214–27. According to Curtius, "Medieval Aristotelianism, which was unacquainted with the *Poetics*, could find Aristotle's theory of poetry only in the *Metaphysics*; hence it could only regard poetry as a human invention and—compared with philosophy—as an *infima scientia*. . . . Scholasticism is not interested in evaluating poetry. It produced no poetics and no theory of art. Hence the attempt to extract an aesthetics of literature and the fine arts from it is senseless and profitless, no matter how often it may be made by historians of art and literature" (221, 224). A careful exegesis of Dante's letter to Can Grande allows Curtius to show how Dante aspired to a *forma tractandi* both philosophical and poetic, and to conclude, "With this Dante claims for his poetry the cognitional function which Scholasticism denied to poetry in general" (225). Curtius therefore illuminates the misunderstanding of a "providential harmony between Dante and Thomas" (224) into which many critics of Dante and many students of Scholasticism have fallen.

cal legitimation and sanction of this mysterious and thrilling cognitive experience that is poetry (let us recall the definition of the "inspiration" as "a mood of great, abnormal in fact, mental acuteness" [L III, 216]), than in Scotus's "first act" and in the *confuse cognoscere?* As Devlin has written, "If the first act is dwelt on . . . then you can feel, see, hear, or somehow experience the Nature which is yours and all creation's. . . . And if you can hold that, then you have a poem 'in petto' to which you must return in order to express it" (Devlin 1935, 114–15). To the extent to which the *confuse cognoscere* precedes (and at once vanishes into and cools down to) a purely intellectual systematization, and is therefore a direct and immediate contact with reality, it meets and corresponds to those exigencies of "immediacy," "palpability," "tactility," "highlighting of particulars" of which I have spoken at length.[23] It corresponds, besides, to two of the most unmistakable linguistic traits of Hopkins's poetry: first, the disordered and tumultuous piling up and literal confusion of images and words, mimetic of sensation; secondly, the absolute necessity of the declaimed reading of his poems, with the mouth and not with the eyes, that Hopkins recommended. But there are further equivalences between Hopkins's "inspiration" and Scotus's *confuse cognoscere:* emphasizing that the *confuse cognoscere* is neither a form of rudimentary and incomplete knowledge nor a secondary moment of the cognitive process, but a sufficiently autonomous and distinct phase, and one even fundamental and primary of the same process, Scotus implicitly suggested to Hopkins—for the above-formulated equivalence—the cognitive power of art and poetry. Opposing *confuse cognoscere* and *distincte cognoscere,* Scotus, far from minimizing the moment of sensation, exalts it and even suggests for some aspects the superiority of intuitive over abstractive knowledge; the former does not certainly arrive at a definition of reality, but although it is only capable of

23. Newman, too, seems to share this Scotist implication when, in *Loss and Gain,* chapter III, while describing Charles Reading "in the season of poetry," he writes that "when we first see things, we see them *in a 'gay confusion,'* which is the principal element of the poetical. As time goes on, and we number and sort and measure things—as we gain views—we advance towards philosophy and truth, but we recede from poetry."

"naming a thing," "naming" a thing needs a greater knowledge of the thing itself than defining it: "We say that something is conceived *confuse* when it is conceived as it were through a name; *distincte* when it is expressed through definition" (*Oxon.*, d. 3, qq. 1 and 2).

The repercussions that these Scotist distinctions exercised on Hopkins's poetics seem to me evident: the abstractive, purely rational knowledge, comes after the intuitive knowledge (in which, as we have seen, sense and intellect are fused) not only chronologically but also hierarchically. This Scotist borrowing seems to me highly important in relation to that simultaneously intellective, emotional, and even muscular and physiological response Hopkins aimed at (so that the poetic meaning should be "felt" rather than understood), and to that transcoding of the meaning, or production of "translinguistic sense" of which I spoke at the end of chapter 2 of Part One. As will be remembered, Hopkins, in a letter to Bridges, spoke of a kind of poetry in which "sometimes one enjoys and admires the very lines one cannot understand" (L I, 50). In another he said that "something must be sacrificed . . . and this may be the being at once, nay perhaps even the being without explanation at all, intelligible" (L I, 265–66).

The genesis of the poetic message as Hopkins intends it thus reveals its kinship with the origin of the cognitive act in Scotus. Yet Scotus, emphasizing that the ideal conclusion of the cognitive process is in the third act, that of the free will summing up in itself and ratifying the tendencies of the two preceding acts, offers Hopkins a further sanction of art, or even a possibility of "sanctifying" it straightaway (one can recall the "connection . . . between prayer and poetry" seen by Devlin). As with the basis of the first act, even when any object whatsoever falls under the senses, there is the confused perception of God's presence under the form of the perfection of created nature, and as God gradually manifests himself as the Object to whom the whole being consciously and freely tends, so poetry, if it really is a form of knowledge, cannot remain for Hopkins a first act and a pure inspiration, but must be intellectually reworked (if only because the poet reconstructs with his word an irremediably lost insight, as Hopkins said in "To R.B."), and must above all be addressed to God through an act of free choice. The insight into nature, in other words, is undoubtedly the perception of a form of beauty, but, as a first act and therefore spontaneous, it belongs, from the moral point of view, to the category of *indifferent acts*: "to admire the stars is in itself indifferent." In order to change it from an indifferent act into a good act, "it must have its positive rightness of justification," that is, there must be "option" and "exercise of right" (S, 166–67). The necessity of orienting the inspiration to God with a voluntary act is also hinted at in a late meditation on the Ignatian *Principium et Fundamentum*:

The sun and the stars shining glorify God. They stand where he placed them, they move where he bid them. "The heavens declare the glory of God." They glorify God, *but they do not know it. . . .* Man was created. Like the rest then to praise, reverence, and serve God; to give him glory. . . . But man can know God, *can mean to give him glory*. (S, 239; Hopkins's italics)

As Devlin has written, "a terror lest natural beauty fade unharvested" (Devlin 1935, 116) is the dominant note of most of Hopkins's poems. Quite appropriately Devlin also quotes "[On a Piece of Music]":

21   Therefore this masterhood,
22   This piece of perfect song,
23   This fault-not-found-with-good
24   Is neither right nor wrong,

25   No more than red and blue,
26   No more than Re and Mi,
27   Or sweet the golden glue
28   That's built for by the bee.

29   For good grows wild and wide,
30   Has shades, is nowhere none;
31   But right must seek a side
32   And choose for chieftain one.

But there is a further, and last, Scotist aesthetic implication of which we can prove the existence, and that regards what hostile critics have often termed Hopkins's *lack of precision* or, worse, *in-consistency* from the point of view of scientific truth and logical consequentiality. My own answer to these charges is, as we have seen, that Hopkins's communication is programmatically con-fused, and to this end I have amply shown above how, having as an almost constant objective the overturning of what is the sense for the world into what is a counter-sense (but most true and au-thentic sense) for faith, it must take on miracular characteristics of a non- and anti-scientific message, of a semantic "confusion" and "diffusion." Medieval philosophies usually assert the superi-ority of faith and theology over reason and pure philosophy; yet, perhaps, in no medieval philosopher other than Scotus are the primacy of theology and at the same time the limits of pure ratio-nality established with such clarity. Hopkins could start from certain contemporary anti-rationalistic trends and arrive at a phi-losophy that, like that of Scotus and so much unlike that of Aqui-nas, not only has recourse to "private inspiration" but also, though obviously "using" reason, "uses" it nevertheless "by hia-tuses" (Devlin 1935, 113) and even in some ways makes it relative and undervalues it.

In the Prologue to the *Oxoniense* Scotus starts from the *quaestio* constituting the almost-constant beginning of the medieval *summae* (Curtius 1953, 222), the investigation of the relationship be-tween philosophy and theology. He states preliminarily: "On this issue there appears to be disagreement between philosophers and theologians. Philosophers maintain that nature is perfect and deny a supernatural perfection. Theologians, instead, affirm the necessity of grace, and supernatural perfection" (q. 1). Philoso-phers maintain that "there is no necessity of such a supernatural knowledge for the present condition of man"; Scotus replies that we know in order to act and that we act in view of an end, and that to be *dispositi* to its achievement we need, the end being su-pernatural, a supernatural knowledge: "One who acts on the ba-sis of knowledge . . . must necessarily have a desire to attain the end toward which he is to act. . . . But man cannot know dis-tinctly his own end from natural things. It is therefore necessary that a supernatural knowledge about it should be revealed to him" (ibid.). Later on Scotus reaffirms the insufficiency of natural reason in these terms:

This at least is certain, that some conditions of this end—which render its search more fervent and desirable—cannot be definitively ascertained by means of natural reason. Even if we were given what natural reason would suffice to prove, that a naked vision and a fruition of God is the end of man, all the same we could not conclude that that would happen to man eternally and in the perfection of the body and soul. . . . And yet the eternity of that good is what makes the end more desirable than if it were merely transitory. It is then more desirable to attain this good in the perfection of nature rather than in the soul [separated from the body]. . . . Consequently it is necessary to know these conditions of the end, and others of this type, to be able to aspire more fervently to this end. But natural reason is not sufficient, and therefore we need a doctrine supernaturally revealed. (Ibid.)

This supernatural knowledge is, in its "prima traditio," the revelation embedded in Scripture, from which theology takes its premises. Scotus then passes on to the treatment of the two following questions: Is theology a science? If so, is it a *scientia speculativa* or a *cognitio practica*? It is impossible here to relate exhaustively the details of Scotus's tortuous argument, but the gist of it is that theology, while it is *in se* and *in God* a science according to three of the four requisites stated by Aristotle ("cognitio certa," "de cognito necessario," "causata a causa evidente intellectui," "applicata ad cognitum per discursum syllogisticum" [q. 3]), cannot be defined, in ourselves and strictly speaking, a science, not only because its conclusions are not syllogistically drawn, but also because its premises, since they are taken from Scripture, are not *causa evidente intellectui* but must be accepted on faith. About the second question Scotus, on the contrary, does not hesitate to maintain that theology is a *cognitio practica*. The truths of theology, in fact, serve to attain man's supernatural aim: "Faith is not a speculative attitude, and to believe is not a speculative act, and the vision following faith is not a speculative, but a practical one. This vision arises in such a way as to be conformable to fruition, and it first occurs naturally in the created intellect, so that a fruition, just and comfortable to it, is elicited" (q. 4). *Praxis* therefore implies "extensio intellectus," and more precisely: (a) an act distinct from intellection; (b) posteriority of such an act; (c) rectitude of such an act according to the rectitude of the intellection. Praxis is therefore "actus voluntatis elicitus vel imperatus" (qq. 4–5). The final pages of the Prologue are devoted to the illustration of the thesis, against Aristotle, of the superiority of theology, *qua* practical, over any other purely speculative science. Such a superiority stems both from the greater *nobilitas* of the act (the will) and from the greater *nobilitas* of the object of theology (God): "On our part we posit that a *cognoscibile operabile*, that is, something that can be attained by action—and this truly is *praxis*—is in itself totally knowable. We also posit that the knowledge of it does not differ from any other, neither according to the quantity of certainty nor according to proportion" (ibid.). Scotus concludes that "[theology] was not invented to abolish ignorance—because many more things could be set down and revealed in this great mass of doctrine than are here communicated. But the same things are frequently repeated to induce more effectively the hearer to perform those things that he is here persuaded to perform."

Everyone can see, from this summary exposition of the Prologue to the *Oxoniense,* what sort of confirmation, encouragement, or sudden intuition some of its statements, emphases, and conclusions could represent to Hopkins, who, at the time when he first read Scotus, was both a poet in the making (who had, however, chosen silence but was gnawed by the desire to utter again the poetic word) and a Jesuit scholastic. The first remark to be made is that Hopkins in 1875 broke that silence and composed "The Wreck of the Deutschland," because he had glimpsed in Scotus the possibility of making poetry a theology, in the sense in which Scotus speaks of it in the Prologue: a theology as a "revelation" of God and as a *cognitio practica,* which "issues" from the intellect and involves the will while leading man toward its ultimate end, salvation (see in particular the final stanza of the "Deutschland"). Secondly, as I said above, there is a close link between the philosophy-theology distinction Scotus makes and the "miracular" characteristics of Hopkins's poetry. Scotus, though he does not say that faith and reason are antithetical, nevertheless goes very far in underlining the limited cognitive power of the *ratio naturalis* regarding man's ultimate destiny. He acknowledges the necessity of a supernatural faith and knowledge (like the one derivable from Scripture) facing which the *ratio naturalis* must bow and make ground. Hopkins strains this distinction and, as we have seen, frequently goes so far as seeing faith's, or even the heart's, knowledge[24] as an exact opposite of natural and rational knowledge. The "thesis" of the "Deutschland" and of many other nature sonnets is a denial of the purely natural perspective and the affirmation of something close to a miracle. It is perhaps useful to remember not only that Scotus was a strenuous advocate of Mary's Immaculate Conception, but that in the Prologue the eighth of the proofs mentioned in order to demonstrate the truth of Scripture is the "miraculorum claritas" (q. 2). If we turn again to the close of the Prologue we will detect in it one of the sources of Hopkins's rhetoric and of many of the communicative exigencies and finalities I have ascribed to it: poetry becomes a new theology, a repetition and reformulation of the divine truths, "to induce more effectively the hearer to perform those things that he is . . . persuaded to perform."

We have so far demonstrated that Scotus's philosophical doctrine (or at least some of its parts) is one of the matrices—under the form both of coincidences and of derivatives and of more or less slight strainings—of Hopkins's most personal and most peculiar aesthetics. We must now see if it is possible to extract from Hopkins's Scotism further aspects, which will allow us to fit the present chapter into the general plan of this Part. In other words, we must see whether Hopkins's Scotism can provide us with further proofs of medievalism to be added to those already found in the foregoing chapters and thus support and corroborate them.

To say that Duns Scotus is a medieval philosopher, and thence to conclude that this is an index of medievalism, would be simplistic and even banal. Besides, on the basis of such a statement,

24. For the cognitive capabilities of the heart see Part One, chapter 2, in particular note 26.

the same might be said regarding a possible Thomism in Hop-kins. The above conclusion ceases, however, to appear gratu-itous when one keeps in mind that Scotus is not only a medieval philosopher but also a British medieval philosopher. This ele-mentary remark was first made by Austin Warren, who men-tioned Scotus, along with Pater, Ruskin, and Newman, among those who were for him the four "real shapers of Hopkins' mind," adding that "all [were] *Britons . . .* all were *British* empiri-cists—all concerned with defending the ordinary man's belief in the reality and knowability of things and persons" (Warren 1945, 74). In the light of what has been said in the preceding chapter about Hopkins's political attitude, this component of a *cultural pa-triotism* (as Ritz 1963 [172–76] has also argued) does not seem to me irrelevant. To this first and nonepistemological (and, on the contrary, purely affective motivation of the Scotist option (which was further fostered by the common links with Oxford) we must add a second, even more illuminating: Hopkins felt such a kinship for Scotus that we may safely speak of a self-identifica-tion at all levels.

Devlin once again paved the way toward such an interpreta-tion. His first essay, a quick investigation of the salient points of Hopkins's Scotism, closed on the statement that "they meet, phi-losopher and poet, rather as *fellow-pilgrims* than as master and dis-ciple" (Devlin 1935, 116). The 1949 essay, "Time's Eunuch," subsequently examined the biographical thread distinctly percep-tible in Hopkins's Scotism. Devlin started from the hypothesis that Scotism was not so much for Hopkins "a body of doctrines, but . . . an attitude to life, a personal dialectic" (Devlin 1949, 304). From 1872 until about 1879 the influence of Scotus (above all in the field of aesthetics) is, as we have seen, profound: Scotus loosens a series of knots, evens out a number of dramatic aporias; Hopkins's first reaction after first reading Scotus is enthusiasm; then peace takes over, both as a spiritual dimension and as some-thing found in nature, which smiles at him and vibrates with him in unison (see the letters and sonnets of the years 1876–79).[25] In

25. Highly relevant is the frequency with which Scotus is associated with *peace*, though in different contexts. Cf. "Duns Scotus's Oxford," "₁₁who of all men

the years 1880–83 Scotism becomes a prevalently theological influence, while after the "last vows" it extends its sphere of influence and becomes the frame of Hopkins's manifold speculative adventures pursued as an alternative to or alongside the poetic activity: "the stem, as it were, through which [his] word was to take shape in the various branches of his learning" (ibid., 304). An example Devlin quotes is Hopkins's invoking "an original thesis of Duns Scotus (that freedom is compatible with necessity—*necessitas spontanea . . . stat cum libertate*—in order to settle a question of rhyme" (Devlin 1949, 304). A passage of a letter to Patmore written in 1884, in which Devlin justly recognizes a "strong autobiographical ring," seems however to mark Hopkins's abrupt farewell to Scotus:

And so I used to feel of Duns Scotus when I used to read him with delight: he saw too far, he knew too much; his subtlety overshot his interests; a kind of feud arose between genius and talent, and the ruck of talent in the Schools finding itself, as his age passed by, less and less able to understand him, voted that there was nothing important to understand and so first misquoted and then refuted him. (L III, 349)

This commemoration slightly precedes the beginning of that period of literary sterility in which Hopkins frequently described himself as a *eunuch,* and one might be thus induced to relate this sterility to a crisis, or even to the *death,* of his Scotism. Scotism becomes unrecognizable as far as textual echoes are concerned, but persists as "a clue to his intimate mental world" and as a "personal dialectic" (Devlin 1949, 307, 309). In the years 1884–86 this personal dialectic takes on the guise of a communion with the whole universe (reminiscent of Scotus's theory of the *natura communis*), a "pan-humanism," a "widen[ed] . . . Christianity" (ibid., 308), and a Franciscan attitude to which Hopkins vainly tries to draw his reluctant friends and interlocutors. After 1886 and the failure of this aspiration, too, Scotism wanes into pure praxis, "self-achievement by correspondence with God's creative grace," beginning "like inspiration, unbidden, in the *spontaneous*

---

most sways my spirits to *peace,*" and the confession of 1875: "I care for him [Scotus] more even than Aristotle and more *pace tua* than a dozen Hegels" (L I, 31).

will as contrasted with the *arbitrary* will, though the arbitrary will must ratify it" (ibid., 310; Devlin's italics). The *terrible sonnets,* to which Hopkins himself refers as "inspirations unbidden and against my will" (L I, 221), are indeed the expression of the "sigh of the *voluntas naturae* . . . which he cannot share" and which makes his frustration similar to that of the "abiding prototype of mediation," Christ (Devlin, 1949, 311).

Devlin's conjectures about the shaping action of Hopkins's Scotism, its temporal extension as well as its metamorphoses along the phases of his biography, seem to me unexceptionable. It is, however, possible to further extend the interpretation of this tight relationship and to maintain what Devlin only hints at: Hopkins's conscious self-identification with Scotus. This is borne out, not only by the sum of purely doctrinal and theological coincidences and extradoctrinal mediations we have amply discussed, but also by Hopkins's appropriation of Scotism even and above all as a personal dialectic, that is, by an actual adaptation, under the form of ways and ideals of life, of purely doctrinal and speculative principles (Scotus's pan-humanism, man's communion with the whole and yet his diversity and singularity, the opposition between *voluntas ut natura* and *voluntas ut arbitrium,* praxis, etc.). In particular, the brief memoir of Scotus quoted above— where Scotus is the one who "saw too far" and "knew too much," in whom "subtlety," "genius," and "talent" were present in such an abundance that his readers became, with the passing of time, "less and less able to understand him"—seems to me the most transparent of self-portraits. And it is a self-identification from which we can derive new aspects, and new confirmations, of Hopkins's opposition to Victorian culture and at the same time of his medievalism. Hopkins's elaboration of a personal theological and philosophical code divergent from and eccentric to the official one of the Catholic church (and, a fortiori, equally heterogeneous to that or those of the Victorians) is an unmistakable index of a profound, deeply-felt and meditated medieval option. What I mean, of course, is not a primitive, "dark," static and self-enclosed Middle Ages, but one "open," ripe, uneasy, vital, and in transformation, though holding fast to the foundations of its faith: a Middle Ages that in Italy found full expression in Dante and that in England, owing to the cultural time lag at which I have often hinted, begins with the dawning of its national culture and ends with the advent of the Enlightenment after the Elizabethan splendor and the Jacobean epilogue. Through its link to and mirroring in Duns Scotus, Hopkins's personality and his oppositional place inside Victorian culture stand out better revealed and individualized. Scotus is on the one hand the "subtlest" and most meticulous and most "baroque" medieval philosopher in the richness—for some, in the Byzantine-like prolixity—of his distinctions and specifications (his "thought," according to De Wulf 1909 [368], is "obscur[e]," characterized by a "long array of divergent opinions," by a "want of equilibrium" and by a "laboured load of arguments and refutations") and on the other, in opposition to St. Thomas, he was one of the first to exalt—even at a biographical level—the diversity and singularity of man: "It was Duns Scotus who . . . gave the studies of the order a distinctly *new orientation*. . . . He brought into fashion a peripateticism that was *sui generis*: his personal genius gave an original stamp even to the earliest scholastic theories that survived in his philosophy. . . . Duns Scotus was a *destroyer of systems*. He attacked most of his contemporaries" (ibid.; De Wulf's italics).

7

Closing a quick survey of the code options of Hopkins's pre-Jesuit period, I hinted above (Part Two, chapter 3) at some aesthetic attitudes he shared with his times (balance, moderation, the truth-beauty pair, etc.); I then interrupted my discussion by quoting some rather disconcerting and unpredictable literary judgments and assessing the global situation of the above-said period as one of a substantial, though increasingly eccentric, adherence to the Victorian cultural model. To reach the ideal conclusion of our investigation we must ascertain whether the medieval codes we have found active in Hopkins (behavioral, signic, political, historical, ethical, philosophical, and theological) are joined, in the Jesuit period, by an equally medieval aesthetic and poetic code and by a medieval conception of the figure of the author.

The truth-beauty pair is, in Hopkins's youthful aesthetics, the ultimate synthesis of art's motivations and finalities. With his entrance into the Society of Jesus such a canon is certainly not dropped, but it undergoes a considerable change, constituted by a strong shift of emphasis on the term *truth,* which means an art prescriptively aiming at a maximum of beauty but within strict limits of morality—for what is written as well as for the writer himself. The different semantic value now given to this term (*truth,* which had been prevalently synonymous, in his youth, with "realism," "adherence to things") is illustrated in the following passage of a letter written to Bridges in 1883:

I agree then, and vehemently, that a gentleman, if there is such a thing on earth, is in the position to despise the poet, were he Dante or Shakspere, and the painter, where he Angelo or Apelles, for anything in him that shewed him *not* to be a gentleman. . . . It is true, there is nothing like the truth and the "good that does itself not know scarce is". . . . As a fact poets and men of art are, I am sorry to say, by no means necessarily or commonly gentlemen. For gentlemen do not pander to lust or other basenesses nor, as you say, give themselves airs or affectations nor do other things to be found in modern works. (L I 175–76; Hopkins's italics)

The literary judgments abounding in Hopkins's letters after 1866 to Bridges, Dixon, and Patmore prove with the greatest transparency that truth and beauty remain the two touchstones of art, but also that the youthful conviction of the supremacy of the latter over the former (J, 74) is literally overturned. Swinburne, one of the most frequently quoted and harassed authors in his letters (L I, 89, 237; L II, 99, 156–57; L III, 228–29) represents very well, for example, the incomplete exploitation of beauty or the lack of truth: "Swinburne has a new volume out . . . a perpetual functioning of genius without truth, feeling, or any adequate matter to be at function on" (L I, 304). Other figures of the past or present receive the same treatment as Swinburne (elsewhere a "plague of mankind" [L I, 39]). Goethe's *Faust* is "fascinating" but also "defective" in unity of action and above all didactic force (L II, 113);[1] in another letter Goethe is coupled to Burns in the category of the "scoundrels" (L II, 25), which subverts a youthful judgment in which Hopkins had seen in him "the . . . union of the classical and the mediaeval" (J, 27). Milton's achievements "are quite beyond any other English poet's," but "he was a very bad man" (L I, 38–39); Browning is admired for his "touches" and "details," but "the general effect, the whole" "offends" him (L I, 137). Of Whitman, Hopkins said: "I always knew in my heart Walt Whitman's mind to be more like my own than any other man's living. As he is a very great scoundrel this is not a very pleasant confession" (L I, 155); and of Blake, that he has "exqui-

---

1. Elsewhere (L I, 225) *Faust* lacks "seriousness," like Dante's *Inferno,* and becomes a farce. On Dante and the *Divine Comedy,* see below.

site freshness and lyrical inspiration" but also "a great deal of rub-
bish, want of sense, and some touches of ribaldry and wickedness" (L II, 153).[2] The same evaluative criteria are to be found
in the judgments regarding figures of the sister arts of painting
and music,[3] both when Hopkins manifests his predilection for the
austerity and realism of medieval and pre-Renaissance art
(Giotto, Della Robbia, Pisano, etc.: J, 237ff.) and when he
touches on artists of other periods: Carl Maria von Weber (together with Purcell), and not Mozart or Beethoven or Bach, is
for him at the top of the scale of values, as "a good man, I believe,
with no hateful affectation of playing the fool and behaving like
a blackguard" (L I, 99).

In this great and potentially unconditioned admiration for the
"brute beauty" and the capabilities of human genius—immediately checked and brought back within moral limits—Hopkins
applies an unmistakably medieval aesthetic code whose vague
Dantesque echoes it is not difficult to perceive.[4] Hopkins follows
Dante not only in the application of this standard of judgment
but also in his constant referring to a specific and precise functionality of art. If, in fact, Hopkins's ideal literary genre throughout
his whole poetic career was—despite the appearances—the dramatic (let us recall his emphasis on "bidding"), and if we keep in
mind that such a dramatic character is equally at the basis of medieval art (let us merely think of the prominence it has in the title
of Dante's poem), one can globally see in Hopkins's poetry a kind
of nineteenth-century morality play.[5] As we have seen, Hopkins

2. See also, for other appreciations of the same tenor, L III, 313–14 (on Ruskin), L II, 143, and L I, 228 (on the Gothic novel).

3. For an excellent, diachronic and comparatistic treatment of the interdependence (even interchangeability) of the three arts (poetry, painting, music), see
Heuser 1958, passim.

4. I refer, in particular, to Dante's "$_{43}$Gran duol" (Inferno 4) in Limbo in front
of the "great spirits," and to the interpretation of Ulysses' journey in Inferno 26,
when Dante, remembering it, once again feels regret (l. 19) and again points out
the necessity to check one's genius "$_{22}$perchè non corra che virtù nol guidi." This
standard of judgment and conduct in the artistic sphere is substantially reaffirmed in Dante's encounters with artists: see above all those with Oderisi from
Gubbio (Purgatorio 11.7–9 and 82–142) and with Statius (Purgatorio 21.82–87 and
22.64–114).

5. Robinson 1978, 108.

aimed at a realistic, immediate art, an art so masculine as to appear even rough, and entirely divested of fripperies and useless decorations: an art, above all, that was not to be an end in itself but rather endowed with a social effect and therefore largely popular. These were characteristics Hopkins did not tire of repeating, and even of proclaiming to his friends Dixon and Bridges, prone in his eyes to "narcissistic" and "aesthetic" faults. We read in a letter written in 1866:

I must tell you he [Savonarola] is the only person in history (except perhaps Origen) about whom I have a real feeling, and I feel such an enthusiasm about Savonarola that I can conceive what it must have been to have been of his followers. I feel this the more *because he was followed by the painters, architects and other artists of his day, and is the prophet of Christian art,* and it is easy to imagine oneself a painter of his followers. (L III, 17–18)

Ironical and singular though it may seem, just the man who in 1868 had voluntarily condemned himself to silence became subsequently the most strenuous champion of the social impact of art (of course in a spiritual and moral sense), and of that didactic end (at the level of *movere* and *docere*) which is much more and much less than Victorian edification, and is indeed the cornerstone of medieval art and rhetoric:

By the bye, I say it deliberately and before God, I would have you and Canon Dixon and all true poets remember that fame, the being known, though in itself one of the most dangerous things to man, is nevertheless the true and appointed air, element, and setting of genius and its works. *What are works of art for? to educate, to be standards. Education is meant for the many, standards are for public use.* To produce then is of little use unless what we produce is known, if known widely known, the wider known the better, *for it is by being known it works, it influences, it does its duty, it does good.* We must then try to be known, aim at it, take means to it. (L I, 231)

Rather than certain requisites at the level of content—which Hopkins never specifies—poetry must have formal requisites. In order to be socially successful and to make the standard of morality effective, poetry must first of all divest itself of all superfluity,

must avoid all empty self-gratifications and formal over-elabora-
tions, and must also adopt, as a primary patent of credibility, the
language of its own time, without indulging in those archaisms
so much in fashion in the Victorian Age—an analogous exigency
of immediacy had caused in the Middle Ages the abandonment
of Latin for the vernacular. Hopkins criticizes, for example, Carlyle's "pampered and affected style" (L II, 59), while he repri-
mands Dickens for having "no true command of pathos . . .
something mawkish" (L II, 73); on the contrary the lack of "fire"
in the Dorset poet William Barnes is amply compensated by the
profound sincerity of his inspiration ("he is a perfect artist and of
a most spontaneous inspiration" [L I, 221]). Swinburne, whom
Hopkins also criticizes for his immorality, is once again the negative model for this defect too, stylistic archaism: "Swinburne is a
strange phenomenon: his poetry seems a powerful effort at estab-
lishing a new standard of poetical diction, of the rhetoric of poetry; but to waive every other objection it is essentially archaic,
biblical a good deal, and so on: now that is a thing that can never
last; *a perfect style must be of its age*" (L II, 99). And Hopkins does
not hesitate to group Swinburne, in this condemnation, and for
the same reasons, with other celebrated literary figures of his
time: "It seems to me that the poetical language of an age shd. be
the current language heightened, to any degree heightened and
unlike itself, but not (I mean normally: passing freaks and graces
are another thing) *an obsolete one*. This is Shakespeare's and Milton's practice and the want of it will be fatal to Tennyson's Idylls
and plays, to Swinburne, and perhaps to Morris" (L I, 89).[6] For
the same reasons, returning to music, Hopkins shows a preference for the severe, essential simplicity of Gregorian chant, of a
Palestrina and of the "old madrigal writers" (L I, 220) as against
the excessive elaboration of a Chopin ("Chopin's fragmentary
airs struggling and tossing on a surf of accompaniment" [L I,
214]).

If we search, in the letters, for Hopkins's predilections in the
circumscribed field of British artistic culture (to the extent to

6. See also, on Swinburne and Morris, L I, 275 and L III, 296.

which this is possible) we should at this point find as a result that Hopkins attributes the approved stylistic components, so far set down "by defect," to British medieval artists. If again we keep in mind Britain's often-mentioned historical and cultural time lag— so that the Middle Ages, the Renaissance, and the Baroque, un- like in continental cultures where these labels and the respective epistemic coordinates are used in a prevalently oppositional sense, cohabit in Britain over an ample time-span—we can say that this does happen. The fact that Hopkins prefers not Low Middle Ages artists but High Middle Ages, Renaissance, late Re- naissance, and even seventeenth-century and "baroque" artists (such, I repeat, according to the current periodizations) is further proof of his exaltation of an evolutionary, open, ripe, and dy- namic Middles Ages, a Middle Ages which in England came to its definitive end only well into the eighteenth century.[7] Shake- speare and Milton in drama and in poetry, Purcell[8] and to a lesser extent Handel in music: these artists best represent those *medieval*[9] characteristics of the art—on the one hand strong and virile and on the other efficacious and captivating—that Hopkins advo- cated. Only in painting Hopkins predictably could not find any British "medieval" genius, and for him the greatest artist was a foreigner, Michelangelo.

Hopkins's Journal shows very well the waning of his infatua- tion with the literary and pictorial Pre-Raphaelitism ("has not

7. On the extension of the "Medieval Model," C. S. Lewis has this to say in his *The Discarded Image:* "The reader will find that I freely illustrate features of the Model which I call 'medieval' from authors who wrote after the close of the Mid- dle Ages; from Spenser, Donne or Milton. I do so, because, at many points, the old Model still underlies their work. It was not totally and confidently abandoned till the end of the seventeenth century" (Lewis 1964, 13). See also Ellsberg 1987, 97–120, for Hopkins and the "baroque . . . tradition": "Considering the atmo- sphere of anti-Catholicism that dominated England after the Reformation period and extended into much of the Victorian age, Hopkins had more in common with a Jesuit of the baroque age than might seem initially obvious" (99). She also says, however, that Hopkins "is baroque in an extrahistorical sense" (ibid.) and illus- trates with examples and analogies (also taken from music and architecture) his "baroque . . . rhetoric and poetic theory [and] aesthetic" (100, 105).

8. Ellsberg 1987, 115–16.

9. In the diaries we read this fragment: "We live to see / How Shakespeare's England weds with Dante's Italy" (J, 48). It might be indicative of the cultural union I am attributing to Hopkins.

Giotto the instress of loveliness?" Hopkins asks in 1868 [J, 168], while Millais is symptomatically "the greatest English painter, one of the greatest of the world" [L III, 201]) and his gradual enthusiasm for the Renaissance art, already veined with baroque streaks, of a Mantegna and a Michelangelo, and even for the baroque pomp of a Rembrandt and a Rubens. The reasons given by Hopkins for such a predilection are illuminating:

Bold masterly rudeness of the blue twelvemonth service of plates or platters by Luca della Robbia. . . . The cartoons and a full sized chalk drawing from the Transfiguration . . . also . . . Michael Angelo's paintings at the Vatican: the *might* [Hopkins's italics], with which I was more deeply struck than ever before . . . *seems to come not merely from the simplifying and then amplifying or emphasising of parts but from a masterly realism in the simplification,* both these things: there is the simplifying and strong emphasising of anatomy in Rubens, the emphasising and great simplifying in Raphael for instance, and on the other hand the realism in Velasquez, but here force came together from both sides . . . (J, 237)

Mantegna's inscaping of drapery (in the grisaille Triumph of Scipio and the Madonna with saints by a scarlet canopy) is, I think, unequalled, *it goes so deep.* (J, 241)

Millais is now significantly "unsatisfying" (J, 245) and Hunt "not very pleasing . . . overglaring" (J, 248). As to music, for the "necessary and eternal" (L II, 13) Purcell one might at once recall the "₇rehearsal / ₈Of own, of *abrúpt sélf*" Hopkins attributes to him in the sonnet by the same title; while of Handel he said (L II, 137) that he could not hear five bars of his music "without feeling that something great is beginning, something full of life."

In the field of stylistic models, the ideally Shakespearean use of Hopkins's poetic language was first asserted and convincingly illustrated in *New Bearings in English Poetry* by F. R. Leavis (who, however, repeatedly and insistently juxtaposed Shakespeare and Milton as the representatives of two antithetical styles). Shakespeare's greatness is for Hopkins so unquestionable that one would have difficulties in quoting more than generic judgments on him (see however L III, 218; L II, 6; L I, 92–93). Recall that in Shakespeare, and also in Milton, Hopkins found the first traces of sprung rhythm ("master of rhythm" [J, 278]).[10] To maintain then that Hopkins reconciles a Shakespearean with a Miltonian linguistic ideal is only apparently a contradiction: if one is willing to see in Hopkins's poetry *only* a "heightening" of common language then certainly "the relation [between Hopkins and Milton] is an anththesis";[11] if instead we keep in mind that along with this aspiration Hopkins's poetry aims to assert itself as an artifact and an autonomous and self-enclosed linguistic organism (as "speech . . . to be heard for its own sake and interest even over and above its interest of meaning" [J, 289]), then Milton's art (which is "incomparable, not only in English literature but, I shd. think, almost in any; equal, if not more than equal, to the finest of Greek or Roman" [L II, 13])[12] proves to be in Hopkins the constant and conscious stylistic model, the ideal incessantly pursued of a classical, balanced diction, drained of any eccentricity: "I hope in time to have a more balanced and Miltonic style" (L I, 66); "Milton is the great master of sequence of phrase" (L II, 8); "I endeavoured in it ["Andromeda"] at a more Miltonic plainness and severity than I have anywhere else" (L I, 87). Hopkins recognized something similar in Dryden, of whom he says in one of his last letters to Bridges, "My style tends always more towards Dryden. What is there in Dryden? Much, but above all this: *he is the most masculine of our poets;* his style and his rhythms lay *the strongest stress* of all our literature on the *naked thew and sinew of the English language* . . ." (L I, 267–268).

Yet no matter how illuminating, Hopkins's predilections for some authors of the past cannot be enough to help us define his medievalism in matters of aesthetics and poetics. On the basis of some acute investigations by Lotman, I have already specified (Part Two, chapter 2) the main foundations of medieval aesthetics and at the same time the most decisive divergences between it and modern aesthetics. If one applies this key to Hopkins's body

10. Milton is, in his turn, "the great standard in the use of counterpoint" (L II, 15).

11. Leavis 1932, 137. It must be recalled, however, that the "heightening" of common language is for Hopkins "Shakespeare's *and Milton's* practice" (L I, 89).

12. See also, for a similar judgment, L I, 38.

of writings, one gets the confirmation that the adherence to a pre-established semantics and the consequent identification of the author as an intermediary of such pre-established text are two principles Hopkins shares with medieval aesthetics. To resume Lotman's terms, this induces us to include Hopkins's production in the sphere of the medieval aesthetics of identity rather than in that of the modern aesthetics of opposition.

I have discussed elsewhere[13] and amply exemplified this important aspect of Hopkins's poetic theory and praxis. I will here merely observe how aesthetically decisive and reverberating Hopkins's entrance into the Society of Jesus proved to be. At that climacteric, Hopkins's aesthetic and behavioral codes reached an admirable adjustment and correspondence. In 1868 the poetic *word,* as an expression of a "pagan" and self-assertive aesthetics tending to pure beauty, was made to yield to a silence optimistically qualified, with revealing irony, "₄The *music* that I care to hear" ("The Habit of Perfection"), that is, a silence equalized to an aesthetic value or surrogate. Of great interest to us is what subsequently pushed Hopkins to resume and permanently to re-adopt the artistic word: the *alibi* that props up, substantiates, and legitimizes the uttering of the word—from the "Deutschland" onward—is a poetry functioning as a "relay word," an expression verbalizing, as in the Middle Ages, the divine messages mirrored by the world:

> *"The Wreck of the Deutschland"*
> 29.1   Ah! thére was a héart right!
> 2   There was single eye!
> 3   Réad the unshápeable shóck níght
> 4   And knew the who and the why;
> 5 Wording it how but by him that present and past,
> 6 Heaven and earth are word of, worded by?—

> *"Hurrahing in Harvest"*
> 5 I wálk, I líft up, Í lift úp heart, éyes,
> 6 Down all that glory in the heavens to glean our Saviour;

13. See Marucci 1977, *passim,* but above all 33–34 and 38–40.

7 ___ And, éyes, heárt, what looks, what lips yet gáve you á
8 ___ Rápturous love's greeting of realer, of rounder replies?

Hopkins's whole production from 1875 practically until the *terrible sonnets* finds its sole and exclusive justification—with respect to a religious code so strict that it sees merely impurity and disorder in art—as an illustration, amplification, comment, gloss of the divine text inexhaustibly "represented" in and by the world (which is, for Hopkins as for the medieval *auctor,* "book of God," God's own word, as we have seen). On the other hand, again with reference to the aesthetics of his youth, one could barely imagine a more effective abolition of art's self-assertive element, of its self-gratification and aspiration to fame (in a word, of the dimension of the author, in the sense of modern aesthetics) than that performed by a man who, though insistently urged, could and would always resist the temptation to publish: the word becomes, even if only as an intention and a project, God's word, a word belonging to Him, and art negates its own autonomy to proclaim its instrumental function and heteronomy. Hopkins's text thus becomes a metalinguistic and "metapoetic" utterance manifesting its genesis, relativity, and dependence on the unique divine Text, a text that in this relation of mediation finds its raison d'être. These indissoluble "iconic" links of a medieval type further help us qualify as structural and systematic elements many of Hopkins's expressive idiosyncrasies and so-called "eccentricities," which are demanded by and are functional to the demonstrative project so frequently underlying the poetic compositions. The richness, not to say the excess of figures of thought, in Hopkins's poetry finds its place in the rhetorical and didactic project and iconic principle presiding over its semiosis. The fact that Hopkins wrote in an age of soaring desemioticization and, in the religious field, of increasing skepticism and agnosticism, accounts for the rhetorical surplus over the medieval norm.

Having already examined at length in the first part of this work the rhetorical and didactic planning—and its necessity and functionality—in Hopkins's poetry, I will here confine my analysis to the illustration of the context of ideally medieval motivations regulating Hopkins's frequent usages of such tropes as parable, allegory, and simile.

We have already seen that Hopkins's poetry subsists and functions as a mediation and amplification of the "divine text," that is, of the theophanic character in man, nature, and the whole cosmos. The changed epistemic coordinates of the Victorian Age with respect to those of the Middle Ages, and as a consequence the sclerosis, insensitivity, and religious skepticism of the Victorian addressee, are such as to make the creation appear to Hopkins (and to a greater extent than in the medieval *auctor*) as a cryptotext, a concealed text, rather than as a manifest text. It is just in the attempt to provide a "bridge" between earth and heaven and between human and divine, and to show men this almost invisible welding—and therefore to fill up the distance between manifest and concealed text—that Hopkins uses in such a conspicuous way the above-mentioned rhetorical devices. They aim, in fact, to prop up, strengthen, and highlight the sense, and are therefore used on the basis of the twofold need to point out in any event the evidence of the divine presence and to verify and make vivid and comprehensible the aridity of dogma and of the hermeneutic passages. These exigencies and procedures Hopkins takes both from the Gospels (in which "Christ's parables [are] all taken from real life" [L III, 374]), and from the *Spiritual Exercises,* where frequently St. Ignatius "clothe[s] . . . a fact of history . . . in [a] parable" (S, 183–84; see also S, 186, 198).

Hopkins's "parallelistic" mind untiringly searches around for traces of God in the multifarious and inexhaustible variety of historical, human and natural phenomenology; it is, in other words, intent on tracing back to God's plan even events and phenomena that are more apparently in contrast with it and seem to be irreducible to it. Such an integral semioticization of cosmos—that is, that *supplementary reading* and that *over-sense* of which I have discussed at length in Part One—makes human life and inanimate nature appear to Hopkins (and to his interlocutors, proportionally to the success of the message) as a great catalogue of parables. A parable is for Hopkins each micro- or macro-event, either whenever it can be read as a divine sign or as bearing the divine imprint, or when it admirably "repeats," "quotes" the parables of the Gospel. The poetry immediately preceding or following his conversion already appears, in an increasingly manifest way, as a re-reading, a re-writing or amplification of the Gospel parables. The parable of the Good Sower and the extended metaphor of the harvest, which are practically ubiquitous in Hopkins, are to be found in a poem with such a revealing title as "New Readings" and also in "See how Spring opens . . ."; that of the Samaritan Woman and of the Weeds among the Wheat in "He hath abolish'd the old drouth"; that of the Wise and Foolish Virgins in "Easter Communion":

> *"Easter Communion"*
> 8   You vigil-keepers with low flames decreased,
> 9   God shall o'er-brim the measures you have spent
> 10   With oil of gladness . . .

The whole group of the nature sonnets following the "Deutschland" is instead an unmistakable parabolic reading, in that reality is taken up as a sign, a text, a manifestation of God, from "God's Grandeur," "The Starlight Night," "Spring," and "Pied Beauty" to "The Windhover" and "Hurrahing in Harvest." While "The Lantern out of doors" quotes again the parable of the Wise and Foolish Virgins and presents Christ as Johannine Light illuminating the world, and "The Candle Indoors" echoes Matthew 7: 3–5 and 5: 5, 13 ("$_{12}$Are you beam-blind, yet to a fault / $_{13}$In a neighbour deft-handed?"; "$_{14}$spendsavour salt"), "Spelt from Sibyl's Leaves" presents a highly dramatic, powerful, parabolic, and "apocalyptic" reading of reality ("$_{10}$Our tale, O our oracle"). The natural evening slowly yielding to night is "$_8$Our evening . . . our night"; death, the secret message of this parable, utters another, the "division" of life into "$_{12}$black, white; I right, wrong". The pastoral images ("$_{11}$pen"; "$_{14}$shelterless") and the "$_{14}$groans" on which the sonnet closes enable us to read in this evening becoming night an echo of the prophecy of the separation of the sheep from the goats in the Day of the Last Judgment (Matt. 25: 31ff.). To read reality as a parable of course implies the adoption of a non-univocal but "multigraded" semantics. Hopkins uses and extensively exploits this process of semantization, which brings him unmistakably close, both in theory and practice, to the major medieval authors, and specifically to Dante and his well-known theory of the four senses and his representation in spatial terms—as a descensional and/or ascensional movement—of semantization and interpretation.[14] Hopkins hints at a spatial conception of sense in this well-known passage (although he refers to the Greek poets and maintains the partially unconscious character of the operation): "In any lyric passage of the tragic poets . . . there are . . . two strains of thought running together and like counterpointed; the *overthought* that which everybody, editors, see . . . , the other, the *underthought,* conveyed chiefly in the choice of metaphors etc. used and often only half realized by the poet himself . . ." (L III, 252).

The medieval way of "reading," as we have seen, "is not the quantitative accumulation of the texts one has read, but a deeper and deeper knowledge of a text, the continuous and repeated penetration into its structure" (Lotman 1973, 45). Hopkins, in a similar way, sees Scripture as a sort of mine from which one never ceases to extract meanings: "Much, much more might be said, for the meaning of the Scripture . . . grows and multiplies as you deal it out" (S, 232). And if the world is God's text, the "reading" of it and the poetic text containing and revealing it cannot but be a deeper and deeper sounding into its meaning. The "Deutsch-

14. "One is called *literal,* and this it is which goes no further than the letter, such as the simple narration of the thing of which you treat. . . . The second is called *allegorical,* and this is the meaning hidden under the cloak of fables, and is a truth concealed beneath a fair fiction. . . . The third sense is called *moral;* and this readers should carefully gather from all writings, for the benefit of themselves and their descendants. . . . The fourth sense is called *anagogical,* that is, beyond sense [*sovrasenso*]; and this is when a book is spiritually expounded, which, although true in its literal sense, by the things signified refers to the supernal things of eternal glory" (*Convivio* 2.1). The "concealed" character of the "truth" demands a "penetration into the sense": Dante not casually says that "the literal sense should always come first, as that whose meaning includes all the rest." It is symptomatic that Dante uses metaphors such as "*venire* a la allegorica sentenza" ["to get at the allegorical formulation"] or "*procedere* alla forma" ["to move toward form"]. See also, for the medieval "multigraded" semantics, Bump 1982, 144.

land" appears the poetic text where Hopkins most extensively and transparently performs this inexhaustible semantic and hermeneutic probing, as will be seen in the next chapter.

The use of a "multigraded" semantics, and more precisely of multiple correspondences between the literal plane and other, nonliteral planes, is in its turn a particular device of a more general expressive procedure, that allegorical construction which is the foundation of medieval poetry and at the same time one of Hopkins's most typical didactic and hermeneutic practices. Allegory is first of all in Hopkins a method of reading and interpreting (one atypical and idiosyncratic) other poets' texts. One easily recalls the exhaustive allegorical reading of Tennyson's "The Vision of Sin" in a letter written in 1862 (L III, 7), or the following retrospective information about the interpretation of an episode of Shakespeare's *A Midsummer-Night's Dream:* "You remember the scene or episode of the little Indian Boy in the *Midsummer Night:* it is, I think, an allegory, to which, in writing once of the play, I believed I had found the clue, but whether I was right or wrong the meaning must have in any case been, and Shakespere must have known it wd. be, dark or invisible to most beholders or readers . . ." (L II, 115). Another judgment, dating back to 1880, contains the following, dogmatic principle of poetics: "I dislike in regular allegory the mixing the parable and the interpretation: it seems to me a great fault in art" (L I, 102).

As a method of composition, allegory presents in Hopkins equally unmistakable occurrences, both under the form of local, circumscribed, embryonic and fragmentary allegories and under the form of self-enclosed, rigorous constructions, such as the hermetic sonnet "Andromeda"[15] and the "Deutschland" itself. Hopkins even forces to this semantic stratification elements that would seem most refractory to it, almost reaching in some cases (as in numerical symbolism) a complexity typical of the Middle Ages. This is particularly evident in his "Marian" poetry, with its complex frame of equivalences and identifications between the

15. The (astrological) key to this sonnet is probably contained in S, 198–202. About allegory in Hopkins, and for an allegorical, and deconstructive, reading of "The Windhover" see Sprinker 1980, 3–19.

gifts of the Holy Virgin and the seasonal cycle ("Ad Mariam"), the variety of flowers and of their colors ("Rosa Mystica") and the beneficent influences of the atmosphere ("The Blessed Virgin compared to the Air we Breathe").[16] Of the political allegory contained in "Tom's Garland" I have already spoken in a foregoing chapter; "Epithalamion," one of the last poems Hopkins wrote, might have become in its turn—had it been completed—the most unmistakable medieval "cast." The allegorical element and the didactic purpose are announced from the outset: ",Hark, hearer, hear what I do; lend a thought now, *make believe*." Here begins what Hopkins, as we have seen in a previous quotation, called the "parable": the description of a leafy wood crossed by a river into which a group of clamoring boys dive. An adult, arrived there by chance, having taken off his clothes, imitates the boys and dives too: ",₄₂Where we leave him, froliclavish, while he looks about him, laughs, swims." It is here that the interpretation, the explanation of the parable—of which, as I was saying, we have only summary hints, sufficient however to make us guess its consistency—begins:

"Epithalamion"

43   Enough now; since *the sacred matter that I mean*
44   I should be wronging longer leaving it to float
45   Upon this only gambolling and echoing-of-earth note—
46   What is .... the delightful dean?
47   Wedlock. What the water ? Spousal love.

    ·   ·   ·   ·   ·   ·   ·

50   turns
51   Father, mother, brothers, sisters, friends
52   Into fairy trees, wildflowers, woodferns
53   Ranked round the bower

    ·   ·   ·   ·   ·   ·   ·   ·

One final figure of style links Hopkins to medieval poetics and aesthetics: the use of similes, comparisons, metaphors. Like and even more than the other figures of speech, tropes help break the

---

16. See Bump 1982, 85–92, for a detailed allegorical reading of "Rosa Mystica."

wall of skepticism in the hearer and thus enhance the credibility of dogmas, of the truths of faith, or of the text in which they appear. If religious faith, as we have seen, is translatable into enunciations that common experience judges as counter-sense or paradoxes, it follows that the more the trope plays on the unusual and the unheard-of (yet, of course, always within the limits of what is empirically controllable), the more its capacities will be strengthened to prop up the sense and increase the probability of success of the message. The conclusion to be drawn—as far as the swarm-like richness of similes, comparisons, metaphors, parallelisms and antitheses, as well as their high degree of estrangement, are concerned—is once again coincident with that reached above: tropes are not in Hopkins purely ornamental and ludic, but are "medievally" didactic supports to clarify, vivify, and thoroughly explain the sense.[17] To be even slightly exhaustive, however, an investigation and classification of tropic functionality would require, if not a volume at least a whole chapter. That lies outside the aims of the present book. (Something of the kind will be carried out, for "The Wreck of the Deutschland," in the next chapter.) This tropic functionality is however at work in the sermons, from which I quote some telling fragments:[18]

In this Gospel *two miracles, not one after the other, but* first the beginning of one, then the other, then the end of the first; as when you drive a quill or straw or knitting needle *through an egg,* it pierces first the white, then the yolk, then the white again. (S, 30; Hopkins's italics)

His [Christ's] hair [was] inclining to auburn, parted in the midst, curling and clustering about the ears and neck as the leaves of a filbert, so they speak, upon the nut . . . (S, 35)

But if God . . . were ever to have kept anyone . . . from falling into any the least sin, still such a man would have the inclination to sin left though

17. For Ellsberg 1987, 105ff., Hopkins's "poetic metaphors" are a "baroque" reworking of "medieval symbolism." She adds that "the dialectical structure of many or most of Hopkins' poems can be seen as either medieval or baroque" (114).

18. Devlin correctly describes Hopkins's tropic technique in the sermons, but fails, in my opinion, to interpret it: "The bad feature of his preaching was a frigid, almost 'euphuistic' playing with conceits and a tendency to chop logic" (S, 9). A similar misunderstanding is found in Warren 1945, 6–7.

he did not yield to that inclination: a watch wound up but kept from going has the spring always on the strain though no motion comes of it. (S, 44)

You have seen at cricket how when one of the batsmen at the wicket has made a hit and wants to score a run, the other doubts, hangs back, or is ready to run in again, how eagerly the first will cry / Come on, come on!—a Paraclete is just that, something that cheers the spirit of man . . . (S, 70)

As the breath is drawn from the boundless air into the lungs and from the lungs again is breathed out and melts into the boundless air so the Spirit of God was poured out from the infinite God upon Christ's human nature and by Christ . . . (S, 98)

❧ "THE WRECK OF THE DEUTSCHLAND": THE MEDIEVAL SYNTHESIS

"The Wreck of the Deutschland," which to me is the keystone and most entropic poem of Hopkins's whole production—and possibly of the poetry of the whole Victorian Age—provides an admirable synthesis of his medievalism and of the series of codes or simply of the aspects into which it is subdivided and in which it is refracted.

A. The Wreck as a "Text" and "God's Text"

Of the circumstances of composition of the "Deutschland" I have spoken in Part One, chapter 3. On one particular, taken from a letter to Dixon, it is useful to pause a little:

But when in the winter of '75 the Deutschland was wrecked in the mouth of the Thames and five Franciscan nuns, exiles from Germany by the Falck laws, aboard of her were drowned I was affected by the account and happening to say so to my rector he said that he wished someone would write a poem on the subject. (L II, 14)

Hopkins, in this letter, immediately goes on to speak of the "new rhythm" which had long resounded in his ears. He does not elaborate in the least either on the kind of affection he had felt or on the orientation possibly advised by the rector. With respect to a pure report of the facts, one of the readiest forms of disautomatizing the avid sensationalism of his contemporaries (see above, Part Two, chapter 1) might have been a sentimentalistic reading or a hagiographic dramatization of the tragedy. Hopkins, as we have seen, chose neither of these possibilities, but launched into the even more arduous task of wringing the event from a purely syntagmatic and aparadigmatic perspective and from the series of the possible and equally "syntagmatic" reactions to it (horror, sorrow, compassion, succor, etc.)—wringing the event, in other words, from its fortuitousness and fragmentariness, and linking it to a different perspective, transforming it into an effect of something, contextualizing, motivating it, and making it a sign, a sign of God. The progressive and systematic reorganization of and search for "rhymes" in the cosmos—in the diaries of his youth and in the Journal—flow into this great hymn to the signic nature of everything created and continually being created by God's will—signic to such an extent as to comprise the seemingly and superficially most refractory and non-signic events and aspects. It is from the "Deutschland" that the more composed signic readings of the immediately succeeding poems (the sonnets) will be generated.

The transformation of the wreck from a non-signic event into a sign shows the activity of a medieval code in the sense in which it has been illustrated in chapters 2 and 4 of this Part. The "Deutschland," too, reproduces both the spirit and the letter of this code, that is, the metaphor of the "book" or "text" of God. The "tempest" of Part the First becomes the language with which God manifests himself to the disbeliever, bent by the "₂lightning and lashed ród":

2.1   I did *say yes*
2   O at líghtning and láshed ród;
3   Thou *heardst* me, *truer than tongue, confess*
4   Thy terror, O Christ, O God;

The silent language of the stars, which in this first part "₃waft[-ing]" Christ (st. 5), is contrasted by the explicit "₈greet[ing]" and

"₈understand[ing]" of the found believer (ibid.), and by the silent revelation of the heart (sts. 7–8). On this laborious recognition of God, with the occurrence of new writing metaphors, Part the First closes: "₈*dark* descending" versus "₅Beyónd *sáying* swéet, past *télling* of *tóngue*" (st. 9). Part the Second, as we have already seen, reduplicates the first: as a language, though a death-language, the tempest, now no longer metaphorical, appears to the desperate crew: "₄storms *búgle* his [Death's] fáme" (st. 11). The correct reading of it coincides again with a passage from a silence, or from a "₇bábble" (st. 17), to a firm and clear word:

17.7   Till a líoness aróse bréasting the bábble,
8   A próphetess tówered in the túmult, a vírginal tóngue tóld.

18.1   Ah, touched in your bower of bone,
2   Are you! turned, for an exquisite smart,
3   Have you! make words break from me here all alone,
4   Do you!—móther of béing in me, héart.

The transformation of the wreck into a sign, word, and text of God begins here to be manifest: in stanza 22 the number of the nuns, *five,* becomes "₂*cipher* of suffering Christ . . . / ₅. . . he scores . . . in scarlet himself on his own bespoken," "₇Stigma, *signal,* cinquefoil token / ₈For *léttering* of the lámb's fleece, rúddying of the róse-fláke." In stanza 29 the "reading" and the metaphor become complete:

29.1   Ah! thére was a héart right!
2   There was síngle éye!
3   *Réad* the *unsh́apeable* shóck níght
4   And *knew* the who and the why;
5   *Wording* it how but by him that present and past,
6   Heaven and earth are *word* of, *worded* by?—

B. *The Ship as a Microcosm*

The literary archetype of the journey, especially as a sea voyage, has proved fairly congenial to English literature. In Hopkins it is even a kind of private archetype. Not only is the "Deutsch-land" the most memorable specimen (within a spectrum ranging from the "crossing" of the youthful "A Vision of the Mermaids" to the solemn landing in the haven of faith in the "Heraclitean Fire"); it also constitutes an important change in the allegorical use of the archetype itself.[1]

Among the numerous allegorical encodings of this archetype in the "Deutschland," one may observe, as in many classical ex-amples, one of a political kind. The nuns and the emigrants leave Germany for America, but actually "land" in England. On this purely factual schema Hopkins superimposes an allegorical one, man's and history's journey. The same thing happens in the twin poem "The Loss of the Eurydice," where, this time explicitly, the wreck becomes an image and symbol of the "₈₈Fast *foundering* own generation." But let us try to document as much as possible the presence of this subterranean political allegory.

The poem closes on the invocation of a "₆ráre-dear Brítain," "inflamed" by the love of Christ, suddenly come back (st. 35). It is not difficult to find in the description of the wreck a parallelism with this hoped-for advent of Christ: in stanza 28 the nun really *sees* Christ coming to her on the waters. The nun is thus identified (in one of the many identifications she undergoes: see below, "The parallelistic web") with England; her sudden vision is identified with the hoped-for sudden vision of England. It is, of course, an England in the making, Catholic and bursting with faith still to come and yet, owing to Hopkins's literal faith in miracles (see, again, below, "Reality of a miracle"), an England that will cer-tainly come into existence in a near future. Stanza 35 not acciden-tally reaffirms both Hopkins's patriotism in its most Victorian terms ("₆More *bríghtening* her, ráre-*dear* Brítain") and the opposi-tion between earthly and heavenly society ("₆as *his réign* rólls") and obviously their hierarchical relation. Of this Augustinian motif there is, I think, incontestable evidence in a series of scattered allu-

1. For a detailed examination of the functions of this archetype in Hopkins's poetry see Marucci 1982.

sions and, above all, in a couple of quasi-parenthetical and digressive stanzas that are very important for our ends.

That Hopkins, in the "Deutschland," is also carrying out an argument on the political division of the contemporary world is easy to see from the epigraph. The specification "exiles by the Falck Laws" almost seems a jarring note or a useless pedantry or a concession to historical exactitude: in fact, it gives us the clue to the argument taking shape in the poem, that about the splitting up of creeds and the fracturing and shattering of the political unity owing also to religious division. On the basis of the frequency of biblical quotations in the poem one may further put forth the hypothesis that stanza 17 conceals an allusion to the biblical episode of the Tower of Babel (Gen. 11:1–9) and the linguistic and political division and dispersion of the earth's population: "₇bábble" ([bæbl]) is a quasi-homophone of Babel ([beibl]). In the following line the metaphor "₈*towe*red" occurs. Furthermore, in stanza 20 and in the first half of stanza 21, Hopkins—in what might seem a gratuitous and unnecessary digression—indirectly reverts to his "dream" of a Christian "pan-civilization" broken with the waning of the Middle Ages and the spreading of the Protestant heresies. One of the many significant coincidences of the poem is that Gertrude, the name of the dauntless nun, of the "₇líoness . . . bréasting the bábble" (st. 17), is also the name of a saint born in the same birthplace as Luther. But the equivalences and the coincidences do not cease here, because they go back to the "original":

20.1	She was first of a five and came
2	Of a coiféd sisterhood.
3	(O Deutschland, double a desperate name!
4	O wórld wíde of its góod!
5	But Gertrude, lily, and Luther, are two of a town,
6	Chríst's líly, and béast of the wáste wóod:
7	From lífe's dáwn it is dráwn dówn,
8	Ábel is Cáin's brother and bréasts they have súcked the sáme.)

21.1	Loathed for a love men knew in them,
2	Banned by land of their birth,
3	Rhíne refúsed them, Thámes would rúin them;

Recall that Luther, in a letter written in 1865, had been contrasted to Savonarola as the "admired author of world-wide heresy in schism" (L III, 18).

C. The Theological and Scotist Frame

In such a way we might re-define the rhetorical frame of the "Deutschland"—which I have discussed at length in Part One from a rigorously synchronic perspective—in the light of the impact and incidence of Hopkins's Scotism. Hopkins, in the "Deutschland," aims not to provide a simple and factual report but to "interpret" the wreck and to share this interpretation with the reader, with all its operative repercussions and implications. Thus the raison d'être of the "Deutschland" is contained, *in nuce,* in Scotus's theology: in the "Deutschland" the poet becomes a poet-theologian using more accessible concepts and notions (the parabolic frame) in order to bring the reader to the truths that are more difficult to grasp (see above, chapter 6, the discussion of the Prologue of the *Oxoniense*). It is not enough, however, to have "understood" the wreck: one should also and above all let Christ enter into his heart and let Him "inflame" it (st. 35). This is the ultimate meaning of the poem in a Scotist perspective.

Scotus's theory of knowledge is in Hopkins the first link in a long chain of borrowings, if not altogether a matrix of a vast and wide-ranging complex of derivations. It seems to me that both parts of the poem present a series of sufficiently unmistakable references to the first and main element of this theory—that is, the distinction between *confused* and *distinct* knowledge (and, one may add, recalling Hopkins's essay on words, between confused and distinct expression)—as well as to the consequent manifestation of God. In Part the First Hopkins arrives at a conscious recognition of God (st. 2, l. 3) starting from a sensation of his presence ("$_7$touch"; "$_8$I feel" [st. 1]). Later on, the perception of the external world, in this case of the marvelous starred vault, is at the same time a perception and recognition ("$_8$understand" [st. 5]) of the Creator. The discovery of Christ as the axis of history—what "₈none would have *known*" [st. 7]—cannot but be, following Scotus, the work first of all of a confused intuition, an intuition of the *heart* ("₈only the heart . . . / ₁Is out with it!" [sts. 7–8]). This process is repeated in Part the Second in the nun, who in the midst of the furious tempest first indistinctly sees Christ ("₃loom" [st. 28]), as in a blurred image, then sees him distinctly and understands and expresses clearly what was initially a simple intuition ("₄*knew* the who and the why" [st. 29]; "₈héard and képt thee *and úttered* thee óutright" [st. 30]).

Another Scotist theory at work in the "Deutschland" is the divine destination of history and the Creation:

The story of the universe is the story of the separation and attempted reconciliation, in time or duration, of two powers which, in eternity, are distinct but never separated: the Mind of God which projects the Divine Idea of Nature, the primordial harmony, and the Will of God which works through matter, through life, but, finally and properly, through the operations of free selves, to re-establish the primordial harmony. The Word of God, the Grace of Christ, working in Nature, is the bridge of re-establishment. . . . (Devlin 1949, 309)

Part the First elaborates this Scotist doctrine where it says that Christ's Incarnation (and Redemption) precede time: the "₂stress" given the Creation "₇rídes tíme like ríding a ríver" (st. 6); the whole Creation, indeed, unconsciously "moves" toward Christ:

8.6   . . . Híther then, lást or fírst,
7   To hero of Calvary, Christ,'s feet—
8   Never ask if *méaning it, wánting it, wárned of it*—mén gó.

This tending of the whole nature to Christ Hopkins called *voluntas ut natura*. The conscious choice of God occurs at the level of *voluntas ut arbitrium,* on which Divine Grace acts, without, however, violating it:

God . . . can shift the self that lies in one [pitch] to a higher, that is / better, pitch of itself. . . . This access is either of grace, which is 'super-nature', to nature or *of more grace to grace already given* . . . ; the action of such assisting grace is . . . threefold . . . (3) elevating, *which lifts the receiver from one cleave of being to another* and to a vital act in Christ: this is truly God's finger touching the very vein of personality. . . . (S, 148, 149, 157–58)

Of this combined action of the will and grace there are in the "Deutschland" almost literal echoes:

1.5   Thou hast bound bones and veins in me, fastened me flesh,
6   And after it almost unmade, what with dread,
7   Thy doing: and dost thou *touch* me afresh?
8   Over again *I feel thy finger* and find thee.

3.6   My heart, but you were dovewinged, I can tell,
7   Carrier-witted, I am bold to boast,
8   To flash from the flame to the flame then, *tower from the grace to the grace.*

Of a final Scotist aspect of the "Deutschland"—the reading of a miracle in the wreck and in the circumstances of the death of the nun, a reading made possible by several synchronic allusions and diachronic supports—I shall speak in the following section.

D. Medieval Aesthetics

Among the medieval aspects I have attributed to Hopkins's textuality, the aesthetic code is undoubtedly the one of which the "Deutschland" offers the most numerous and cogent proofs.

A. THE WRECK AS A PARABLE.   Christ's parables in the Gospel are "all taken from real life" (L III, 374). It is by now beyond dispute that the whole "real life" can become for Hopkins, as a "medieval" author, a religious parable, a coded message of God. The shipwreck, though in itself an exceptional occurrence, does not escape this rule; indeed, its exceptional nature serves to "demonstrate" the most arduous of the truths of faith: the wreck becomes a new parable illustrating how death can be transformed, through faith, into life and salvation. I do not want to insist, after what I have said in Part One, on this specific form of parable; what I here want to point out is how the parabolic nature of the text also manifests itself in the guise of a scriptural and evangelic intertextuality, a quotation, repetition and replica of motives and situations that are already, from the point of view of faith, paradigmatic. It is a further index of what Lotman defines as an aesthetics of identity.

The poem teems with scriptural echoes and quotations—patiently collected and signalled by critics and commentators[2]—ranging from Genesis to the Book of Job, to the Psalms, to the Pauline letters, to the Gospels. This is—owing to the nature of the poem—normal and even predictable, but not in itself very important in the poem's general plan. Such an intertextuality, however, becomes a primary and structural fact once we observe that the "Deutschland" is entirely modelled on two similar episodes in the Gospel; both are referred to in the text, one explicitly and the other cryptically: Christ's calming the tempest and his walking on the water:

And the same day, when the even was come, he saith unto them, Let us pass over unto the other side. And when they had sent away the multitude, they took him even as he was in the ship. And there were also with him other little ships. And there arose a great storm of wind, and the waves beat into the ship, so that it was now full. And he was in the hinder part of the ship, asleep on a pillow: and they awake him, and say unto him, Master, carest thou not that we perish? And he arose, and rebuked the wind, and said unto the sea, Peace, be still. And the wind ceased, and there was a great calm. And he said unto them, Why are ye so fearful? how is it that ye have no faith? And they feared exceedingly, and said one to another, What manner of man is this, that the wind and the sea obey him? (Mark 4: 35–41)

And straightway Jesus constrained his disciples to get into a ship, and to go before him unto the other side, while he sent the multitudes away. And when he had sent the multitudes away, he went up into a mountain

2. See for example Gardner's notes in P II, 254–63, *passim*. In addition to the references already found, I suggest that lines 7–8 of stanza 12 probably contain an allusion to the parable of the Lost Sheep (Matt. 17: 12–14), that "₇heaven of desire" and "₈treasure" of stanza 26 contain another to Matt. 6: 19–20 (the treasure on earth gnawed by rust versus the treasure in heaven, incorruptible), and line 6 of stanza 28 ("₆He was to cure the extremity where he had cast her") "quotes" Christ's frequent healing actions (and also Lazarus's resurrection) in the Gospel.

apart to pray: and when the evening was come, he was there alone. But the ship was now in the midst of the sea, tossed with waves: for the wind was contrary. And in the fourth watch of the night Jesus went unto them, walking on the sea. And when the disciples saw him walking on the sea, they were troubled, saying, It is a spirit; and they cried out for fear. But straightway Jesus spake unto them saying, Be of good cheer; it is I; be not afraid. And Peter answered him and said, Lord, if it be thou, bid me come unto thee on the water. And he said, Come. And when Peter was come down out of the ship, he walked on the water, to go to Jesus. But when he saw the wind boisterous, he was afraid; and beginning to sink, he cried, saying, Lord, save me. And immediately Jesus stretched forth his hand, and caught him, and said unto him, O thou of little faith, wherefore didst thou doubt? And when they were come into the ship, the wind ceased. Then they that were in the ship came and worshipped him, saying, Of a truth thou art the Son of God. (Matt. 14: 22–33)

A comparison of these passages with our poem proves not only the numerous lexical echoes and recurrences but also that Hopkins had them in mind in the "Deutschland," and that he built up the poem on the equivalences and differences he detected in and superimposed on the event he described. The explicit textual echo of this Gospel schema occurs in stanza 25:

5 They were élse-mínded then, áltogéther, the mén
6 Wóke thee with a *We are périshing* [text's italics] in the wéather of
   Gennésaréth.

It is clear from these lines that the five nuns, and more generally the passengers of the ship, repeat the experience of the disciples on the ship in the lake under the storm; also, Sister Gertrude in particular "is" at the same time Peter and Christ. The final lines of stanza 17 and stanza 19 contain the cryptic Gospel quotation (from Matthew) and establish the equation between the nun and Christ. Christ, with his voice, calms the storm, and the same is done by the nun, to whom two of the most traditional of Christ's epithets are given ("₇líoness" and "₈próphetess"):

17.7   Till a líoness aróse bréasting the bábble,
   8   A próphetess tówered in the túmult, a vírginal tóngue tóld.

19.6   . . . she rears herself to divine
  7   Ears, and the call of the tall nun
  8   To the men in the tops and the tackle rode over the storm's
          brawling.

Peter and the other disciples at the end of the Matthew passage
make their profession of faith: so does the nun when in stanza 30
she "₈heard and kept thee and uttered thee outright," and when
in stanza 29 Hopkins hails her as "₇The Simon-Peter of a soul!"
Christ, in Matthew, reassures his dismayed disciple walking on
the water. His "Lord, save me!" matches the nun's "₇'O Christ,
Christ, come quickly' " (st. 24), a cry that, like Peter's, Christ
hears. The celebrated series of aposiopeses of stanza 28 beats the
measure of his approach:

28.1   But how shall I . . . Make me room there;
  2   Reach me a . . . Fancy, come faster—
  3   Strike you the sight of it? look at it loom there,
  4   Thing that she . . . There then! the Master,
  5   Ipse, the only one, Christ, King, Head:

The time lag between the Gospel episode and the wreck of the
"Deutschland" necessitates a didactic use, and consequently a
modification, of the model: in the time of the disciples Christ really transforms the storm into a calm and materially brings about
salvation; man, now, can "awaken" Christ or call him to help (so
that the storm is becalmed, and death is transformed into life)
only at the bottom of his conscience, spiritually.

  B. REALITY OF A MIRACLE.   The two Gospel episodes
that are the model, cryptic but altogether crucial, of the
"Deutschland" are two miracles: this allows us to discuss, before
analyzing another important form of scriptural intertextuality in
the poem, an aspect at which I have frequently hinted in this
work, Hopkins's literal faith in the supernatural and in miracles.
There are good reasons to maintain that the nun's "vision" and
"knowledge" of Christ of stanza 28 (ll. 1–5) and 29 (l. 4) are not
merely for Hopkins hyperbole, something imagined, but on the
contrary something absolutely real. I am in complete agreement,

regarding this interpretation, with E. Schneider, who has first formulated it:[3]

The drift of this stanza [st. 28], then, clearly is that the nun saw Christ's very self; and it seems to me equally clear that what is implied is a super-natural event, not an ambiguous "vision" or a hallucination. . . . Much of what is said about the nun before and after this stanza can be justified, as to what is said and at what length, only if a miracle is pointed to. (Schneider 1968, 29, 31)

It is useful to recall what Hopkins wrote in a sermon: "And in general you will find that what Christ aimed at in his miracles was to breed faith in him [the public] or it being bred to nurse it; to breed it and to nurse it, I say, both in the receiver of the miracle and in all who should witness it or hear of it" (S, 30–31). As Schneider again has written:

Not only did biblical and the early saints' miracles move him [Hopkins] deeply, but he also eagerly sought reasons to believe any accounts of contemporary miraculous healing or other supernatural signs of grace. . . . Miracles enter prominently into the *Deutschland,* and the whole poem really turns on the hint of a miraculous presence through which the wreck and the conversion of England are brought within a single focus. (Schneider 1968, 18–19)

Hopkins himself authorizes these suppositions when in a letter to Bridges he feels the need to make it clear (although he refers to the first, autobiographical part of the poem) that everything "is . . . *literally* true and did all occur" (L I, 47), and when, in another letter, he admits to having been "not over-desirous that the meaning of all should be quite clear, at least unmistakeable" (L I, 50). But even in the absence of this internal evidence, Hopkins's faith in visible divine interventions in the present time is proved by numerous hints, confessions, and allusions in the diaries and in the letters, above all in relation to the dilemma between poetic

3. And with A. Sulloway, who in her turn has elaborated it (Sulloway 1972, 182–83). The point is hotly debated: Cotter (1972, 148) and Downes (1985, 52) resolutely deny that a miracle is implied, while Robinson (1978, 116) agrees with both Schneider and Sulloway.

silence and the writing of poems and the hoped-for conversion of England.

For 6 November 1865 we read in the diary the following entry: "Nov. 6. On this day by God's grace I resolved to give up all beauty *until I had His leave* for it . . ." (J, 71). It is the first of a series of entries that confirm the expectation of (and therefore the faith in) special signs of divine assent or disapproval. Years later, in 1879, Hopkins, answering Bridges's encouragements to publish, wrote:

> I cannot in conscience spend time on poetry, neither have I the inducements and inspirations that make others compose. Feeling, love in particular, is the great moving power and spring of verse and the only person that I am in love with seldom, especially now, *stirs my heart sensibly* and when he does I cannot always "make capital" of it. . . . (L I, 66)[4]

In 1881, with the anniversary of the death of some English Catholic martyrs imminent, Hopkins wrote: "For the 1st of December next is the 300th anniversary of his [Campion's], Sherwin's and Bryant's martyrdom, from which *I expect of heaven some,* I cannot guess what, *great conversion or other blessing* to the Church in England" (L I, 135–36). The last confirmation comes from the private notes of the years 1883–85:

> Also in some med. today I earnestly asked our Lord to watch over my compositions, not to preserve them from being lost or coming to nothing, for that I am very willing they should be, but they might not do me harm through the enmity or imprudence of any man or my own; that he should have them as his own and employ or not employ them as he should see fit. *And this I believe is heard.* (S, 253–54)

I will support this with only one extratextual proof: Hopkins's interest in the French mystic and seer Marie Lataste (1822–47) and the frequency of quotations from her writings in his commentary to the *Spiritual Exercises* (see S, 129 151, 175, 185, 200 and the biographical information and anthological selection provided by Devlin in S, 325–37).

---

4. Sulloway (1972, 184–85) also remembers Hopkins's admiration for Plato and Wordsworth, as men having experienced what "does not happen to other men, as having *seen something*" (L II, 147; Hopkins's italics).

C. THE APOCALYPTIC PREMONITION. To prove further the extent of the scriptural intertextuality in the "Deutschland," and at the same time its entropy (or the prodigiously multigraded character of its semantics), one cannot fail to signal another biblical model unmistakably active in the poem, that of Revelation. A. G. Sulloway deserves full credit for having synthesized and convincingly developed an investigation that was not new but had been only superficially pursued by previous critics.

An accurate inspection of Hopkins's texts establishes his familiarity and even obsession with apocalyptic themes and allusions. This is an element that, for Sulloway, Hopkins shares with the literature and homiletics of an age dominated, for various cultural and social phenomena, by an acute and widespread feeling of uncertainty about the future of mankind and by the expectation of an imminent end of the world. Echoes of this are traceable in several poems: "Heraclitean Fire," the fragment "The times are nightfall . . . ," and, with absolute evidence, "Spelt from Sibyl's Leaves." Yet, while in other Victorians and in all these texts we have an "elliptical treatment of the second Advent" (Sulloway 1972, 178), the "Deutschland" is, on the contrary, a "complete Apocalypse" (ibid., 159) "consciously based upon Revelation from beginning to end" (227, note 56). Hopkins starts from a certain number of "factual details" but subsequently subjects them to an allegorical and symbolic transfiguration in an apocalyptic sense, "translates the factual outlines of the *Deutschland*'s ordeal into apocalyptic language" (186, 191). The demonstration of this assertion is carried out on several registers and levels of comparison. Apart from some analogies that may appear strained or debatable, Sulloway's general analysis and single findings are absolutely correct and convincing.

Between Revelation and the "Deutschland" there are, first of all, parallelisms and analogies of a general character:

Both the Apocalypse and *The Wreck of the Deutschland* move from terror to joy, and from a private vision to the public catastrophe that was prophesied in the vision, and finally to a harvest of souls raising their voices in adoration of the "Lord of living and dead" (stanza 1). Like the Apocalypse, *The Wreck of the Deutschland* is divided into two parts: a short prologue embodying the private vision of one of God's seers, full of swooning terror and comfort; and a long section to follow, in which the series of ghastly punishments and warnings function as analogues for the potential fate of all mankind. (Sulloway 1972, 191–92)

Having established this general schema, Sulloway finds a series of exact equivalences: the "swooning" of stanza 2, line 6, the "escape" toward Christ of stanza 8, lines 6–8, the trumpets, the drums, the swords, the deluges and the flames of death of stanza 11, which are as many "voices" of the "usual apocalyptic catalogue of deaths." "In both works of prophecy," furthermore, " 'the shipwrack' or the destruction becomes a 'harvest' of saved souls as well as a pile of bodies awaiting damnation: the 'tempest' carries the 'grain' for Christ" (ibid., 193). Sulloway also notices that the "colour scheme" of the poem (red, white, gold) is the same as, and has the same symbolic values as, the Apocalypse, and that, within this contextual parallelism, the death of the nuns takes on the semblance of a "divine repetition of the death of the Apocalyptic martyrs"; the death of the passengers is a "copy of the deaths of the careless sinners in Revelation" (187, 188). The nuns' "₇sisterly séal[ed]" (st. 23), concomitant with the arrival of the seraphim, and the trumpets spreading death in stanzas 11 and 12 are other elements with counterparts in Revelation. The nun's invocation to Christ, too, resembles for Sulloway "Christ's loving admonitions to the suffering martyrs in Revelation" (189).

In conclusion, the Apocalypse undoubtedly has in the "Deutschland" a very high modelling capacity. This makes the poem unique in Victorian literature:

By means of prophecy, Hopkins has translated a contemporary "ordeal of the waters," which took place on 7 December 1875, into a mystical event. . . . *The Wreck of the Deutschland* is a pivotal work in Victorian literature because it is the only major Victorian work in a distinctively aesthetic form—as opposed to a sermon—that treats the Apocalypse as indisputable prophecy. . . . Lay writers like Tennyson or Morris . . . placed no comprehensive dogma before the public. They did not take the prospect of the second coming literally. . . . And so, because *The Wreck of the Deutschland* is the only major Victorian work in a lay form that presents the matter and the symbols of the Apocalypse to the public as absolute dogma, it is also the only one that is totally shaped by the Apocalypse. (Sulloway 1972, 194–95)

D. NUMERICAL SYMBOLISM. It is an absolutely singular phenomenon of medieval aesthetics—and *qua* medieval, markedly foreign to post-medieval cultures—that sense in literary works springs not only from the linguistic signs of which they are made but also from supplementary channels, such as the number of lines and metrical and stanzaic units and other partitions of which they consist. Moreover, owing to the high semiotic spirit pervading all aspects of its organized life and culture, a marked sense of proportion and partition reigns in the literary works of the Middle Ages, while certain numbers take on a supplementary meaning and even certain symbolic values according to an elementary theological and religious code. This phenomenon is carefully studied by Curtius with an analysis of "numerical composition" in Dante (above all, at the level of the groupings of the characters in the three realms: Curtius 1953, 374–78) and with a survey of the most recurrent numbers in medieval authors (see, ibid., excursus XV, "Numerical Composition," 501–9). Concerning the origins of this numerical symbolism, Curtius mentions the authority enjoyed in the Middle Ages by a versicle of the Book of Wisdom (11: 20), "omnia in mensura et numero et pondere disposuisti" (ibid., 504): "Through this verse, number was sanctified as a form-bestowing factor in the divine work of creation" (ibid.). It is in the light of these premises that there are good reasons to maintain that Hopkins exploited numerical symbolism to a far greater extent than the average of post-medieval authors and literatures.

The fortune of certain numbers in the Middle Ages may depend, simply, on their "aesthetic significance," or their "theological significance" (3, 7, 9, 12, 33). We find probatory examples of numerical significance in Hopkins even before or outside the "Deutschland." In a youthful medieval "cast," "The Queen's

Crowning," the number 3 recurs almost obsessively; 7, else-where, indicates, along with 6 or 5, paradigmatic measures:

> *"A Vision of the Mermaids"*
>
> 34   I gazed unhinder'd: Mermaids six or seven

> *"A Voice from the World"*
>
> 6   Now like the bird that shapes alone
> 7   A turn of seven notes or five,

The same can be said of 10 or 12:

> *"Binsey Poplars"*
>
> 20   Tén or twélve, ónly ten or twelve
> 21   Strókes of havoc únsélve
> 22   The sweet especial scene,

> *"As kingfishers catch fire . . ."*
>
> 12   . . . For Christ plays in ten thousand places.

There is a decidedly symbolic numerical use in "The Half-way House": "$_{12}$Peace and food cheered me where four rough ways meet," where the "four ways" may represent the Cross.

An investigation of Hopkins's numerical symbolism in the "Deutschland" may be carried out along two lines: (1) the symbolism of the total number of lines, parts, and stanzas, and of the number of stanzas in each part; and (2) the symbolism of the occurrences of numbers in the poem. As to the first, the 280 lines of the poem, the 35 stanzas (10 in the first part, 25 in the second) seem but to point to a medieval predilection for "round figures" (5, 10 or multiples) and the proportionality and symmetry of parts (a predilection so well highlighted in a letter to Dixon: L II, 71–72). About the second line, on the contrary, one can observe that Hopkins "interprets" and/or "adjusts," in a symbolic sense, several pieces of objective numerical data (taken from the reports of the wreck) and makes them support the religious demonstration he is undertaking in the poem that describes that very wreck.

For certain numbers the symbolic use is tenuous as well as conventional: 3 is for example explicitly referred to the Trinity (st.

9, l. 2 and st. 34, l. 5). Not so 2, which, as in "Spelt from Sibyl's Leaves," connotes dualism and opposition (st. 20: Gertrude versus Luther = Abel versus Cain). Stanza 12 is *par excellence* the stanza of numbers. There is here both an adjustment of figures and a care for symmetry and proportion:

12.1   —On Saturday sailed from Bremen,
    2   American-outward-bound,
    3   Take settler and seamen, tell men with women,
    4   *Two hundred* souls in the round—
    5   O Father, not under thy feathers nor ever as guessing
    6   The goal was a shoal, of *a fourth* the doom to be drowned;
    7   Yet *did* [text's italics] the dark side of the bay of thy
                   blessing
    8 Not vault them, the *million* of rounds of thy mercy not reeve
       even them in?

(In "The Loss of the Eurydice" we find ",₂Three hundred souls, O alas! on board"). The number 12 recurs in the "Deutschland" in stanza 15: "₄Hope was twelve hours gone." The number 5, however, is the most symbolically loaded in a medieval sense, and in a perfectly consequential way if we keep in mind the allegorical and argumentative plan of the poem:

22.1   Five! the finding and sake
    2   And cipher of suffering Christ.

23.5   . . . and these thy daughters
    6   And five-livèd and leavèd favour and pride,
    7   Are sisterly sealed in wild waters,

The "cipher of suffering Christ" had already appeared in "Barn-floor and Winepress":

13   For us the Vine was fenced with thorn,
14   Five ways the precious branches torn;

in "New Readings":

11   From wastes of rock He brings
12   Food for five thousand . . .

and several times in "Rosa Mystica":

37   How many leaves had it?—Five they were then,
38   Five like the senses and members of men;
39   Five is their number by nature, but now
40   They multiply, multiply who can tell how?[5]

E. THE PARALLELISTIC WEB. The presence in the "Deutschland" of an allegorical and demonstrative schema similar to that of the rhetorical discourse with its canonical partitions is already a formal though not decisive characteristic of *medievalism*.[6] This is reinforced by the assortment of tropes: we find harvest metaphors ("$_8$is the shípwrack then a hárvest" [st. 31]), kinship metaphors ("$_4$móther of béing in me, héart" [st. 18]), food metaphors ("$_2$giver of . . . bread" [st. 1]), nautical metaphors ("$_3$heaven-háven of the rewárd" [st. 35]), sexual metaphors ("$_7$here was heart-throe, birth of a brain" [st. 30]), metaphors implying writing on others' dictation ("$_3$make words break from me here all alone, / $_4$Do you!" [st. 18]), "inexpressibility *topoi*" ("$_5$Beyónd sáying swéet, past télling of tóngue" [st. 9]).[7] Yet, to reduce the "Deutschland" to a collection of medieval *topoi* does not do full justice to the aesthetic value and originality of the poem, because it implies a controlled and mechanical use of certain stylistic devices. It is our objective, as always, to point out both the letter and the spirit of Hopkins's operation. The argumentative plan of the poem has as its generative nucleus a formulation that, unsupported, could hardly pierce the average credibility of the addressee. Within that plan the tropic uses provide the "translation into images" and substitutive enunciation that, as in the great poetic works of the Middle Ages, collaborate in rendering that formulation and demonstration more credible and less irritating. Tropes function in the "Deutschland" both in a quantitative and

5. For the symbolism of number 5 as also a Tractarian element see L. Strachey's *Eminent Victorians*, chapter I, "Cardinal Manning."

6. On rhetoric in the Middle Ages, and on the penetration of its rules into the literary works, see Curtius 1953, chapter 4, "Rhetoric" (62–78) and chapter 8, "Poetry and Rhetoric" (145–66).

7. On the medieval origins of these *topoi* and for a vast exemplification see again Curtius 1953, chapter 5, "Topics" (79–105), and chapter 7, "Metaphorics," 128–44. For the "inexpressibility *topoi*" see 159–62.

a qualitative sense: we have both a tropic accumulation and disautomatization. In stanza 4 man's irresistible gravitation toward Christ—with which death is ultimately subverted and annulled—is signified through a rapid succession of four heterogeneous metaphors, "$_7$a vein / $_8$Of the góspel próffer, a préssure, a prínciple, Chríst's gíft." In stanza 22, similarly, Hopkins submits to the credibility of his addressee the symbolism of the number of the nuns, using another figure of tropic accumulation:

22.1	Five! the finding and sake
2	And cipher of suffering Christ.
	....
7	Stigma, signal, cinquefoil token
8	For léttering of the lámb's fléece, rúddying of the róse-fláke.

The same occurs in stanza 28, where the addressee witnesses the real apparition of Christ: "$_4$There then! the Master, / $_5$*Ípse,* the ónly one, Chríst, Kíng, Héad." The heart's sudden intuition, or the exultation of man appropriating Christ, "$_2$best or worst / $_3$Word last," is illustrated in stanza 8, by a well-known metaphor:

3	. . . How a lush-kept plush-capped sloe
4	Will, mouthed to flesh-burst,
5	Gush!—flush the man, the being with it, sour or sweet
6	Brim, in a flásh, fúll! . . .

Concerning tropic uses (analogies, similes, comparisons, etc.), the aspect of medievalism that decidedly claims our attention is, however, a different one. We have seen in a previous chapter that the Journal of the years 1866–75 shows the progressive reorganization and harmonization of a cosmos perceived as a chaotic and discontinuous whole—shows, we said with another metaphor, the "rhyming" of out-of-tune and dissonant elements, one with another and all with their common denominator and "original," God. The "Deutschland," the first poetic fruit after seven years of silence, proves in this sense to be the natural and ideal prolongation of the Journal, in that it shares its search for "rhymes" and even makes it more systematic, detecting as it does in the wreck a meshing of coincidences, syntagmatic similarities and ana logues and paradigmatic references indeed prodigious and in any case inconceivable for the Victorian audience.[8]

Hopkins's "rhyming" action in the "Deutschland" develops along two planes: (1) union and identification of as many normally distinct and disunited or simply neutral aspects as possible; (2) fresh discovery—in a dazzling paradigmatic crescendo—of the original of each single copy. The original nucleus, the general and archisemic parallelism of the poem is DEATH ~ LIFE. It is announced in stanza 4, line 4, and is periodically reaffirmed: in stanza 7, "₃Warm-laid grave of a womb-life grey"; in stanza 23, "₂Drawn to the Life that died"; in stanza 28, "₇Do, deal, lord it with living and dead." It is reformulated, and transposed into images, in stanza 31: ₈SHIPWRACK, ₈TEMPEST ~ ₈HARVEST. The whole first part of the poem can be said to be an effort to transcend appearances and to see the coincidence and unification, at the bottom, of what on the surface is opposition: "₄Lord of living and dead" (st. 1), "₂best or worst / ₃Word," "₅sour or sweet," "₆lást or fírst" (st. 8), "₆lightning and love," "₆winter and warm" (st. 9). In the following stanzas we have "₈Storm flákes" which become "₈scróll-leaved flówers, lily shówers" (st. 21), and Christ defined "₈wild-worst Best" (st. 24). It is principally in Part the Second that we witness an increase of the parallelistic links in the main "actants" of the wreck: I, SHIP, PASSENGERS, NUNS, NUN (GERTRUDE). The "redoubling" between the two parts of the poem includes first of all the parallelism I-NUN (visible in sts. 19, ll. 1–2 and 24, ll. 1–4); but the experience of Part the First has two paradigmatic copies (ST. PAUL and ST. AUGUSTINE [st. 10, ll. 5–6]), besides a syntagmatic one. The representative function (and therefore the parallelism of a synecdochic type) performed by the NUNS in relation to the PASSENGERS, and by the NUN in relation to the other NUNS, is quite evident. As regards the SHIP, and above all the NUN, stanza 20 is an exemplary running fire of nonconventional parallelistic links. The SHIP is the symbol of the country of which it bears the name, doubly "desperate" because also a sym-

8. As we have seen above (Part Two, chapter 2), Bump (1982) links this search with the biblical typology of the Tractarians. Motto (1984) too notices how Hopkins "recovers meaning for otherwise disconnected events" (127).

bol of religious division; we have furthermore: ₅GERTRUDE (nun of that name) ~ SAINT GERTRUDE, then CATHOLICS ~ ₅GERTRUDE ~ SAINT GERTRUDE ~ ₈ABEL on the one hand, and on the other PROTESTANTS ~ ₅LUTHER ~ ₈CAIN. The greatest parallelistic supply is however found in the NUN. Not only is she a homologue of the "I" of Part the First and, as we have just seen, of SAINT GERTRUDE, but she takes on, in Part the Second, ever-different identifications, stanza after stanza. In stanzas 17 and 24 the NUN is first identified with ST. JOHN THE BAPTIST (she is a "₈prophetess" [st. 17] and she "₈christens her wild-worst Best" [st. 24]); then in stanza 23 she chooses, like ST. FRANCIS, the way of the Cross (ll. 1–2) and in stanzas 25 (while the PASSENGERS repeat the crossing of the Apostles in the lake of Gennesareth under the storm) and 29 she is identified with ST. PETER ("₇The Simon-Peter of a soul!"). The last two paradigms of the NUN are CHRIST and the VIRGIN. The NUN's death gains her the stigmata of a SACRIFICE and of CRUCIFIXION ("₆The appealing of the Passion is tenderer in prayer apart" [st. 27]), and the recurrence of the feast of the Immaculate Conception—on the eve of which the wreck occurred—exhibits its profound motivation in its telltale coincidence with another birth of Christ:

30.3   What was the feast followed the night
4   Thou hadst glory of this nun?—
5   Feast of the one woman without stain.
6   For so conceivèd, so to conceive thee is done;
7   But here was heart-throe, birth of a brain,
8   Word, that heard and kept thee and uttered thee outright.[9]

9. On the "comprehensive . . . role" of the nun in the "Deutschland" Sulloway (1972, 190–91) makes observations quite similar to mine. She also notes, with reference to the imagery of stanza 7 (where the Passion is ambiguously described in terms of birth) and to stanza 30 quoted here, that "by a series of linked metaphors, Hopkins suggests a divine analogy between three archetypal scenes of suffering, the birth of the Christ Child, the agony on Calvary, and the nun's death as a symbol of God's wrath and man's martyrdom" (190).

Collections

1945 *Gerard Manley Hopkins by the Kenyon Critics.* New York: New Directions. Page references are to the reprint, 1973.
1966 *Problèmes du langage.* (Special issue of *Diogène* 51). Paris: Gallimard.

General Bibliography

Abbott, C. C. 1935. "Introduction" to *The Letters of Gerard Manley Hopkins to Robert Bridges.*

Alighieri, Dante. *Tutte le opere.* Firenze: Sansoni, 1965.

Altick, R. D. 1957. *The English Common Reader: A Social History of the Mass Reading Public, 1800–1900,* Chicago: University of Chicago Press.

Aristotle, *Poetics.* Translated by I. Bywater. Oxford: Clarendon Press, 1909.

———. *Rhetoric.* Translated by J. H. Freese. Cambridge, Mass.: Harvard University Press, 1926.

Arnheim, R. 1959. "Information Theory. An Introductory Note." *Journal of Aesthetics and Art Criticism* 17.

Augustine, St. *De civitate Dei.* 2 vols. Corpus Christianorum. Series latina. Turnhout: Brepols, 1955.

———. *The City of God.* 2 vols. Translated by M. Dods. Edinburgh: T. & T. Clark, 1871.

Barthes, R. 1970. "L'ancienne rhétorique." *Communications* 16.

Bender, T. K. 1966. *Gerard Manley Hopkins: The Classical Background and Critical Reception of His Work.* Baltimore: The Johns Hopkins University Press.

Bense, M. 1965. *Aesthetica.* Baden-Baden: Agis Verlag.

Bergonzi, B. 1977. *Gerard Manley Hopkins.* London: MacMillan.

Bottalla, P., G. Marra, and F. Marucci, eds. 1991. *G. M. Hopkins. Tradition and Innovation.* Ravenna: Longo.

Bottrall, M., ed. 1975. *Gerard Manley Hopkins: Poems. A Casebook.* London: MacMillan.

Boyle, R. 1961. *Metaphor in Hopkins*. Chapel Hill: University of North Carolina Press.

Brémond, A. 1934. "La poésie naïve et savante de Hopkins." *Études* 5.

Bridges, R. 1918. "Preface to Notes" in *Poems of Gerard Manley Hopkins*.

Briggs, A. 1968. *Victorian Cities*. Harmondsworth: Pelican Books. Reprint.

———. 1977. *Victorian People*. Harmondsworth: Penguin Books. Reprint.

Buckley, J. H. 1966. *The Victorian Temper: A Study in Literary Culture*. London: F. Cass and Co.

Bump, J. 1977. "Hopkins' Imagery and Medievalist Poetics." *Victorian Poetry* 15.

———. 1982. *Gerard Manley Hopkins*. Boston: Twayne.

Cohen, J. 1966. *Structure du langage poétique*. Paris: Flammarion.

Collins, J. 1947. "Philosophical Themes in Gerard Manley Hopkins." *Thought* 22.

Coogan, M. 1950. "Inscape and Instress: Further Analogies with Scotus." *PMLA* 65.

Coons, E., and D. Kraehenbuehl. 1958. "Information as Measure of Structure in Music." *Journal of Music Theory* 2:2.

Cotter, J. F. 1972. *Inscape: The Christology and Poetry of Gerard Manley Hopkins*. Pittsburgh, Pa.: University of Pittsburgh Press.

Cox, R. G. 1968. "The Reviews and Magazines." In B. Ford, ed. 1968.

Croce, B. 1937. "Un Gesuita inglese poeta." *La Critica* 35:2.

Curtius, E. R. 1953. *European Literature and the Latin Middle Ages*. Translated by W. R. Trask. London: Routledge and Kegan Paul. Originally published as *Europäische Literatur und lateinisches Mittelalter* (Bern: Francke, 1948).

Davie, D. 1952. *Purity of Diction in English Verse*. London: Routledge and Kegan Paul. Page references are to the reprint, 1967.

Devlin, C. 1935. "Hopkins and Duns Scotus." *New Verse* 14 (April 1935). Page references are to the partial reprint in M. Bottrall, ed. 1975.

———. 1946. "An Essay on Scotus." *The Month* 182.

———. 1949. "Time's Eunuch." *The Month* N.S. 1.

———. 1950. "The Image and the Word." *The Month* N.S. 3.

———. 1967. "Scotus and Hopkins." In *The Sermons and Devotional Writings of Gerard Manley Hopkins,* ed. C. Devlin.

De Wulf, M. 1909. *History of Medieval Philosophy*. Translated by P. Coffey. London: Longmans.

Downes, D. A. 1960. *Gerard Manley Hopkins. A Study of His Ignatian Spirit*. London: Vision Press.

———. 1961. "The Hopkins Enigma." *Thought* 36.

———. 1965. *Victorian Portraits: Hopkins and Pater*. New York: Bookman Associates-Twayne.

———. 1983. *The Great Sacrifice: Studies in Hopkins*. Lanham, Md.: University Press of America.

———. 1985. *Hopkins' Sanctifying Imagination*. Lanham, Md.: University Press of America.

Duns Scotus, Johannes. 1968–69. *Opera Omnia*. 16 vols. Foreword by Tullio Gregory. Hildesheim: Georg Olms Verlagsbuchhandlung [facsimile reprint of the Lyon edition, 1639].

Eco, U., ed. 1972. *Estetica e teoria dell'informazione*. Milan: Bompiani.

Eliot, T. S. 1934. *After Strange Gods. A Primer of Modern Heresy*. London: Faber.

Ellsberg, M. L. 1987. *Created to Praise: The Language of Gerard Manley Hopkins*. New York: Oxford University Press.

Empson, W. 1930. *Seven Types of Ambiguity*. London: Chatto and Windus.

Faccani, R., and U. Eco, eds. 1969. *I sistemi di segni e lo strutturalismo sovietico*. Milan: Bompiani.

Ford, B., ed. 1968. *The Pelican Guide to English Literature*. Vol. 6, *From Dickens to Hardy*. Harmondsworth: Penguin Books.

Foucault, M. 1966. *Les mots et les choses*. Paris: Gallimard.

Gallet, R. 1984. *G. M. Hopkins ou l'excès de présence*. Paris: FAC Editions.

Gardner, W. H. 1949. *Gerard Manley Hopkins (1844–1889). A Study of Poetic Idiosyncrasy in Relation to Poetic Tradition*. 2 vols. London: Secker and Warburg [Vol I, 1944; vol. II, 1949]. Page references are to the reprint (London: Oxford University Press, 1969).

Gardner, W. H., and C. Devlin. 1950. "Correspondence." *The Month* N.S. 4.

Génette, G. 1966. *Figures*. Paris: Editions de Seuil.

Gérard, A. 1946. "Duns Scot et Hopkins." *Revue de langues vivantes* 12.

Greimas, A. J. 1983. *Structural Semantics. An Attempt at a Method*. Translated by D. MacDowell, R. Scleifer, and A. Velie. Lincoln and London: University of Nebraska Press. Originally published as *Sémantique structurale* (Paris: Larousse, 1966).

Grendi, E. 1970. *L'Inghilterra vittoriana*. Firenze: Sansoni.

Grigson, G. 1955. *Gerard Manley Hopkins*. London: Longmans.

Groupe μ. 1970. *Rhétorique Générale*. Paris: Larousse.

Harris, D. A. 1982. *Inspirations Unbidden: The Terrible Sonnets of Gerard Manley Hopkins*. Berkeley and Los Angeles: University of California Press.

Hartman, G. H. 1954. "The Dialectic of Sense-Perception." In G. H. Hartman, *The Unmediated Vision: An Interpretation of Wordsworth, Hopkins, Rilke, and Valéry*. New Haven, Conn.: Yale University Press. Page references are to the reprint in Hartman, 1966.

———. 1966. "Introduction: Poetry and Justification." In G. H. Hartman, ed., *Hopkins: A Collection of Critical Essays*, Englewood Cliffs, N.J.: Prentice Hall.

Heller, E. 1952. *The Disinherited Mind*. London: Bowes and Bowes.

Heuser, A. 1958. *The Shaping Vision of Gerard Manley Hopkins*. London: Oxford University Press. Page references are to the reprint (London: Archon Books, 1968).

The Holy Bible, King James Version. New York: American Bible Society, n. d.

Ignatius of Loyola, St. *Exercitia Spiritualia*. Literal version from the Spanish autograph, annotated by R. P. J. Roothan. Ratisbon: F. Pustet, 1920.

Ingarden, R. 1960. *Das literarische Kunstwerk*. 2d ed. Tübingen: Niemeyer.

Jakobson, R. 1963. *Essais de linguistique générale*, Paris: Editions de Minuit.

Johnson, A. L. 1991. "Phonetic and Syntactic Patterning in G. M. Hopkins's 'God's Grandeur'." In P. Bottalla, G. Marra, and F. Marucci, eds. 1991.

Johnson, W. S. 1968. *Gerard Manley Hopkins: The Poet as Victorian*. Ithaca, N.Y.: Cornell University Press.

Kempis, Thomas à. *Imitation of Christ*. Translated by E. Daplyn. New York: Sheed and Ward, 1978.

Kierkegaard, Søren. 1944. *Either-Or*. Translated by W. Lowrie. 2 vols. Princeton, N.J.: Princeton University Press.

Klingopoulos, G. D. 1968. "Notes on the Victorian Scene" and "The Literary Scene." In B. Ford, ed. 1968.

Kristeva, J. 1969. Σημειωτική. *Recherches pour une sémanalyse*. Paris: Seuil.

———. 1970. *Le texte du roman*. The Hague-Paris: Mouton.

Landow, G. P. 1980. *Victorian Types, Victorian Shadows: Biblical Typology in Victorian Literature, Art, and Thought*. Boston: Routledge and Kegan Paul.

———. 1989. "Elegant Jeremiahs. The Genre of the Victorian Sage." In J. Clubbe and J. Meckier, eds., *Victorian Perspectives*. London: MacMillan, 1989.

Lausberg, H. 1982. *Elemente der literarischen Rhetorik*. 7th ed. Munich: Hueber.

Leavis, F. R. 1932. *New Bearings in English Poetry*. London: Chatto and Windus. Page references are to the reprint (Harmondsworth: Penguin Books, 1967).

Lewis, C. S. 1964. *The Discarded Image*. Cambridge: Cambridge University Press.

Lichtmann, M. L. 1989. *The Contemplative Poetry of Gerard Manley Hopkins*. Princeton, N.J.: Princeton University Press.

Longinus (Cassius). *On Sublimity*. Translated by D. A. Russell. Oxford: Oxford University Press, 1965.

Lotman, J. M. 1969. "Il problema di una tipologia della cultura." Italian translation of "K probleme tipologii kul'tury," *Trudy po znakovym sistemam* 3. Tartu, 1967. In R. Faccani and U. Eco, eds. 1969.

———. 1973. "Il problema del segno e del sistema segnico nella tipologia della cultura russa prima del XX secolo." Italian translation of "Problema znakovosti i znakovoy sistemy v tipologii russkoj kul'tury pervoj poloviny XX veka." In J. M. Lotman and B. Uspenskij, eds. 1973.

———. 1977. *The Structure of the Artistic Text.* Trans. G. Lenhoff and R. Vroon. Ann Arbor: The University of Michigan. Originally published as *Struktura chudozestvennogo teksta* (Moscow: Iskusstvo, 1971).

———. 1990. *Universe of the Mind. A Semiotic Theory of Culture.* Translated by A. Shukman. London: I. B. Tauris.

Lotman, J. M., and B. Uspenskij. 1973. *Ricerche semiotiche. Nuove tendenze delle scienze umane nell'URSS.* Italian translation of *Semioticeskie issledovanija.*

———. 1975. *Tipologia della cultura.* Edited by R. Faccani and M. Marzaduri. Milan: Bompiani. Italian translation of *Stat'i po tipologii kul'tury.* Tartu, 1973.

———. 1978. "On the Semiotic Mechanism of Culture." *New Literary History* 9:2. English translation of "O semioticeskom mechanizme kul'tury," *Trudy po znakovym sistemam* 5. Tartu, 1971.

MacChesney, D. 1968. *A Hopkins Commentary: An Explanatory Commentary on the Main Poems, 1876–89.* London: University of London Press.

MacLuhan, H. M. 1945. "The Analogical Mirrors." In Collections 1945.

MacKenzie, N. 1968. *Hopkins.* Edinburgh: Oliver and Boyd.

———. 1981. *A Reader's Guide to Gerard Manley Hopkins.* Ithaca, N.Y.: Cornell University Press.

Mariani, P. L. 1970. *A Commentary on the Complete Poems of Gerard Manley Hopkins.* Ithaca, N.Y.: Cornell University Press.

Marucci, F. 1977. *Gerard Manley Hopkins. Il silenzio e la parola.* Pisa: Giardini.

———. 1982. "Gerard Manley Hopkins. Poesia e parabola." In *Profili di scrittori.* Milan: Edizioni "Letture."

Melchiori, G. 1956. "Two Mannerists: James and Hopkins." In G. Melchiori, *The Tightrope Walkers. Studies in Mannerism in Modern English Literature,* London: Routledge and Kegan Paul.

Miles, J. 1945. "The Sweet and Lovely Language." In Collections 1945.

Miller, J. Hillis. 1963. *The Disappearance of God. Five Nineteenth-Century Writers.* Cambridge, Mass.: Harvard University Press.

Milroy, J. 1977. *The Language of Gerard Manley Hopkins.* London: André Deutsch.

Mizener, A. 1945. "Victorian Hopkins." In Collections 1945.

Moles, A. A. 1958. *Théorie de l'information et perception esthétique.* Paris: Flammarion.

———. 1960. "L'analyse des structures du message poétique aux différents niveaux de la sensibilité." In *Poetics,* Proceedings of the I International Congress Devoted to Problems of Poetics, Warsaw, 18–27 August 1960, ed. by the Polska Akademia Nauk and the Institut Badau Literackich, Paustwowe Wydawnictvo Naukowe, Warsaw. Italian translation in *Il Verri* 14 (1967).

Morghen, R. 1968. *Medioevo cristiano.* Bari: Laterza.

Motto, M. 1984. *"Mined with a Motion." The Poetry of Gerard Manley Hopkins.* New Brunswick, N.J.: Rutgers University Press.

Murry, J. Middleton 1919. "The Poetry of Gerard Manley Hopkins." *Athenaeum* (June 1919). Page references are to the partial reprint in M. Bottrall, ed. 1975.

The New Cambridge Bibliography of English Literature, ed. G. Watson. Cambridge: Cambridge University Press, 1969. Vol. 3, 1800–1900.

Newman, J. H. *An Essay in Aid of a Grammar of Assent.* Notre Dame: University of Notre Dame Press, 1979. First published 1870.

———. *Loss and Gain.* Oxford: Oxford University Press, 1986. First published 1848.

Noon, W. T. 1949. "The Three Languages of Poetry." In N. Weyand and R. V. Schoder, eds. 1949.

Ong, W. J., 1949. "Hopkins' Sprung Rhythm and the Life of English Poetry." In N. Weyand and R. V. Schoder, eds. 1949.

———. 1986. *Hopkins, the Self, and God.* Toronto: University of Toronto Press.

Pagnini, M. 1976. *Shakespeare e il paradigma della specularità.* Pisa: Pacini.

———. 1988. "La critica letteraria come integrazione dei livelli dell'opera." In M. Pagnini, *Semiosi,* Bologna: Il Mulino, 1988.

Pater, W. *Marius the Epicurean.* Harmondsworth: Penguin Books, 1985. First published 1885.

Perelman, C., and L. Olbrechts-Tyteca. 1971. *The New Rhetoric. A Treatise on Argumentation.* Translated by J. Wilkinson and P. Weaver. Notre Dame and London: University of Notre Dame Press. 2d printing.

Peters, W. A. M. 1948. *Gerard Manley Hopkins. A Critical Essay toward the Understanding of His Poetry.* London: Oxford University Press.

Pick, J. 1942. *Gerard Manley Hopkins. Priest and Poet.* London: Oxford University Press.

Piper, D. 1965. *Painting in England 1500–1880.* Harmondsworth: Penguin Books.

Praz, M. 1968. *Storia della letteratura inglese.* Florence: Sansoni.

Read, H. 1933. "The Poetry of Gerard Manley Hopkins." In H. Read, *English Critical Essays, Twentieth Century.* London: Oxford University Press, 1933. Page references are to the partial reprint in M. Bottrall, ed. 1975.

Richards, I. E. 1926. "Gerard Hopkins." Page references are to the partial reprint in M. Bottrall, ed. 1975.

Ritz, J.-G. 1963. *Le poète Gérard Manley Hopkins s.j. (1844–1889). Sa vie et son Oeuvre*. Paris: Didier.

Roberts, G., ed. 1987. *Gerard Manley Hopkins. The Critical Heritage*. London and New York: Routledge and Kegan Paul.

Robinson, J. 1978. *In Extremity: A Study of Gerard Manley Hopkins*. Cambridge: Cambridge University Press.

Sapir, E. 1921. "Hopkins." *Poetry* (September 1921). Page references are to the partial reprint in M. Bottrall, ed. 1975.

Šaumjan, S. K. 1966. "La cybernétique et la langue." In *Collections* 1966.

Schneider, E. W. 1968. *The Dragon in the Gate: Studies in the Poetry of Gerard Manley Hopkins*. Berkeley and Los Angeles: University of California Press.

Scotus. See Duns Scotus, Johannes.

Serpieri, A. 1969. *Hopkins Eliot Auden. Saggi sul parallelismo poetico*. Bologna: Pàtron.

Sprinker, M. 1980. *"A Counterpoint of Dissonance": The Aesthetics and Poetry of Gerard Manley Hopkins*. Baltimore: The Johns Hopkins University Press.

Strachey, L. 1918. *Eminent Victorians*. London: Chatto and Windus.

Sulloway, A. G. 1972. *Gerard Manley Hopkins and the Victorian Temper*. London: Routledge and Kegan Paul.

Thomas, A. 1968. "Was Hopkins a Scotist Before He Read Scotus?" In *Studia Scholastico-Scholastica, 4. De doctrina Johannis Duns Scoti*, vol. 4, *Scotismus decurso saeculorum*. Rome.

―――. 1969. *Hopkins the Jesuit*. London: Oxford University Press.

Tillotson, K. 1954. *Novels of the Eighteen-Forties*. Oxford: Oxford University Press.

Toporov, V. N. 1969. "Le strutture dei livelli inferiori in poesia." Italian translation of "K opisaniju nekotorych struktur, haracterizujuscich preimuscestvenno nizsie urovni, v neskol'kich poèticeskich tekstach," *Trudy po znakovym sistemam* 2. Tartu, 1965. In R. Faccani and U. Eco, eds. 1969.

Trevelyan, G. M. 1945. *English Social History*. London: Longmans.

Turner, V. 1944. "Hopkins: A Centenary Article." *Dublin Review* 215 (1944). Page references are to the reprint in M. Bottrall, ed. 1975.

Warren, A. 1945. "Gerard Manley Hopkins (1844–1889)" and "Instress of Inscape." In *Collections* 1945.

Webb, R. K. 1968. "The Victorian Reading Public." In B. Ford, ed. 1968.

Weyand, N., and R. V. Schoder, eds. 1949. *Immortal Diamond: Studies in Gerard Manley Hopkins*. New York: Sheed and Ward. Page references are to the reprint (New York: Octagon Books, 1979).

Whitehall, H. 1945. "Sprung Rhythm." In *Collections* 1945.

Winters, I. 1949. "The Poetry of Gerard Manley Hopkins." *The Hudson*

258 BIBLIOGRAPHY

Review 1: 4 (Winter 1949). Page references are to the reprint in I. Winters, *The Function of Criticism*. London: Routledge and Kegan Paul 1962.

Zareckij, V. A. "Obraz Kak informacija." *Voprosy Literatury* 2 (1963). Italian translation "La 'figura' come informazione," in U. Eco, ed. 1972.

Žolkovskij, A. K. 1969. "Dell'amplificazione." In R. Faccani and U. Eco, eds. 1969. Italian translation from *Strukturno-tipologičeskie usledovanija*. Moscow, 1962.

INDEX OF WORKS CITED

INDEX OF NAMES

263

The Fine Delight That Fathers Thought: Rhetoric and Medievalism in Gerald Manley Hopkins was composed in Bembo by World Composition Services, Inc., Sterling, Virginia; printed and bound by BookCrafters, Chelsea, Michigan; and designed and produced by Kachergis Book Design, Pittsboro, North Carolina.